WHO
RULES
JAPAN?

The Inner Circles of
Economic and Political Power

Harold R. Kerbo

AND

John A. McKinstry

PRAEGER

Westport, Connecticut
London

Library of Congress Cataloging-in-Publication Data

Kerbo, Harold R.
    Who rules Japan? : the inner circles of economic and political
power / Harold R. Kerbo and John A. McKinstry.
        p.   cm.
    Includes bibliographical references (p.   ) and index.
    ISBN 0–275–94903–6 (alk. paper)
    1. Elite (Social sciences)—Japan.   2. Japan—Social
conditions—1945–   3. Japan—Politics and government—1945–
I. McKinstry, John A.   II. Title.
HN730.Z9E444   1995
305.5'2'0952—dc20   95–7988

British Library Cataloguing in Publication Data is available.

Library of Congress Catalog Card Number: 95–7988
ISBN: 0–275–94903–6

First published in 1995

Praeger Publishers, 88 Post Road West, Westport, CT 06881
An imprint of Greenwood Publishing Group, Inc.

Printed in the United States of America

The paper used in this book complies with the
Permanent Paper Standard issued by the National
Information Standards Organization (Z39.48–1984).

10 9 8 7 6 5 4 3 2 1

Contents

Preface

This story is about the ruling elites that guided Japan's reemergence as a major economic power in this new world economy. These were elites who were determined to move their people to prosperity and well-being after the destruction of war; elites who were made up of the best and brightest Japan had to offer; elites who, if not totally free of personal greed, at least had enough dedication and self-sacrifice to temper any greed with behavior designed for the common good of their people. An explanation of who some of these key Japanese elites were and are is based on information seldom if ever brought to the reading public, especially outside of Japan. Equally important is a description of how these elites are selected, how they are organized, and why they are unified to a far greater extent than found in any other post-industrial society.

The story then turns to the process of change among elites in Japan in recent years, change in a direction that if continued will be detrimental to the future of the Japanese people. There are distinct signs that Japan's elites are becoming more inbred, more self-serving, and even somewhat less talented than those of the post-war generation. As a result of the most severe economic recession since World War II, and with unprecedented political turmoil in the first half of the 1990s, Japan is presently facing up to the necessity of change. How such change will proceed, and if such change will proceed, will not only determine the place of Japan in the new world order, but also influence prospects for North America and Europe in meeting the challenge of Japan in the new world economy.

We thank several people in the United States and Japan for their help.

This is certainly not a story we could have told without their help and encouragement. Asako McKinstry was instrumental in many stages of our research and writing, from aiding us in securing Japanese-language material and helping John McKinstry in translating some of the most difficult parts, to providing comments and corrections on the final manuscript. We owe much to Elke Wittenhagen who responded to our writing with comments making the book more readable and understandable. We thank Professor Leonard Broom and Mr. Frank Gibney for giving us encouragement on the project over the years, and we especially thank Professor G. William Domhoff, who suggested we should write this book in the first place.

When not in Japan, we were allowed complete use of the Hoover Institute collection on Japan at Stanford University. Ms. Emiko Moffitt was invaluable in helping us locate much of the material, as were Professors David Grusky and Szonja Szelenyi, the former even walking through a heavy rainstorm to help us secure books when we needed them on short notice. Professors Chikako Usui and Jeffery Broadbent provided us with comments and materials for many parts of the book. Finally, professors Nakao Keiko and Morioka Kiyoshi have been very helpful in responding to our ideas by providing us with insights and saving us from some embarrassing mistakes. As usual, we owe much to our families for support and tolerance during the many months of research and writing that went into this book.

CHAPTER 1

The "Iron Triangle": The Nature and Impact of Japanese Elites

The pages of this book present two interrelated themes: an explanation of who and what rules Japan today, and the effects of this rule on post-war Japan and its future. As for the first, it is common to ask the question: Who rules? But power in modern industrial societies is never created out of a vacuum, out of sheer will or talent. There are institutional arrangements behind who rules, institutions which set the rules, opportunities, and limitations of human action. Of course these institutions must be examined. Still, on top of these institutions are real people who benefit from the status quo, and no doubt rather enjoy their privilege. The personal side of the people and families who make up these elites are also our subject.[1]

The nature and organization of these Japanese elites are very much tied up with the many calls for change in the 1990s: corruption is widespread, the economy has slowed, democratic prerogatives seem endangered, and the appearance of growing inequality has produced much anger. But Japan, we will argue, is not really changing, at least as much and in the direction that most Japanese desire. In contrast to the pre-war situation (as we will see in Chapter 3), the organization of elites Japan found itself with after World War II was instrumental in bringing about rapid recovery and the much-discussed Japanese "economic miracle." But while this new organization of elites was needed for such a recovery, they are not now what Japan needs to move to the next levels of individual prosperity and social well-being for the Japanese people. It is the interlocking network and power of current elites, as outlined in coming chapters, that will make the needed changes and reforms sluggish and at best very limited.

One of many specific examples of these elites is one of the corporate elite, Hirose Gen, chairman of Nippon Life Insurance Company.

Financial institutions such as banks, investment firms, and insurance companies, are among the most influential corporations in all industrial nations. In Japan, financial institutions are even more powerful because of their size *and* extensive ownership of stock in other corporations. Japan's largest 100 industrial firms, for example, count forty-seven insurance companies or other non-banking financial institutions among their number one stockholders. Of the top twenty-five banks in Japan, twenty-one have an insurance company as their number one stockholder.[2]

Nippon Life Insurance Company is the biggest of them all. This alone makes its chairman a member of the most powerful corporate elites in Japan.[3] But Hirose Gen also sits atop a company which has major stock control in many of the biggest corporations in Japan. The steel industry can be taken as a random example: Nippon Life is the fourth largest stockholder in the biggest steel company in Japan (Nippon Steel), third largest stockholder in the next largest (Kawasaki Steel), fifth in the third largest (Nippon Kokan), third in the next (Sumitomo Metal), second in the fifth largest (Kobe Steel), and the list continues like a broken record for the top ten steel companies.[4]

Like the chairman of any big corporation, Hirose is no longer much involved with the day-to-day running of his company, but is responsible for bigger, long-term decisions. Hirose has time for involvement with other cross-corporate organizations that benefit Nippon Life and Japan's broader business community. For example, Hirose sits on an organization of insurance providers in Japan and has served on several advisory boards appointed by recent prime ministers. Perhaps most important, however, Hirose is a key member of both Sansui-kai and Keidanren. Sansui-kai, "Three Waters Club," is a *shachō-kai*, or presidents' club, for one of the biggest groupings of Japanese corporations—the famous *keiretsu*. The Sanwa *keiretsu* to which Nippon Life belongs has forty-four main companies as members and twenty-four other large affiliates. Among the main members are corporations such as Sanwa Bank, Hitachi Metal, Hitachi Manufacturing, Sharp Electronics, and Daihatsu Industries. The Sansui-kai brings together the chairmen and presidents of all these corporations for weekly meetings to deal with common problems, plan for future needs, and organize for political influence.

Keidanren is a kind of congress of top business executives in Japan, with about one thousand members from the biggest corporations. Operating through many committees, Keidanren has considerable influence over every aspect of industrial policy in Japan, far more than any organization of private business in any other country in the world. Many of its activities, in fact, would no doubt be illegal in the United States because of anti-monopoly laws. Keidanren is often called the parliament of big business, with its chairman, now Toyoda Shoichirō, still chairman of Toyota Motor Corp. as well, called the prime minister of big business and perhaps the single most influential man in Japan. As an important member of Keidanren, Hirose of Nippon Life commonly takes time away for his leadership of Nippon Life to work on several committees within Keidanren which often require him to attend several meetings a month.

Across town from where Hirose conducts his corporate meetings, in a maze-like building located in Kasumigaseki, the government center of Tokyo and recently the site of sarin gas terrorism, Ozaki Mamoru conducts his own meetings. Specifically, in the early weeks of 1993, Ozaki was busy with meetings to decide what to do about Japan's declining stock market. Ozaki had just taken over as Vice-Minister of Finance in the summer of 1992 after a term as Director General of the National Tax Administration, which is attached to the Ministry of Finance.[5] Ozaki joined the elite track at the government Ministry of Finance in 1958 when he, like Hirose Gen, graduated from the elite Tokyo University, where more than 80 percent of the other top officials at the Ministry of Finance received their university degrees, along with the top officials at most other ministries and almost as many of the corporate elite.[6]

Along with the Ministry of International Trade and Industry (MITI), the Ministry of Finance can justifiably be called one of the most powerful agencies in Japan.[7] A position with the Ministry of Finance "is considered the most prestigious career track in government." Also, "MoF men are some of the world's most incorruptible and indefatigable civil servants. They are bureaucrats' bureaucrats: accountants' accountants."[8] And it is the administrative vice-minister position that is the most powerful: as with the other main government agencies in Japan, the minister of the agency is a politician, an outsider with little experience in the agency, and only there for a brief period. There were, for example, three different Ministers of Finance during 1991 and 1992 whom Vice-Minister Ozaki had to put up with.

During early 1993, Ozaki's problem was a big one: since 1990 the Japanese stock market had dropped by 60 percent.[9] Ozaki had to step in to prevent a real stock market crisis. Along with other top Ministry of Finance officials, such as Teramura Nobuyuki, chief of the Banking Bureau, and Ogawa Tadashi, chief of the Securities Bureau (both also Tokyo University graduates), Vice-Minister Ozaki decided to act decisively. They began by ordering many Japanese corporations not to sell shares of stock, while putting extensive pressure on the big financial institutions to buy shares. Hirose, at Nippon Life, was likely subjected to these pressures himself. These Ministry of Finance officials then put aside $22 billion in public pension funds which they control in order to buy shares of stock.[10] The stock market began its slow recovery.

As we will see in more detail, elite bureaucrats such as Ozaki have the power to do such things. The hand of the market place in Japan is not so hidden: it is guided by elite bureaucrats, such men as Ozaki. In response to criticism from Japanese corporate elites that the Ministry of Finance waited too long before acting decisively, one top official in the Ministry of Finance said, "We tried the free-market approach [for awhile] . . . it didn't work."[11]

While Hirose of Nippon Life was busy keeping the *keiretsu* running and attending Keidanren meetings, and Vice-Minister Ozaki was trying to organize Japan's stock market recovery, Kanemaru Shin was in big trouble. Until the fall of 1992, Kanemaru was the head of the most powerful faction of the Liberal Democratic Party, the party that had controlled Japan's Diet (parliament) from 1955 until 1993. In this position Kanemaru was the key person deciding who becomes Japan's prime minister, as well as most other top political positions.

In late 1992, however, Kanemaru was implicated in the Sagawa Express bribery scandal and forced to resign his position. Then, on March 9, 1993, police checked his home for further evidence and found $50 million in cash and gold bars in his safe. His son's home was also checked that day, where the police found another $34 million in cash and gold. Months after his first arrest (months!) he still had the money stashed away in his home. In reference to Kanemaru, a *New York Times* article stated that this "seemed to drive the point home that Japan's ruling class lives in a world of its own."[12]

The New York Times didn't quite have it right: Kanemaru is *not* such a central member of what can be called the "ruling class." Of the three main elite groups in Japan today—the corporate elite, the government bureaucratic elite, and elite politicians—the latter, despite all of its money and supposed political power, is not nearly as influential as most people assume. If this were not the case, one would certainly wonder how Japan has been able to survive the antics of its politicians in recent years. Nor would there be reason for the United States and Europe to worry about future economic competition from Japan. As we will see in coming chapters, Japan's government functions are mostly controlled by the unelected bureaucratic elite—a situation which, with characters such as Kanemaru afoot, has been somewhat fortunate for the Japanese people.

Hirose, chairman of Nippon Life, Vice-Minister Ozaki, and to a lesser degree political elites like Kanemaru, are members of Japan's inner circle of elites. Together with a relatively small and highly interconnected group of other members of this elite, these men can be said to rule Japan's economy and government. These are the men who sit atop the most central institutions within the economy and government, have extensive interpersonal ties, and have attended the same academic department within the same universities, mostly Tokyo University. A majority of these elites, in fact, belong to one or more of approximately forty extended families, called *keibatsu*, either through birth or marriage.[13] Throughout this book we will show how few if any subjects related to the Japanese Government and economics can be understood without reference to this network of elites in Japan today.

THE NATURE OF ELITES

One can describe the process of social evolution to modern industrial societies as a history of emerging elites and their power.[14] Only in recent times (roughly the last 200 years) has the trend toward ever more powerful and wealthy elites been somewhat reversed in democratic industrial societies. But even in modern industrial societies, elites continue to dominate the economy and governmental institutions. Compared to others in the society, these elites will always obtain more of whatever is valued, such as income and wealth, and have more influence over most aspects of the society.

However, questions such as these—Will there always be elites?, Will there always be the rich and poor?—are meaningless. More significant questions are, How rich are the rich? How poor are the poor? How powerful are the elites? To what extent are they able to exploit others? How effectively do elites rule? Throughout history, and certainly today, societies differ considerably with respect to how these questions are answered. The answers have profound effects on what happens in these societies.

Specifically, we must consider at least seven interrelated sets of questions to understand elites in Japan.[15] First, we need to know where the most important elite positions are located in the society. For example, does one gain more power and rewards from being a prime minister, a top government minister, the head of a major corporation, or a senior military official? In other words, is Hirose Gen more influential in the Japanese society because he is chairman of Nippon Life than is, say, Ozaki Mamoru as Vice-Minister of the Ministry of Finance, or the prime minister of Japan? These questions do not involve personalities as much as institutional positions, and what these positions bring in the way of opportunities for influence and rewards.

Second, we need to know the extent of elite power in Japan. There are a number of questions here, involving such things as whether or not elites are checked by some democratic influences from below; whether or not there are other elite groups creating checks and balances; or whether or not different elite groups cooperate to dominate those below, and therefore increase their power. In other words, to what extent does Hirose of Nippon Life work behind the scenes with Ozaki at the Ministry of Finance to make sure his company gets everything it wants? Or, to what extent does Ozaki at the Ministry of Finance restrain the activities of Nippon Life for some wider national good and the protection of other people in the society?

Third, we need to know the extent to which there are interpersonal networks within elite groups and across elite groups. Generally it can be said that extensive contact among elites brings them more influence due to a greater potential for cooperation and consensus.[16] In other words, we need to know the extent to which Hirose gets together with other corporate executives in Japan to share information, become aware of their common interests, and organize to further these common interests. We also need to know the extent to which people like Hirose from the corporate sector get together with people like Ozaki of the Ministry of Finance, or elite politicians. And in all of these cases, to what extent do we find people moving from one position to another during their careers, thus forming interlocking personnel within and across these elite sectors?

Fourth, we need to know something about elite backgrounds. That is, where do the elites come from in the society? Do they tend to come from certain classes, regions of the country, a few prominent families, or do they have diverse backgrounds? For example, if people such as Hirose and Ozaki often come from similar prominent families in an upper class, it is quite likely that they will understand the needs, interests, and worldviews of the upper class much more than they do those of other people in the society.

Fifth, how are these elites selected? Are they selected upon some objective measure of merit, talent, and integrity? Or are they selected through "an old-boy network" and family background? Related to this, is there a system of sponsored mobility in which, whatever their background, people are selected for elite positions because they are believed to serve the interests of people already in powerful positions or the interests of the whole nation?

Sixth, because the center of economic activity and influence in advanced industrial societies is found in the biggest corporations, we need to know who owns and controls these corporations. Are these corporations owned and controlled by wealthy families, individual corporate managers, the government, or a cross-corporate business elite which is able to influence several big corporations at the same time?

Seventh, to what extent are elites able to manipulate or exert influence over the general population? If the masses are not kept in their place or to some degree rather passive, elites, who are always a small minority, will find it difficult to maintain their dominance. The American founder of the power elite concept and theory, C. Wright Mills, had much to say about a "mass society" in the United States which he believed was manipulated by elites, and for the most part kept ignorant of much of what elites were doing so as to protect elite interests. While this manipulation may be overstated, we need to know the extent to which Japanese elites are able to manipulate their citizens to produce this "mass society."

All of these questions will be considered in coming chapters. The answers will help us understand the impact of elites in the Japanese society, along with such things as what gets done in the society and why. But the answers will help us understand more than just which groups are favored and which groups are exploited: the answers to these questions are related to a country's vitality, international competitiveness, and survival.

Elite Rule in Japan: Puzzles and Contradictions

Uncovering the nature of Japanese elites, however, is no simple task: these elites defy many of our preconceptions and present many apparent puzzles and contradictions. A few examples of these puzzles we must consider in coming chapters are in order.

To begin with, if these men are so powerful, why aren't they rich? Japan has one of the lowest levels of income inequality among major industrial nations, much lower than the United States.[17] By American standards, Japan's corporate elite average only modest incomes. And, we might add, no one has found any of them with $50 million stashed away at home. There is corruption among corporate executives in Japan, but it is primarily restricted to executives from smaller corporations, below the corporate elite level.[18]

The contrast to American corporate executives was shown most dramatically during former President George Bush's trip to Japan in January of 1992. The average yearly income of the eighteen executives accompanying Bush was at least $1.2 million, not even counting stock options, with one of these executives, C. J. Silas of Phillips Petroleum, making over $5 million. While in Japan these American executives met with their Japanese counterparts, running some of the most competitive corporations in the world, who had incomes closer to $500,000.[19] A 1991 survey of top executive incomes in the biggest 838 corporations in Japan and the United States found an average income of about $378,000 in Japan, compared to an average of $1.2 million in the United States. More generally, several studies indicate that the income gap between corporate presidents and average workers in Japan is around seventeen to one, in contrast to an eighty-five to one gap in the United States.[20] And it is interesting that comparative studies show that in the post-war years Japanese elites voice more support for low inequality and limiting top incomes than elites for other industrial nations, especially compared to the United States.[21]

Hirose, chairman of Nippon Life, is again a good case in point. Hirose will soon be stepping down from his position: he is approaching retirement. With retirement, he will not be able to reside for the rest of his life in a huge mansion as do many American top executives: he never had one. Hirose will most likely continue to live in his modest house (less than 2,000 square feet) about a half-hour drive from the center of Osaka, where he has lived for the past fifteen years, when away from his much smaller apartment closer to the corporate headquarters in Tokyo. Like other top executives in Japan, Hirose owns very little corporate stock to fall back upon in his retirement, and what stock he does own was paid for out of his own pocket, without benefit of stock options, which are prohibited in Japan. Hirose is likely to miss some of his perks of office upon retirement, such as his entertainment expense account and golf club membership. But we know that Hirose will not miss trips on the company jet, meals in the private executive dining room, or the huge private office with executive washroom: he never had any of these things to begin with. Like the vast majority of his Japanese corporate peers, Hirose will be comfortable, but unlike American chief executives, certainly not wealthy after his retirement as chairman of the biggest life insurance company in Japan.

Japan's top government bureaucrats, on the other hand, could barely be considered upper-middle class by American income standards. These individuals have gone to the same prestigious universities as the corporate elite, in particular Tokyo University, and often have more power over the Japanese economy and society than their classmates who took corporate positions. Their old classmates now in the corporate world may visit them in their government offices, bow deeply, and speak to them in formal, honorific language while asking favors. But the top 100 members of the bureaucratic elite seldom make more than $60,000 a year.[22] And the surprising answer to the question which has likely just come to mind is, no, there has been very little corruption among this bureaucratic elite since World War II. Corruption involving bureaucratic elites has occurred in recent years, to the shock and surprise of the Japanese people: so far, however, corruption is still centered among politicians.

Another puzzle: neither are there many families in Japan which are truly wealthy by the standards of other mature capitalist economies. Today there are few Japanese equivalents to the wealthy Rockefellers, Mellons, Fords, or Morgans. The Mitsui, Nomura, and Fuji families, for example, who would have been equivalents, had most of their wealth taken away after World War II. A few of the world's most wealthy individuals are Japanese. But these new rich are seldom very influential or most highly respected inside Japan. In fact, over 90 percent of the most important form of wealth in a capitalist nation, corporate stock, is not even owned by private individuals, families, or groups of individuals in Japan at all: about 80 percent of corporate stock is owned by other Japanese corporations—not pension funds or trust funds for other people, but owned by the corporations![23] In one sense it can be said that Japan is a capitalist society, but with few true capitalists.

Another atypical aspect of the Japanese elite pertains to how they got to the top. The post-war elites in Japan have had the image of a sort of deserving meritocracy in the eyes of many ordinary Japanese citizens because they have passed the litmus test of higher education in one of Japan's extremely selective universities. Especially since World War II, the first step to elite status in Japan has been admittance into one of the elite universities, most importantly Tokyo University. As is commonly known, matriculation at these top universities is restricted to those few young people able to pass very difficult entrance exams: money is of little importance in going to these universities.[24] Soon after World War II, and on into the 1960s and 1970s, for example, a far greater percentage of Tokyo University students were from working-class backgrounds, by about 30 percent, than was the case at places such as Harvard, Yale, or Oxford universities. These working-class sons, in other words, were well positioned for future elite status.

In seeming contrast to all of this, however, there are powerful family groups in Japan today, called *keibatsu*. But in another contrast to Western industrial nations, a tradition of arranged marriage (through meetings called *omiai*) has made these *keibatsu* families accessible through marriage: bright young graduates from the elite universities, starting promising careers in major corporations or the powerful government ministries, are likely to become members of *keibatsu*.[25] There is even a rather good chance for some of these young men from humble origins to become a *yoshi*—a son-in-law who is then legally adopted as a son in one of the *keibatsu*, with the rights of a natural male heir. Hirose Gen, chairman of Nippon Life, provides an example of how this all works.

Hirose, whose original family name was Naruse, has reason to feel satisfaction when he thinks back over his career as he nears retirement. True, his is not a rags to riches story. Although Hirose's family circumstances were by no means affluent as he grew to adulthood, his father, Naruse Ryūzō, had been one of the managers of Mitsui family enterprises before the war. Hirose's brother, Naruse Tatsu, preceded him as a recruit into the ranks of Nippon Life Insurance Co. following his own graduation from Tokyo University. In fact, Naruse Tatsu, after reaching the level of president of Nippon Life, and until his retirement a few years ago, actually had more day-to-day responsibilities in the organization than did his younger, but more powerful brother as chairman.

Nothing was simply handed to Hirose on a silver platter. The whole family knew that regardless of the accomplishments of his father and older brother, he could not wear the mantle of success unless he could manage to enter either Tokyo University or another university in the top four or five ranking. To this goal he dedicated his entire conscious youth. Even during the war when he was forced to move in with relatives in the countryside, he had to study, study, study. Hirose's mind needed to be crammed with thousands of facts in order to pass the entrance examination to a top university. Of course he had help—tutors, special cram school sessions, sympathy and encouragement from his family; but in the end he had to pass the examination all by himself, as he did with great success.

The next step was of course to marry well, to extend *keibatsu* family alliances, and in this endeavor, Hirose was extremely lucky. Shortly after joining Nippon Life, Hirose Jotarō, the company president at the time and son of the company founder, let Hirose Gen (still Naruse Gen) know through a superior that after careful examination of his background and close observation of his character while at the firm, he had decided to have someone arrange a meeting between the young man and his own daughter. This meeting would be an *omiai*, a traditional Japanese method of arranging marriages, to see if the two young people would consider themselves appropriate marriage partners. It is also important to note at this point that Hirose Jotarō, the son of the company founder and then president of Nippon Life, did not have a son and heir. The *omiai* went well, and soon afterward wedding plans were announced. And, it was also announced that the man known until then as Naruse Gen would be adopted into the family of his bride as legal heir (becoming a *yoshi*) and be transformed into Hirose Gen. Over the next several years, Hirose Gen worked hard for the company as he moved up the ranks, but everyone knew that, as de facto grandson of the founder of the company, he was destined for a top post. And in the age-ranked society of Japan, this is the only reason that Hirose Gen could become the chairman of Nippon Life while his older biological brother, Naruse Tatsu, was under him as the president of the company.

By the time he was moving to the top of Nippon Life, Hirose Gen and his wife had their own children, and of course wanted them to have the kind of success Hirose Gen enjoyed. He knew that relentless study for his son and the right kind of preparation for marriage for his two daughters were pivotal to passing on elite status to the next generation. Their son Gentarō was a winner on both counts: he was able to get the right kind of university affiliation as well as to marry the granddaughter of the late Matsukata Masayoshi, a former count and pre-war prime minister. The Matsukata family was no longer wealthy, but it was the right kind of pedigree for the family of a business executive.

The real coup de grace, however, came a few years ago when it was time for Hirose Gen's granddaughter to find a suitable husband. A great deal of preparation and thought had gone into the matter. Through his adopted father's contacts, Hirose Gen was able to arrange an *omiai* between Masako, his granddaughter, and Matsushita Masayuki, grandson of Matsushita Kōnosuke, founder and then still president of Matsushita Electric Company, one of the largest consumer electronics manufacturers in the world. He was no doubt rather pleased when he heard that the couple had hit it off, and that Matsushita Konosuke had agreed to the union. And he was no doubt equally pleased when the great man himself, the emperor of consumer electronics, sat at the same table with Hirose Gen, toasting each wedding speech with him, behaving for all the world like his old friend. With the exception of Vice-Foreign Minister Owada, whose daughter married Crown Prince Naruhito in June of 1993, *keibatsu* family ties don't get any better.

Elites and the Rise and Fall of Nations

Ideas about how elites affect a nation and its survival go back at least to Aristotle and Plato. Aristotle thought strong elites were good for us all, while Plato thought we "will never have rest from their evils. . . ."[26] In more recent times, which is to say in the past 100 years or so, several philosophers and social scientists have constructed grand theories about the nature of elites and their effects. For example, the German scholar Robert Michels coined the phrase "iron law of oligarchy" to suggest there will always be elites who dominate the rest of us. Another German, Karl Marx, believed that dominant elites now come from private ownership of the means of production, and would therefore eventually be eliminated with collective ownership. The Italian social scientist Gretano Mosca more or less agreed with Michels, and wrote that there will always be two classes of people, "a class that rules and a class that is ruled." (Mussolini rather liked Mosca.) But the work of another Italian, Vilfredo Pareto, is famous for his exploration of the "circulation of elites" and the need for differing types of elites in different stages of a society's development. Pareto agreed that societies will always have elites in some form or another, but he stressed that it is important that there be a circulation of elites so that the most talented in the society are able to rise, new ideas and interests can be represented, and the elites don't stagnate or become overly exploitative.

History is full of societies which declined and fell in large part because of their elites. For example, the Roman Empire fell by 500 A.D. However, most people don't realize that the Roman Empire fell not because of the "moral fiber" of the common people, but because Roman elites became shortsighted, exploitative, and more and more rich compared to the common people.[27] In the end, nomadic raids from the likes of the Vandals and Attila the Hun met little resistance from a Roman population fed up with the exploitation.

Another clear example can be found closer to our age. As the eighteenth century began, both England and France were already in competition to replace the Netherlands as the preeminent power in the world economy. In the previous century, France actually had been in a stronger position economically and militarily than England: but after more than 100 years of war and economic conflict, the eighteenth century ended with England in the dominant position, and an empire beginning to stretch around the world. In contrast to France, the landed nobility in England were able to cooperate with, and even join, the new merchants and industrialists who were becoming more important as industrialization became the future. France, on the other hand, was mired in domestic violence and chaos from the massive revolution which began in 1789, in large measure brought about by the ineptitude and greed of the French aristocracy, who tried to hold on to their wealth and power while forcing merchants and peasants to pay for their costly ventures against the British.[28]

Looking back from the end of the next century, will historians record that Japan moved into a dominant position in relation to late twentieth-century competitors in part because of its elite network established after World War II? Or will history record that the post-war Japanese elite structure which helped produce their economic miracle in the 1960s was short-lived, and Japan was unable to continue its economic gains into the twenty-first century? We will return to this question primarily at the end of this book. For now we must first consider briefly what was different about this post-war Japanese elite before we expand upon this theme again in Chapter 3.

THE TRAUMA OF DEFEAT AND POST-WAR ELITES IN JAPAN

There is a simple truth which one can learn only through suffering: in war not victories are blessed but defeats. Governments need victories and the people need defeats. Victory gives rise to the desire for more victories. But after a defeat it is freedom that men desire—and usually attain.

> Aleksandr Solzhenitsyn, *The Gulag Archipelago*[29]

At the end of World War II Japan lay in ruins, with a large part of the population living on the brink of starvation.[30] Production was less than 20 percent of what it had been just five years before.[31] Hiroshima, of course, was leveled, with at least 140,000 dead soon after the bomb blast. In Nagasaki about 70,000 died, but the center of the city suffered less complete destruction because the bomb missed its target. Pictures taken at the end of World War II, however, show that Tokyo and many other cities looked much the same as Hiroshima—the main difference was that it took many months to do in Tokyo what took seconds in Hiroshima.

It is Hiroshima, however, that stands for the stupidity of war in the minds of the Japanese people. Every year many thousands of junior high and high school students come to Hiroshima for their annual school trip. They spend two or three days touring the Peace Park, and listening to lectures on what happened there on August 6, 1945.[32] There is a museum in the Peace Park where these children can see things such as granite steps with the shadow of a person vaporized by the bomb. Walking around the many monuments in the park outside, these children can see one mound, today covered with grass, which contains the ashes of "tens of thousands" of people who died during the bomb blast.

The key point is that Japanese elites, past and present, experienced the same misery. Most still alive after the war lost everything, or almost everything. The very rich had their remaining property taken away. And many of Japan's future elite, like Mieno, head of the Bank of Tokyo, suffered from the same poverty as others at the end of the war. Many of those now moving into elite positions were young children at the end of the war and carry with them personal stories of suffering. These are men such as Satō Takahiko, head of Ube's corporate operations in Germany during 1992. He was six years old in August of 1945, living just outside of Hiroshima in the city of

Kure. Satō remembers climbing one of the mountains around the city with his mother on that day because they thought the bomb might have contained poison gas.[33] And there are men such as Professor Tominaga Ken'ichi, senior professor at elite Tokyo University in 1992, who remembers the destruction and hunger. But he was lucky, having been transferred to another high school in June of 1945, away from the Hiroshima Military High School located, until August 6 anyway, on the castle grounds near the center of Hiroshima.[34]

General statements such as Solzhenitsyn's are often simplistic and limited in their application. But his observation becomes more impressive when we reflect upon the number of times history has recorded a rise from the ashes after the trauma of military devastation. Defeat in war can sometimes clear away obstacles to progress, and cause a radical recirculation of elites. In Japan, the suffering shared by elites, future elites, and the masses was a leveling experience which had profound effects on attitudes for many years.

In fact, revolutions often occur when nations having outdated forms of social organization, with high levels of exploitation by elites, are forced to compete militarily and economically with nations already transformed to more modern, efficient forms of social organization.[35] The French Revolution of 1789 was one of the best examples; there have been many others.

Violent revolution did not follow Japan's defeat in World War II, but many of the changes which followed were quite revolutionary in scope. These changes were in large part made possible by popular anger directed toward old elites, in many ways seen as responsible for the war and its destruction. It was the Occupation under General MacArthur, however, that pushed through many of the basic changes which set the stage for Japan's later economic "miracle." Many of the most important changes affected Japanese elite organization.

Before World War II, for example, ten families in Japan controlled about 75 percent of all corporate assets: just four families owned about 25 percent of these assets.[36] There was a rigid class system with little mobility into top positions. Exploitation was extreme. In contrast to today's small income gap between corporate elites and workers noted earlier (about seventeen to one), the gap before the war was around 100 to one.[37] Extensive starvation was not uncommon in the pre-war countryside, where parents sometimes sold their daughters into prostitution rather than see them starve.[38] Taxes took about 35 percent of the crop, and rents paid to landowners usually took another 50 percent. There were many peasant revolts and violent urban strikes during the 50 years that preceded World War II, all violently suppressed.[39] In short, Japan was not the country of harmony, relative equality, and cooperation which is often depicted today.

The Occupation reforms after World War II created many changes for elites, elite organization, and the relationship between elites and masses that will be examined in detail in Chapter 3. For example, the richest families noted above had most of their wealth taken away, and land was distributed to the landless. These wealthy families no longer controlled the big corporations. Corporate organization itself was altered: the now famous *keiretsu* corporate groups emerged due to the redistribution of corporate assets and other changes brought about by, or later stimulated by, the Occupation reforms. Finally, there were major changes in class relations in a more general sense. Income and wealth inequalities were drastically reduced. A very educated and relatively affluent middle class was able to emerge within a decade or so after these reforms. After a period of post-war repression and labor violence, compromises were eventually made with labor which brought the famous labor-management cooperation to today's Japan. And not least important, we will show how humiliation and hardship brought by defeat, and commonly experienced by the previously rich and poor alike, helped forge a sense of unity, common interests, and cooperation.

THE FUTURE OF ELITES: A THREAT TO JAPANESE ECONOMIC POWER?

Through most of the post-war years there seems to have been a vague notion of fairness felt by the Japanese people in regard to the way the economic system operates.[40] There was an awareness that inequality was not exceptionally high and that elites were people who had attained their positions through talent and hard work. With the exception of a few scandals involving politicians, corporate and government elites were viewed as honest and soberly at the helm of the ship of state, even though rather haughty at times.[41]

All of this, however, is potentially in flux today. Japanese newspapers of late are full of stories about corruption by politicians like Kanemaru. But in a few cases, which is the real shock to many Japanese people, it is not just the politicians. Also, the Japanese people are increasingly unhappy about their situation in life, and feel that something is not right about belonging to one of the richest nations in the world, if not the richest, while being individually rather poor when considering their standard of living and how hard they work. And specifically there is a growing sense of unfairness directed toward the more affluent and powerful. A government "White Paper on National Life" in 1988 found new popular concern over what was perceived to be increasing income and wealth inequality in Japan.[42]

We can find no Japanese social scientist who has any data clearly showing that income inequality has increased in Japan in recent years, but the Japanese people feel this nevertheless. There is certainly visual evidence of growing wealth inequalities due to the "bubble economy" of the late 1980s: rapidly rising real estate and stock values gave many Japanese the ability to flaunt wealth not seen since before World War II. Throughout the 1980s one could see an ever increasing number of expensive German cars on the streets, more Japanese men going to very expensive golf clubs, and lavish amounts spent by businessmen on entertainment.[43]

In the context of all this, there are other things happening which may have effects on future elites. We noted above that there was a surprisingly high percentage of students in the elite tracks at Tokyo University from middle-and working-class backgrounds after the war. In recent years this percentage is not much higher than the percentage of working-class students attending Harvard (Ishida 1993). There is also evidence of growing inter-marriage among young people from elite families in Japan today, also re-ducing elite circulation and upward mobility for the most talented.

We earlier pointed out that in some ways the changes experienced by Japan after the war were revolutionary in scope. As with the aftermath of revolution, Japan experienced a rapid circulation of elites and reduced in-equality, among other political and economic changes which laid the foun-dations for the strong recovery to follow. Lessons from the study of revolutions can be considered again, this time in relation to Japan in the 1990s.

An overwhelming conclusion from the study of revolutions through his-tory is that reduced inequality, greater circulation of elites, and the ideolog-ical dedication of elites to serving the people sometimes found in the years immediately after a revolution, cool in the next generation.[44] There is even a special name for this phenomenon, the "Thermidorian reaction," with original reference to what happened after the French Revolution of 1789. The next generation of elites find ways to increase inequality, making sure they are at the upper ranges of the inequality growth. They also try to make sure their sons and daughters obtain positions among the next generation of elites, thus slowing the previous circulation of elites.

Is Japan again following the pattern of revolutions with their own Ther-midorian reaction? Will this Thermidorian reaction work against the forces producing the "Japanese miracle" in the years after World War II? These are questions to be considered throughout coming pages, but most directly in our last chapter after we have had a chance to consider all of the char-acteristics of Japanese elites in more detail.

JAPANESE ELITES TODAY: A CONCLUSION AND BEGINNING

No one can say that elites are all-powerful or that they rule just as they please, especially in complex modern societies today. The three elite groups in Japan do not always get their way. At times they lose to other interest groups. Neither are they united on all important issues, which is to say they sometimes have conflicting interests. These divisions among the elites often reduce their power.[45] But despite all of this, more often than not, and more often than any other group in Japan, especially when they are relatively united over important issues, the iron triangle of elites get their way.

In what follows we will show that since World War II there has been a triumvirate of elites ruling Japan—the corporate elite, the government bureaucratic elite, and the political elite.[46] For each of these elite groups, however, we must not only ask "who rules?" but also "what rules?" It is not just the people on top, but the institutional arrangements which give them the power, define their limitations, and create demands on these elites themselves.

These elites are extensively interrelated through *keibatsu* family ties and through personnel exchanges, business organizations, clubs, and old school ties. These ties are important in creating the elite consensus and cooperation which have been important in building the strong economy and maintaining their nationalistic united front to the outside world since World War II. Elites have worked to maintain a "mass society" in Japan, in various ways keeping the Japanese population from threatening the status quo. Consideration of all of these factors allows a better understanding of why call for change in Japan is likely to fall very short of popular expectations for some time to come.

CHAPTER 2

Japan: Some Key Aspects of Social Structure and Culture

No other society has been described by so many people as unique, mysterious, and even unknowable by outsiders, as has Japan. Likewise, with no other country has there been so much disagreement over the degree to which the country is unique or mysterious, or if these words even apply at all. No attempt to analyze and explain any aspect of Japan can escape or ignore this controversy.

In considering concepts such as culture, individualism, conformity, and the nature of groups in the Japanese society, we must step back from our specific focus on such members of elites as Mr. Hirose, Mr. Ozaki, and Mr. Kanemaru to present an overview of Western views and contacts with Japan throughout history and to put the idea of uniqueness in perspective. After doing so we will analyze the concept of culture as it relates to our subject of the power and formation of elites, and finally present some key aspects of Japanese culture and social organization which shape the nature of elite formation and power in Japan today.

EARLY WESTERN VIEWS OF JAPAN

Despite modernization in Japan, the old images of Japan held by Westerners, and among Japanese themselves, persist. Among Europeans, Japan was not even known to exist until the accounts of Marco Polo described "Cipangu," an island full of "idolaters" with great amounts of gold. The first account of Japan in English came in 1577 with Richard Willie's *The History of Travayle in the West and East Indies*.[47] It was at this time and soon after that many of today's Western stereotypes of Japan began. Recent research and a new collection of articles[48] written by Europeans—mostly British, German, Dutch, and French—during the eighteenth century show that already the Japanese were labelled as obedient, group-oriented, and hard-working, but not so creative.[49]

During the time of these early writings by Europeans, of course, Japan was basically a closed country, since the new Tokugawa Shogun expelled foreigners in the early 1600s, restricting the few foreign contacts that remained to a small island off the coast near Nagasaki. When Japan was forced to open its borders by the United States in 1853, the outside world began getting somewhat more inside information about the Japanese culture and society.[50] One of the central figures in providing this information was Lafcadio Hearn, an American journalist who fell in love with Japan, moved there permanently in 1890, and became the first Westerner allowed to take Japanese citizenship.[51] In books such as *Kokoro: Hints and Echoes of the Japanese Inner Life, Glimpses of Unfamiliar Japan, Exotics and Retrospectives,* and *In Ghostly Japan,* we find even more of what Europeans had been writing about the Japanese almost two centuries before, plus much more: Hearn tells of the "real" Japan which is often "mysterious and strange" to the Western civilization.[52]

The new trend among Japan scholars is to show that many of the explanations of Japanese society and culture by these previous Japanologists, as well as many current ones, have been overly positive toward Japan, and at best misleading, but quite often simply wrong.[53] Without going as far as many of these critiques in rejecting the ideas and works of earlier Japan scholars, it is possible to show that their works do contain some inaccuracies and biases that make the understanding of Japanese elites more difficult. Most generally, these scholars have neglected the extent to which unequal power, conflict, and divisions are important aspects of Japanese society and culture, along with the group cooperation, obedience, and consensus commonly described in Japan. Examining the concepts of culture and social organization will help to make these points most clearly before considering these specific aspects of Japan in more detail.

CULTURE AND EXPLANATIONS OF JAPANESE BEHAVIOR

One of the most used and abused concepts is "culture." Culture, it seems, can explain everything. Why does one country have higher birth rates than another? "It must be because of cultural differences." Why does one country have more cooperation between labor and management? Again, "it must be their cultural propensity to respect authority."[54]

Japan, we are told, has a value system emphasizing the group which leads to cooperation, self-sacrifice, economic strength, and a lack of many social problems. This group orientation is then commonly explained with reference to the principles from Buddhism, Confucianism, and Shintoism which are found in Japan's history.

There are certainly cultural differences, and cultural values certainly affect what humans do. Many differences found in Japan, when compared to Western societies, are related to culture. A few decades ago most social scientists believed that Japan would eventually end up being almost identical to the West with respect to cultural values. Most simply put, it was believed that the process of industrialization and modernization would eventually make all societies basically alike. Special attention was given to Japan in the 1960s because it was the first Asian society to industrialize fully.[55] By the 1980s, however, the old views of modernization were being debated again, with more scholars now saying something like, "well, not exactly."[56] There are cultural influences in Japan which, for example, make work in groups more valued and extended families remain more important than in Western nations.[57] Still, culture can't explain everything.

Problems for Cultural Explanations of Japanese Behavior

Explanations citing culture, as indicated above, are useful and should not be overlooked, but at the same time we must recognize significant limitations in these explanations. First, cultural values are rather vague: in practice they need interpretation to show how they apply. One reason for the need of interpretation is the fact that values can be contradictory. For example, all would agree that freedom is a stated American value. But freedom can include the freedom to discriminate against others, as well as the freedom from such discrimination. Thus, how are the broad values to be interpreted, and by whom? Simply put, cultural values and beliefs can be, and certainly have been, manipulated for selfish interests. In this case we must ask who has the influence and motivation to shape cultural values in a certain direction throughout a society's history.

Second, values are certainly subject to change, and they are not so deeply ingrained within individuals and societies as is often assumed. One of the most fascinating natural experiments of this has recently been completed: a personal observation I made while in Germany is that former East and West German cousins hardly recognize each others' values after something like one generation of separation.[58]

All of these problems with the concept of culture apply to Japan and Japanese history. There has been much more change in Japanese history than most accounts have indicated. For example, women have not always been so subservient, and the divorce rate not always so low. In fact, a few centuries ago Japan had a matrilineal society (with women more dominant than men), and in some rural areas this was the case as recently as a century ago.[59] Also, much about the Japanese economy which is admired, such as "lifetime employment," low inequality between managers and workers, and practices promoting teamwork, did not exist before World War II. In other words, these things cannot be primary aspects of Japanese culture if they have existed less than fifty years. In addition, major aspects of Japanese cultural values were clearly and intentionally shaped and directed by Japanese elites in the late 1800s and early 1900s to control the behavior of the Japanese people.

There is another point: even to the extent that cultural values influence such things as economic success, consensus, teamwork, and so forth, these cultural values are not alone in producing such outcomes. Cultural values may provide the potential for such outcomes, but social arrangements from political and economic systems, to name only two, are also involved. How else can we explain the fact that people of Chinese descent tend to be the most wealthy and successful business leaders in almost every Southeast Asian nation today, while people in China have remained poor throughout this century, and are only now starting what seems to be sustained economic development? Inside China, opportunities and motivations for amassing wealth and running businesses were restricted, first by major political disruptions, and then by the political and economic system put in place after 1948. But take the Chinese out of China, and chances are rather good that many of them will become successful in economic activities.

This point must be extended to Japan: the Meiji Restoration of the late 1800s, and then again the major changes soon after World War II, must be seen as more important in shaping Japan today than any deeply ingrained Japanese culture. And many of these changes in the last century have involved the nature of Japanese elites.

KEY ASPECTS OF JAPANESE SOCIAL ORGANIZATION AND CULTURE

For centuries, and certainly long before Japan became a focus of interest, the vaguely defined Orient has been considered by Westerners to be the cultural contrast to the West, or Occident. Much like the "mysterious" label pinned on Japan, however, this cultural contrast has been overstated. Still, the contrast cannot be completely rejected: considered with prudence and caution, we can use some of what has been described as cultural contrasts between the East and West in an analysis of the nature and power of elites in Japan. It will be useful to begin with one of the most general cultural contrasts between these variants of East and West, make these more applicable to Japan, and then later consider more specific characteristics of Japanese culture and social organization for what they can tell us about elites.

At the most general level of value preferences, the West is commonly described as having an individualistic value system, while Asia is described as having a collectivist value system. Most simply this means that the group is more important in Asia, while the individual is more important in the West. Such things are never quite so simple, of course, but it is useful to think of these polar opposite values as being on a continuum, with individualism at one end and collectivism on the other. No nation or culture can be found completely at one extreme or the other, though they do tend to fall further to one side or the other, with Western nations more to the individualistic end and most Asian nations more to the collectivist end.

As industrialization was rapidly changing European societies in the eighteenth and nineteenth centuries, many of the best social scientists of the time—such as Emile Durkheim, Max Weber, Ferdinand Tommies, and Georg Simmel—were speculating about how societies would survive: the previously strong bonds linking individuals to small groups in preindustrial societies were breaking as people became more mobile, thus leaving small villages for big cities. A totally individualistic society, one with everyone going his or her own way, considering only his or her own selfish interests, these social scientists knew, would not work: there would be only destructive conflict and anarchy. However flawed some of his ideas, the great interpreter of the Western mind, Sigmund Freud, also outlined this dilemma of human societies in one of his greatest books, *Civilization and Its Discontents*, in 1930. Some means of organization and compromise must be attained between the conflicting interests of the group and the individual.

The Western industrialized societies evolved toward allowing ever more freedom to the individual. The individual, of course, must continue to have responsibilities toward, and even make some sacrifices for, important groups—the family, and work groups, for example. But in these Western nations, and to the greatest extent in the United States,[60] value preferences suggest that individuals should be given as much freedom and independence as possible. Asian collectivist cultures, in contrast, require more sacrifice for group needs and place more restraints on what the individual may do in satisfying individual desires. All of this not only affects the individual's relation to small groups, but also the individual's relation to the broader community and nation.

The standard explanation for differences between the more individualistic West and the more collectivist East is worth considering briefly. This standard explanation is also worthy of brief consideration because it is used to describe how and why Japan differs to some extent from its Asian neighbors.

At base, the explanation may seem simplistic, perhaps even absurd, because it has to do with what people eat, the food people in the West versus the East have most depended upon for survival over the centuries.[61] It is not, however, the nutrients or even chemicals in this food, but rather, how the food must be produced. In contrast to the cultivation of cereal crops such as wheat in Western civilizations, a long history of wet rice cultivation in Asia has helped establish a collectivist value orientation. Wet rice cultivation is labor intensive, requiring group cooperation in community projects to get the water in and out of the fields at the right time during the growing seasons. Thus, out of necessity, values favoring more group unity and control over the individual developed over the many centuries of dependence upon wet rice cultivation for food.

Not all Asian societies, however, have equally developed this collectivist value orientation. While Japan did develop this collectivist value orientation, the Japanese did not do so to the same degree or in the same way as, for instance, China. The explanation for this is again related to geography and agriculture: because of the far greater abundance of water coming down from mountains in Japan, wet rice farming did not require such large group projects or large groups working together as in China.[62] Thus, Japan came to have values favoring groups, but relatively small and more independent groups compared to many other Asian nations. And neither did Japan have the early development of a strong overarching state to organize irrigation projects which resulted in powerful political elites as in China.

These "hydraulic empires," such as those found in early Chinese history, are also said to have led to more rigid social stratification and a powerful political elite able to block changes that were needed for industrialization. Most importantly, this meant blocking the emergence of a merchant class with the wealth and influence to threaten political elites favored by the old agricultural economy. Even before Japan was finally opened to the West through pressure from the United States in the 1850s, there was less resistance to changes setting the stage for industrialization because the powerful state was less in evidence, and, therefore, Japan's feudal system, which predated industrialization, was more like that of Europe than other Asian nations.[63] For the present discussion, however, it is Japanese values stressing smaller groups and more loyalty to these smaller groups which is most important.

The Group

With all of this in mind, there is little need to emphasize the importance of the nature of groups in modern Japan. Elite formation and power would be decidedly different if the traditional group structure was altered.

Sociologists divide groups into two basic types. Primary groups are those to which the individual is more strongly attached, where emotional ties are greater, more time is spent with other group members, and where a diverse set of personal needs are met. Secondary groups, on the other hand, are more temporary: there is less time spent with others in the group, emotional ties between members are less strong, and the group primarily exists for some specific tasks. The best examples of the first are families and close friendship groups, the best example of the second is a work group.

Sociologists of the nineteenth century, concerned with the effects of industrialization, discovered that people were coming to attach themselves more often to secondary groups, while primary groups were becoming fewer and weaker. The Western individualistic orientation is no doubt both a cause and an effect of this change in the nature of groups in these societies.

In Japan, even the industrialized Japan of our day, by contrast, primary groups remain comparatively more important. More precisely, we can say there remains less distinction between primary groups and what would in some other societies be considered secondary groups at work. While it is certainly an overstatement to call the Japanese corporation an "extended clan" or family, the tendency for Japanese groups to remain primary groups with respect to many characteristics means that people usually have stronger attachments, more loyalty, and even more willingness to undergo some self-sacrifice for the work group than is found in the United States.

There is now extensive research supporting what Japanologists have been saying for decades. For example, in a massive study of fifty corporations in the United States and fifty corporations in Japan, with questionnaire data from about 5,000 workers in each country, Lincoln and Kalleberg found that Japanese workers have more satisfaction with their jobs when working alongside others, and even feel more freedom when working with others compared to Americans. Japanese workers were also much more likely to say that they should sacrifice for their work group, and that they had more trust and confidence in their coworkers.[64] There is change in Japan: as many studies and polls indicate, while fewer Japanese compared to Americans say the family is more important than the work group, there is a growing generation gap. Younger Japanese are more likely to say that the family is more or equally important, that they feel it is alright to change jobs, and want to sacrifice less of their time to work.[65] Still, compared to other industrial nations, and especially the United States, ties to small groups of many kinds, including the work group, remain far stronger in Japan.

These group attachments have many implications for the power of Japanese elites. Certainly there are many implications for the power of corporate elites: but there are many other implications which do not come to mind as readily, such as the low tendency among Japanese people to join groups other than those most important to them. This means, for example, that protest groups have more difficulty building a broad popular base, therefore keeping such groups on the margins of society, and less threatening to the status quo.

Personal Ties and Vertical Groups

The above implies that interpersonal ties between group members are relatively more important in Japan. But there is another dimension of these group ties that is important in understanding Japan: vertical ties are said to be more important than in other industrialized nations, which is to say that links between superiors and subordinates are of extreme importance. And most of all, it is a bonding of pairs of junior and senior partners which is said to be important—the *kōhai-sempai* relationship. Horizontal links between people of equal rank in the group are certainly present, but in contrast to Western industrial nations, these horizontal relationships are less likely to bring people together in the absence of people with vertical relationships in the group, superiors. The boss, in other words, is more ever-present. A result of this is that vertically based conflicts within a group are comparatively rare, while horizontally based conflicts are not so rare.

Because of this vertical group structure there is greater need for sponsorship in Japan, to have a particular person of higher rank who will show the ropes to the subordinate, take care of the junior, speak for the junior person, and protect him. In return, the senior partner in the bond will receive loyalty and support from the junior partner. Both parties, therefore, have duties and responsibilities toward the other which are important for advancement and protection.

With these characteristics in mind, one of Japan's leading social scientists, Chie Nakane, argues that Japanese groups are formed through multiple inverted "Vs": that is, subordinates are more strongly tied upward with specific superordinates, who in turn are tied to specific superordinates, with the inverted "Vs" stacked one upon another all up and down the society.[66] As for another implication of this, attachments to individuals are more important than attachments to principles. That is, it is said that Japanese people are less likely to fight for principles—such as fairness, democracy, unjust exploitation by elites—which again makes protest groups weaker—but Japanese people more willing to support and even sacrifice for respected people even when they may agree that what these superiors do is wrong.

Critiques of this view charge that Japanese people socialize no less with co-workers of equal rank than in other countries, that there is identification with the common interests of co-workers, and that the worker versus manager line of conflict is as likely to occur in Japan as elsewhere. It seems, however, that most of the controversy has come because of overemphasis on the vertical nature of the Japanese group. Vertical groups are relatively more important in Japan, but horizontal ties certainly do exist, even if in somewhat weaker form. There is increasing evidence for this statement. Again we can turn to Lincoln and Kalleberg's study for empirical support. The Japanese in this study had more frequent interactions with superiors and less with equal co-workers compared to Americans, they were more likely to prefer help and advice from superiors, more likely to say their boss was involved in many aspects of their lives, and to say they liked it this way. In the United States, in addition to the contrast with all of the above, Americans more often said their jobs are more rewarding when their boss leaves them alone, and they preferred to interact much more with equal co-workers.[67]

Because of the nature of vertical groups in Japan, there is a tendency toward factions even within important groups. For example, Toshiba Electric may be very important to workers from this corporation, but the work group they form with their boss at the top is even more important. Likewise, a political party may be important, but the overall party and even principles the party stands for are less important than particular individuals to whom individual party members are strongly attached for sponsorship and protection. Thus, extended groups in Japan have a tendency to split and break apart and they contain important divisions which must be recognized in understanding the company, party, family, or nation as a whole. And, as we will explore more fully below, here lies an important stimulant to conflict in the Japanese society, which in contrast to the image many people have of Japan, is present in many forms.

Conformity

It is quite likely that more inaccuracies have been written about "conformity," "obedience," and "lack of conflict" in Japan than about any other subject. The Japanese have been described as "obedient ants." A recent French prime minister actually said, "The Japanese [are] ants imbued with a single-minded devotion to vanquish the Western world," and people who "blindly follow authorities."[68] One Japanese writer even claimed that Japan lacks "good novels" because "novelists need people [and] the problem for the Japanese novelist is that there is no general acknowledgement in his culture that noticeable personalities should be allowed to exist." During World War II, Robert J. Smith, an American writer, claimed that, "The Japanese are difficult to understand, not because they are complicated or strange, but because they are so simple . . . no conflict is felt to exist [among] them."[69]

Implied in the assumed Japanese characteristic of conformity is a lack of social conflict: the Japanese society is often seen by Westerners as orderly to the extreme, with everyone afraid to get out of line, producing the smooth labor-management relations which seem to come "naturally" for the Japanese.

Pressure to conform in Japan *is* great, but the pressure to conform is not as highly successful as usually thought in the West, nor does the conformity which does exist come easily, naturally, or without any unhappiness for Japanese people. And neither can it accurately be said there is no individuality, no personalities worthy of novels due to the blind conformity or lack of individual inner conflicts. This, in fact, is the real stuff of classic Japanese novels from the Meiji period and turn of the century. Most of the characters in the great novels of Sōseki, for example, are rebels—they defy authorities, they face inner conflict, and they struggle against the pressure to conform. In *Sore kara* (And Then . . .) the main character defies accepted tradition and morality in his personal life; in *The Miner* the main character rejects his rigid middle-class world and escapes to the dirty, dangerous, but for him, "free" world underground in the mines. In *Kōjin* (The Wayfarer) the main character struggles against conformity, and produces the famous line, "To die, to go mad, or to enter religion—these are the only three courses left open to me"; in *Mon* (The Gate) the main character defies the authority of his parents to marry for love and is rejected by friends and family.

The main point is that the theme of rebellion against society, parents, and others can be found throughout Japanese literature. Because the pressure on Japanese people to conform is great, the characters of Sōseki's novels (and those of others) frequently express a desire to rebel, but alas, the character usually "gets it" in the end, which also expresses an inner dread for Japanese people.

In contrast to the Western proverb stating that "the squeaky wheel gets the grease," the commonly heard Japanese saying is "the nail which sticks out gets pounded down." Psychotherapy in Japan is said to have the "chief aim [to] . . . reintegrate individuals into the family and their small part of the objective social world."[70] The point is that the pressure to conform is great, and it produces inner conflict, at times individual trauma, and is often resisted, otherwise so much effort to try to enforce conformity would be unnecessary. This is not the stuff of "ants." Another important characteristic of Japanese society is that outward appearances of conformity are quite often misleading. Authorities, including political and economic elites, must work hard to maintain a relatively conforming, obedient, or at least not openly rebellious population. How it is achieved must be considered in presenting a complete picture of who or what rules Japan, and how.

Group Conflict

Japanese history has been full of conflict, and not only the conflict of samurai armies, with one feudal lord against another or against the shogun. No, peasants have rebelled, workers have rebelled, students have rebelled, and the list can go on and on.[71] With respect to strikes and labor protests from the 1970s to the present Japan has recorded some of the lowest rates in the world, but a look through Japanese history, and especially since the 1860s, shows the present to be rather atypical.

The group nature of Japanese society and culture misleads people about conflict in Japan. Outsiders have often assumed that in a society where group attachments are very strong there will be little conflict. Especially in the case of Japan, the opposite can in fact be the case. Classic and contemporary social science theory and research show that a strong sense of "in-group" almost certainly produces an equally strong sense of "out-group."[72] In addition to the unacknowledged but humanly normal psychological tension resulting from attempts to assure obedience in Japan, a strong sense of in-group is also likely to produce conflict with the out-group. The main question is where are the lines between the in-group and out-group to be drawn?

Many scholars are now aware of the fact that Japan is atypical among Asian nations in the mixture of conflict and cooperation/order in the society. Equally atypical is that conflict in Japan can come and go at different levels within the society.[73] Thus, Toyota, Nissan, and Mazda can be in deadly competition with each other, while at the same time coming together for common corporate class or national interests. Try to visit a Mazda factory, for example. A background check is likely required to see some of the operations, not because they suspect CIA connections, but because they fear Toyota or Nissan connections. The city of Yoshi, near Mazda headquarters in Hiroshima, has a test track for development of new Mazda autos: at one time the windows of the hotels facing this track were blacked out to prevent easy access to Toyota or Nissan spies. At the same time, Mazda, Toyota, and Nissan executives are equally strong members of the most important big-business organization in Japan, Keidanren, working toward common interests of Japanese big business.

The reason for Japan's somewhat different mixture of order and conflict is in part attributable to the nature of Japanese rice agriculture. In the less centralized political system existing during the centuries of feudalism in Japan, while the shogun might have some influence on the national level, the local feudal domains and their overlords the daimyo, were in consistent conflict and competition.[74] The unity in Japanese history, in fact, has more often been stressed at the level of the patriarchal linage, the *ie*, and the local feudal domain, with conflict beyond these levels. National unity is rather recent in Japanese history. And finally, there is the contribution some scholars attribute to interpretations of Confucianism peculiar to Japan's history. Confucianism has not produced the same kind of rejection of conflict and competition found in some other Asian societies. This point will be considered more fully below.

THE ASIAN CONCEPT OF POWER

To understand the nature and power of elites in Japan, it is necessary at least briefly to consider the meaning of power in general before returning to Japan more specifically. The concept of power, according to some political scientists, such as Lucian Pye, is shaped by cultural definitions. The most important element of Asian culture influencing the image of power is the ideal of a benevolent, paternalistic leader, and the legitimacy of dependency for those below the elites.[75] Thus, it is said, ancient traditions and Asian religions, shaped by centuries of agricultural cooperation in most of Asia, have resulted in a relationship of obligation, duties, responsibilities, and mutual protection between leaders and followers. This relationship, of course, is broken from time to time, changes occur over the ages to alter some definitions of the obligations and responsibilities of both sides, and there have certainly been revolutions throughout Asian history to redefine the obligations, though more often than not these have been meant to strike back when old obligations have been violated. While the concept can be exaggerated, and all Asian nations are by no means identical, there *is* a different concept of power and the relationship between ruler and ruled throughout most of Asia.[76]

In addition to all of this, Pye states that power through most of Asian history has been a dimension of status or honor, something to be attained as a badge of respect rather than for other purposes, such as to promote specific policy goals, attain more wealth, or control people per se. In other words, power in Asia has been something to attain in its own right, simply for the status of having it, rather than for other, utilitarian goals. It is just here, however, where Japan is said to differ from many of its Asian neighbors. The concept of power in Japan has historically carried a more utilitarian component, it is to be used for something other than just the status of having it.[77]

This deviation of the Asian concept of power in Japan is combined with some other important Japanese features, including multiple levels of group attachments and authority, and a tradition of family divisions or splits. As noted above, there are in-groups and out-groups at various levels in Japan— the family, the work group, the corporation, the nation. This is in contrast to the more unified and all-powerful authority exclusively at the highest level found in most other Asian nations throughout history. These divisions of authority relations are related to the nature of Japanese feudalism and agriculture as already described, but also to differences in the *ie*, or extended family system in Japan. Compared to most other Asian nations, in Japan it has long been acceptable, even preferred, that new extended family lines break off from the main family, or *ie*, from time to time. A younger son, in contrast to the firstborn, who inherits control over the lands and possessions of the *ie*, can break from the *ie* to form a new family line, or *gosenzō*. Here is another mechanism promoting authority divisions, or the proliferation of subgroups in Japan, and a tradition of acceptable transfer of loyalty from one group to another.

We can now put these elements together for what they collectively mean for Japanese power: Japan's utilitarian concept of power and differing levels or divisions of authority relations help produce competition between the leadership of these differing groups to use their power for utilitarian purposes, often resulting in innovation and change. It is perhaps this situation which allowed new elites in Japan to open the country and industrialize during the Meiji Restoration in the late 1800s. But most importantly and in contrast to most other Asian nations, it is this feature which is said to be related to a greater sense of meritocracy in selecting and retaining Japanese elites. Power can be used for utilitarian purposes, and elites or would-be elites can be judged on objective criteria of success, and subgroups can compete to see whose leaders become elites. This situation may seem natural by Western ideals in industrialized nations, but it is actually rare in the history of human societies, and even more rare in many Asian nations.

There is a final, important aspect of the conceptualization of power in many Asian nations. As van Wolferen writes, "To put it simply: whereas power in the West is masked by the illusion of principle, in Japan it is masked by the illusion of benevolence."[78] The implication, of course, is that people can be dominated and exploited in the name of benevolence; there is a tradition of paternalism which can be manipulated to make people think what is good for elites is also good for the people. Pye, however, adds complexity to this idea:

Asian forms of nationalism, racial identity, and company loyalty constitute new forms of authoritarianism. They are new in the sense that they are built out of the complex personal bonding ties of superiors and subordinates, of patrons and clients—ties in which it is often obscure who is manipulating whom, and for what purpose.[79]

As anywhere else, in Japan there is much accuracy in the statement "power corrupts, and absolute power corrupts absolutely." But we must examine more carefully when and how power corrupts, despite complicating factors.

THE JAPANESE FAMILY SYSTEM

The family system, its forms and traditions, everywhere shapes many other aspects of a society. This is especially true in today's Japan where, as in other Asian nations, old family traditions have yet to be altered as much by modernization and industrialization as they have in the West. Again, however, it must be stressed that all Asian nations are certainly not identical with respect to their family traditions.

The image most Westerners have of the Asian family as male-dominated, extended to several generations and degrees of blood relationship, with extensive authority over all family members, and strong in-group unity is not so accurate. In some countries, such as Thailand, the family is not male-dominated and is rather more democratic. And as we have already seen in the case of Japan, while the *ie* is certainly an important unit of identity and authority, it is less extended than in other Asian nations due to the possibility of new families branching off from the original *ie* line. We can add that in Japan the father tends to be somewhat less dominant and in the modern era more warm and in recent decades personal with children. But there are other features of the traditional Japanese family which are of more concern for our subject of elites and elite formation.

In contrast to other Asian nations, it is said that the Japanese family is more of an economic unit and puts less emotional stress on blood relations. What this means is that Japanese family alliances, expansions, or additions for reasons of power, wealth, or whatever intent, are more possible.[80] One important example of this has already been briefly introduced in the first chapter. The practice of adopting an unrelated son into the household, especially after an arranged marriage to a daughter, is rather common among all classes in Japan. Most commonly, because of the male-dominated society today, families without a son will adopt their son-in-law, who then becomes a *yōshi*, with the full rights of inheritance of a biological first son. Among the higher classes in Japan such adoptions are even more common, not just in the case of families without sons, but also when other political or economic interests make such an adoption attractive.

Finally, with respect to elite families, there is the common problem of expanding wealth and power, or at least trying to prevent its decline through "unfortunate" marriage partners for sons and daughters. It is always nice for those involved when, say, a Rockefeller can marry a Du Pont or a Mellon rather than some "commoner." For the American upper class, however, this has always been something of a problem. As one upper class American put it, "the democratic whims of romantic love often play havoc with class solidarity."[81] Japanese elites have much less of a problem in this regard; there is a long tradition of what can be called arranged marriages in Japanese society, and this practice is still common, especially among the rich and powerful. But we must expand the description to avoid misconceptions and oversimplification.

It is not quite correct to call what commonly takes place in Japan today an "arranged marriage," and more than 60 to 70 percent of all Japanese young people today have *renai kekkon*, the standard Western ideal of a romantic love marriage, i.e., they find their own marriage partner. Still, about 30 to 40 percent of young Japanese find their marriage partner through what is called an *omiai*, which is a formal meeting between potential marriage partners arranged by a third party. The process involves, in sequence, inquiries by the third party matchmaker to both parties, exchange of pictures and résumés if there is initial interest, then a meeting between the potential couple and all of their family members. After this, if there is continued interest on both sides, a private detective agency is hired to check out the other family, and if mutual interest remains between the young people involved, they will begin dating, and very soon the assumption is that they are "engaged."[82] As this suggests, even the *miai kekkon*, or "arranged marriage," today seldom involves the old practice of many Asian nations where the young couple has no choice in the matter. However, Japanese people of all social levels are still more likely to view marriage as a rational arrangement for more than just love and sex.

It is important to point out, however, that the above applies most accurately to the average Japanese today. For elite families it is rather different. Among elite Japanese families, arranged marriage, with or without the consent of the young people involved, is more common.[83] It seems this is easier for parents in elite Japanese families, less plagued by "democratic whims of romantic love" because of Japanese traditions continuing, although weaker, in the form of *omiai*. From this tradition of marriage, then, come powerful family alliances and mergers creating what are called *keibatsu*.

APPEARANCES VS. REALITY, OR KEEPING FACE

Finally, it will be useful to bring up an issue which is not necessarily vital to understanding Japanese elites, but can help keep outsiders from misunderstanding Japanese society, or from being misled. It will be useful to begin with examples from recent research involving personal interviews with Japanese corporate executives and their German employees in thirty-one Japanese corporations with operations in Germany.[84]

To the surprise of many people, this research indicates that relations between Japanese managers and German employees are generally positive. In contrast to many countries with Japanese transplant corporations, including the United States and England, German workers have extensive protection through German labor laws and strong labor unions.[85] Thus, in Germany there is less conflict with Japanese managers over issues such as wages, working hours, and work organization. This also means that German workers are less likely to feel mistreated. If the Japanese do business in Germany, it is on terms highly influenced by German workers. However, the relationship between Germans and Japanese are not without problems. In the process of this research we heard again and again from Japanese executives that Germans are sometimes "rude, rather blunt, and at times arrogant." The Germans, on the other hand, often complained that the Japanese do not communicate well with them, do not give them straight answers, and sometimes do not tell them what they really mean or feel.

Most Japanese are anything but blunt, while Germans do have this stereotype even among other Westerners. Germans say it is better to be direct, to "get things out from the beginning," not to hide true feelings. Japanese, on the other hand, are taught to be subtle, indirect, or even hide true feelings when these true feelings can cause someone to "lose face" or create tensions. Some important Japanese concepts are related to these cultural differences: *omote*, meaning facade or false front; *tatemae*, meaning something like "the official version of events"; and *honne*, meaning basically "the blunt truth."[86] Japanese tradition suggests that it is not dishonest to give the *omote* or *tatemae* version of something or some situation if it can reduce conflict and help both parties "save face." This is not really what Westerners would consider a lie, though what some call a "white lie" is close in meaning. Also, among Japanese people themselves, clues may at the same time be given indicating that it is the *omote* or *tatemae* version. The understanding by both parties is something like, "I know I am not telling the truth, and I know the other person knows I know that I am not telling the truth," and thus both parties pretend in order to avoid conflict. To Germans, or anyone else not aware of the cultural differences, the situation can be maddening and can provoke quite a negative reaction. Conversely, of course, German "bluntness" can do the same thing to the Japanese.

The important point for research on Japan, and not only research by outsiders, is that things are not necessarily what they appear, or what is given by the *tatemae* version. This is by no means to say that research on controversial issues in Japan, such as elite dominance, is impossible. But it is to say that caution in taking first appearances or first impressions is in order.

CONCLUSION

Which brings us back to the introductory comments in this chapter. Japan has often seemed mysterious to Westerners in the past because these people didn't look deeply enough into the society, and/or were misled. Many Japanese themselves take pride in what they think are unique and "mysterious" aspects of Japan, and may tell outsiders that it will be impossible for them to understand Japan. There is a billion-dollar publishing industry developed around popular books on the subject of *Nihonjinron*—the study of the Japanese. Many claims in these books are wild: Japanese brains are different, Japanese stomachs will not allow them to digest Western beef, Japanese people do not use the same logic as Westerners when thinking. Other claims sometimes suggest that Japanese people are superior.[87]

In reaction to these extreme claims of Japanese "uniqueness" there is now division and debate among Japan scholars. The new side can roughly be described as the "Japan is not so unique crowd." In sometimes more politically charged terms, especially in the United States, these groups of Japan scholars overlap with what are often called the new "revisionists" versus "the chrysanthemum crowd." It is the "revisionists" who argue that Japan is not so unique, and that such arguments of uniqueness have been used by the Japanese and their supporters to obtain special treatment in relations with the United States, mainly with respect to economic relations.[88] They refer to the other side as the "chrysanthemum crowd" of "old Japan hands" who are "in love with the country," have overlooked Japan's "faults," and have been taken in through their "naïveté."[89]

We must agree with the "revisionists" that in the past most Japan scholars have missed many negative aspects of Japan. Yes, the Japanese heavily discriminate against Koreans, *burakumin* outcastes, aboriginal Ainu people, women, and others; yes, common practices of the Japanese police and criminal justice system in Japan would be unconstitutional in most Western societies. What is interesting and rather discouraging about Japan for Westerners, and especially Americans, is that much of what can be admired about Japan—such as low inequality, low unemployment, children who are able to score at the top of almost every international test of math and science skills, a very low crime rate, and a strong competitive economy—is often the product of basic features Westerners would not admire about Japan if they understood them.

It is certainly correct as well to say that the older Japan scholars from the West have missed the importance of power, conflict, and oppression in Japanese society. Things in Japan are not always so nice, with happy citizens supportive of everything, and always loyal because they agree with what is being done in their country or company. The lack of extensive overt conflict in Japan is often because people have little choice in the matter and protest is strongly suppressed.

Still, we are *not* necessarily suggesting that Japan is any worse with respect to much of this when compared to Western industrial nations, especially the United States; the mix of "good and bad" is simply different. Japan does have much less poverty, the Japanese robbery rate is more than one hundred fifty times less than the U.S. rate, and Japan at least provides jobs for its people—*and* at livable wages. We could go on and on, but the main point is this: often the "revisionists" go too far in the other direction because of political values—their political orientations push them to assume the U.S. is "good," while Japan represents the "bad." We hope that the reader will soon find that we have no illusions about either country.

Finally, to restate one of the main points of this chapter: power and conflict, among some other important characteristics, have been neglected by Japan scholars in the past. This is a key point because the subject of this book is primarily Japanese elites. Nevertheless, the "Japan is no different crowd" has often gone too far. Every nation has many differences when compared to others, and there is much evidence to indicate that Japan is somewhat more unique compared to other industrial nations, and even compared to other Asian nations. *But*, at the same time, these differences and unique characteristics found in Japanese society and culture must be viewed realistically and not overstated.

CHAPTER 3

From *Bakufu* to *Keiretsu*: The Making of the Japanese Upper Class

Before the end of World War II, the Mitsui family was the richest in Japan, indeed, one of the world's most wealthy. The eleven branches of this family owned major interests in at least 130 large corporations, including one of the largest banks, life insurance companies, mining companies, and a trading house, along with many industrial firms producing everything from ships and airplanes to steel and chemicals. The Mitsui holding company, Mitsui Gomei, was worth some one-half billion yen itself, and it controlled companies accounting for more than 1.6 billion yen. Along with Mitsui, three other *zaibatsu* family groups held 25 percent of *all* corporate assets in Japan. But the Mitsui family, by the end of the 1920s, was already the biggest *zaibatsu* of them all: they alone controlled 15 percent of all Japan's industrial assets.[90]

On October 8, 1945, two trucks under U.S. Army escort pulled up at the Mitsui headquarters in Tokyo. The drivers got out, and with the help of some Mitsui employees, loaded onto the trucks some forty-two wooden cases containing $281 million in Mitsui securities. Soon, the securities were gone, and with them the Mitsui *zaibatsu* which had dominated Japan's pre-war economy. About one year later, the new United States-backed Japanese Government placed an extensive tax upon the remaining wealth of the leading *zaibatsu* families. The head of the main Mitsui family at the time, Mitsui Hachirōemon, was forced to give up 91 percent of his remaining family wealth. He, along with the rest of the Mitsui clan, was never to dominate a company, let alone the country, again. Mitsui Hachirōemon used some of his remaining money to buy a little schoolhouse where he spent his last years running his own small kindergarten. And while he continued to have some property in Japan, Mitsui Hachirōemon's total income in 1970 was reported to have been $28,000. As for the future of the Mitsui family, "Younger members . . . have taken ordinary white-collar jobs (a few with Mitsui companies), apparently without receiving any special consideration or showing any special abilities. One occasionally meets a Mitsui in other Japanese business offices, but if they have any distinction it is as minor curiosities of yesteryear rather than as men of tomorrow."[91]

The history of the Mitsui family flows through some of the most dramatic changes in Japan over the period of 150 years since its forced opening to the outside world in 1852. It was a period of unprecedented economic development, collapse, and rebirth from the ashes to become the world's second largest economy. Rich *zaibatsu* families like the Mitsui, however, did not rise from the ashes; their wealth and power was gone. Out of the ashes a new type of upper class emerged, though remarkably little else about the economy and political system of Japan experienced much change when it was all sorted out and functioning once again.

Every society has particular historical forces shaping the present, making that society at least somewhat different from all others, despite pressures from industrialization and modernization for convergence. In understanding Japanese elites in particular, the country's centuries of relative isolation, feudal traditions, and especially the long, rigid control of the (Tokugawa) shogunate must be considered. But for the modern era, particular attention must be paid to how Japan began rapid industrialization during what is called the Meiji Restoration. The group of mostly samurai who took charge of this "restoration" from the 1860s helped form what became one of history's most powerful and wealthy collection of upper-class families, called *zaibatsu*. And though the major *zaibatsu* families did not retain their wealth and power after the war, the economic structure they helped create, and even some of their old companies, reemerged to lead Japan to even greater economic influence than before. It is the history of all this we must now consider at least briefly to understand the nature of the people and families who dominate Japan in the present.

THE LEGACY OF FEUDAL JAPAN

Most people are no doubt somewhat familiar with feudal Japan from novels and movies such as *Shogun*. Even before the 1600s depicted in the novel *Shogun*, Japan had a feudal system closer to that of preindustrial Europe than did any other Asian country. The economy was dominated by a landed aristocracy called daimyo, who owned most of the land, which was worked by landless peasants. The samurai were the "knights," or military men of high status who were attached to the daimyo for the protection and expansion of the daimyo clans. The shogun, in turn, was at the top of this system, ruling over the daimyo, with a government of retainers, and his own samurai, all together referred to as the *bakufu*. The emperor ruled in name only, and since the eighth century A.D. was more a figurehead in his Kyoto palace than a real ruler.

So it was this feudal system with a shogun and *bakufu* on top that the European colonizers, particularly the Dutch and Portuguese, found when reaching out to exploit Asia in the late sixteenth century. In the next 200 years these Europeans came to dominate all of the countries of East Asia and Southeast Asia except Thailand and Japan. It was the luck of geography which helped Thailand escape when the British, French, and Dutch agreed to leave old Siam nominally free so as not to fight over it as they closed in from all sides. Japanese rulers, however, took matters more into their own hands when they closed the country in the beginning of the 1600s. It was not only colonization they feared, but also disruption to a social order which kept merchants powerless. Too much trade with the West could have changed all of this by making the merchants more important and wealthy. With the exception of a small island off the coast of Nagasaki in southern Japan, foreigners were kept out, and ordinary Japanese themselves were not allowed to leave or have any contact with the outside.

The next 250 years brought a period of stability to Japan that had not been experienced for centuries. There was rule by one clan, the Tokugawa clan, with relatively few of the violent battles between various daimyo clans vying for power that had dominated Japan's history for several centuries before this time. Two aspects of the Tokugawa period are most important for an understanding of Japanese elites today. It was a time when Japan could maintain its racial and cultural homogeneity while forging the political unity and national identity so lacking before. It was also a time of rigid social order enforced in large part by a formal system of status ranking instituted by the Tokugawa shogunate.

Soon after taking power, Tokugawa Ieyasu established a system of social stratification in some ways not unlike the caste system of India. This *shi-nō-kō-shō* system of hierarchy created four primary status ranks, with the 266 daimyo families under the shogun and *bakufu*, followed by the samurai, peasants, and merchants in the lowest formal rank. The real bottom, however, was occupied by *burakumin* or *eta* outcastes, like the outcastes or untouchables of India, so "unclean" and despised that they had no formal position. Few individuals could move from their status position of birth, and many rituals and symbols of rank were required to be present at all times. Only samurai, and those above in rank for example, could wear silk as outer clothing, and only samurai could carry swords, which theoretically could be used on any peasant or merchant whenever individual samurai felt the lower orders were not showing proper respect. Only the merchants could carry on what the ruling class defined as the dirty job of commerce, while only the peasants could tend the fields. The samurai, no matter how poor they might become, could do neither.

All of this lasted, relatively stable and unchallenged, until the system began to deteriorate noticeably in the early 1800s. The problems were internal and relatively manageable at first, but then the Americans arrived in 1853 to thoroughly mess things up for the Tokugawa ruling elite.

THE RISE OF MERCHANTS, AND CRACKS IN THE TOKUGAWA ORDER

Toward the late 1700s, and certainly by the first few decades of the 1800s, strains in the feudal order came to be more pronounced. The reasons were varied—economic stagnation, increasingly extravagant spending by the shogunate, the expenses of maintaining a samurai class that served little function after 200 years of relative peace, and more and more taxes on peasants and lesser daimyo. In many ways it seemed a repeat of the years before the French Revolution of 1789. And like the French Revolution, the bellwether of coming trouble was indicated by a wave of peasant revolts around the turn of the new century—by some accounts over 1,000 such revolts.[92]

More directly related to our story of elites, however, was the charade of feudal pretence in the face of a new economic reality. By the early 1800s, Japan was not the backward society living in a time warp of the early middle ages it has been previously assumed.[93] There was more and more economic activity outside of agriculture, and even some industrialization. But more than anything, what made the feudal order and the *shi-nō-kō-shō* system of ranking a facade was the wealth of the merchant class by the first decades of the 1800s. By some accounts, the merchant class held 95 percent of wealth in Japan by the mid-1800s. Though low in status (only the untouchable *burakumin* were lower) the merchant class was free to engage in all kinds of non-agricultural economic activity. The daimyo and samurai, on the other hand, were prevented from doing so by the Tokugawa status order. Thus, while the peasants were harmed more and more by economic stagnation, rising rents, and higher taxes, the upper classes were going deeply into debt to the merchant class in an emerging post-agricultural economy. The merchants had no political power, nor could they wear silk, have family names, carry swords, or engage in many activities reserved for the higher classes: but they were getting very rich.

From the earliest sociological works we know that humans generally strive for three things in the community—economic gain, political influence, and what can simply be call prestige, or status-honor.[94] Likewise, people and families in all societies are commonly ranked with respect to economic standing, political clout, and status-honor. And in most places and times in human societies, the three dimensions of rank have tended to overlap or converge: that is to say, the people with wealth tend to have extensive political influence and high status. It is uncommon for the three dimensions of hierarchy to diverge as radically as they did in mid-nineteenth century Japan, but when they do there are inevitable strains and tensions setting the stage for dramatic change in the social order. In other words, when those with all the political power and formal status are broke and completely in debt to a politically powerless class looked down upon by everyone except outcastes, something is going to happen. Such was the situation when Admiral Perry steamed into Tokyo Bay in 1853 with orders from the president of the United States to open the country to American ships seeking trade and safe harbor.

It will be helpful to step back in time to the origins of the Mitsui clan that fell in shambles with the social collapse and change following World War II. Most of the *zaibatsu* families of the early twentieth century were relatively new among the rich. But a few, primarily the Mitsui and Sumitomo families, had roots among the wealthy merchants who emerged during the Tokugawa period. We can therefore better understand the transition from Tokugawa Japan and the next stage of Japanese development through a brief look at the early experiences of this most important *zaibatsu* clan.

THE HOUSE OF MITSUI

Family records indicate that the Mitsui clan held samurai status as far back as the 1400s. However, the family business began in 1616 when the family head, Mitsui Sokubei, returned from a trip to Edo (Tokyo) where he saw the growing material wealth of the city and some Japanese merchants. Gathering the family before the clan shrine in Ise, he explained to them and the souls of their ancestors: "A great peace is at hand. . . . The shogun rules firmly and with justice at Edo. No more shall we have to live by the sword. I have seen that great profit can be made honorably. I shall brew sake and soy sauce, and we shall prosper."[95] With that prophetic vision, Mitsui Sokubei took the remarkable step of giving up the honor of samurai status which prevented any merchant activity: the House of Mitsui had begun.

Things turned out as Sokubei foresaw, except that it was not he who achieved the first real success in business activities. Sokubei's cultured samurai education made him fit for poetry and calligraphy, but "he was clumsy with figures and even worse at drumming up trade."[96] With his early death, the business was saved by his wife, Shuho, the daughter of a successful merchant, who also saw to it that their sons received good training from other merchants. It was the eldest son, Hachirōbei, who really started the business empire which came to dominate Japan's economy in the early twentieth century.

Mitsui business activities became much more prosperous in the second half of the 1600s, especially after Hachirōbei was able to build connections to the Tokugawa government, helped considerably by their former samurai status. By the end of the 1600s, the Mitsui enterprises included an appointment as merchant supplier to the military government and permission to engage in a crude form of banking previously nonexistent in Japan.

Hachirōbei's legacy, however, was most important for the innovative family enterprise group that he created. He allowed his sons to engage in their own business activities with his financial backing, but they had to agree to pool family funds for common needs, and accept only a limited salary for themselves. After Hachirōbei's death, his will established the basis of a formal family constitution in 1722 which spelled out rules and obligations for the family business empire. This Mitsui family constitution remained very much in effect and unaltered until the realities of industrialization forced a revision in 1900, and the Occupation finally disbanded the *zaibatsu* and outlawed such family constitutions in 1945.

From the early 1700s, the Tokugawa years were generally good for the Mitsui clan, until the strains and conflicts of Tokugawa decline in the nineteenth century became inescapable. Like many other merchants, by the early 1860s the House of Mitsui was almost broke. There were more restrictions on commerce and increasing demands for tax payments and new loans by the faltering Tokugawa government, which they seldom repaid. It was at this time that the Mitsui clan hired a non-family business manager, Minomura, who saved them through shrewd deals with all sides in the coming revolution.

Through Minomura's connections to the Tokugawa leaders a deal was made by which the House of Mitsui would in effect become the government's banking house, which also gave the government a stake in reversing the Mitsui decline because of high taxes and forced loans. But while Minomura was dealing with Tokugawa Government leaders, Mitsui family members and employees were forming strong ties with the Satsuma-Chōshū rebels, and giving them money—*lots* of money. These ties paid off handsomely: with the rebellion successful after 1868, Mitsui again became a semi-official government banking house, now for the new Meiji government, and was extremely well positioned for many government favors in the coming drive for industrialization which was directed by this new Meiji government. By the late 1920s the Mitsui clan was valued at more than 1.5 billion yen, and the Mitsui *zaibatsu* included 130 major corporations, making it more than double the size of second place Mitsubishi.

There was a familiar pattern in the crisis years of the 1930s. While the Mitsui clan was not in favor of the war with China that eventually brought Japan into war with the United States, they eventually went along with the increasingly military-dominated government. With mounting rightist movements in the 1920s and 1930s against the increasing inequality and Western orientation of Japan, the *zaibatsu* families and corporations were common targets. For example, Baron Dan, the head of the huge Mitsui Trading

Company, was assassinated by rightists in 1932. But at the same time, Mitsui family members and employees were secretly building ties with the rightist groups and offering them cash. This again served Mitsui well when the military came more fully to dominate the Japanese government. The government's wars called for more military production, and their conquests, especially in the puppet state of Manchukuo in Northern China, created many new investment opportunities. While others, especially some "new *zaibatsu*" such as Nissan, were actually more favored by the military government, in the eyes of many people, the leading *zaibatsu* such as Mitsui came to be strongly identified with the military and war devastation. Such perceptions helped bring about the end of these dominant *zaibatsu* clans.

THE MEIJI RESTORATION AND A NEW UPPER CLASS

In 1868, when the rebellious army from the Satsuma and Chōshū regions of Japan marched into what is now Tokyo, the revolution, or what is called the Meiji Restoration, had finally come. In the typical pattern for political elites new and old, there was a call for popular legitimation through political symbols and national images. In this case the neglected emperor system was used. What was in effect a relatively bloodless, top-down revolution made by one faction of the samurai class came to be called a restoration when the emperor was brought from political isolation in the old capital of Kyoto to the new capital in Edo, renamed Tokyo.

A primary concern of the new Meiji Government was the threat of either European or American colonization and economic exploitation. Indeed, this had been a major issue bringing about the fall of the Tokugawa shogunate in the first place. The new *genrō*, as the revolutionary leaders behind the new government were called, wanted industrialization, and they wanted it fast. As they correctly ascertained, only a powerful economy and military of their own would bring them security and equal treatment with the Western powers. To achieve this modernization and industrialization they eliminated most of the old feudal institutions: for example, land was taken from the daimyo, the samurai lost all of their rights and privileges, and anyone who so chose could involve themselves in commerce. Then they went about creating new institutions.

In effect, a kind of forced industrialization and modernization took place, all orchestrated by the new government, which has since been described as a "capitalist development state."[97] They first sent many of their best and brightest to Europe to study the institutions of the West, and these emissaries later reported back what might best work for Japan. (They especially liked and copied many aspects of Bismarck's Germany.) They then set about to create a capitalist industrial economy—the first attempt at that time by a state to create a capitalist economy, skipping many stages of the more gradual development which had occurred in the West.

It was this state-sponsored capitalism which also established a new upper class for Japan. This new upper class was a capitalist upper class, to be sure, but it was also one with many different features due to Japanese traditions, late economic development, and state-sponsored capitalism. Though among the biggest, the houses of Mitsui and Sumitomo were in some ways untypical. Most of the new capitalist upper-class families and their *zaibatsu* corporate groupings did not predate the Meiji Restoration. Consideration, therefore, of how and in what form modernization and industrialization was carried out during the Meiji period is necessary to understand the nature, organization, and power of the new upper class that was created as part of the process of modernization.

RISE OF THE *ZAIBATSU*

In his detailed study of the *zaibatsu*, Morikawa refers to the largest and most successful as "political merchants."[98] All of the big *zaibatsu* houses in one way or another developed and grew through sponsorship and protection by the political elites. In some cases the government granted them exclusive rights to certain economic activity, as with Mitsui's first role as banker to the new government. In other cases the new government started its own industries, especially when it was judged that these industries were most important for rapid industrialization. As the government was rather unskilled in this activity, however, the government-run industries usually did not operate efficiently, and were soon sold. Few Japanese, of course, had the money or access to government loans for such purchases, but some of the old merchant families had enough money, as did many former daimyo and samurai who were given government compensation after losing their old positions. Thus, through *very* low cost deals on struggling government companies, then more government protection, others were added to the list of wealthy *zaibatsu* families.

Along with Mitsui, other powerful *zaibatsu* who emerged in the Meiji period as "political merchants" included Yasuda, Ōkura, Fujita, Iwasaki, Sumitomo, Furukawa, and Asano.

Like Mitsui, though without the long merchant traditions, the Yasuda *zaibatsu* was started by Yasuda Zenjirō as a privileged purveyor of financial services to the new government. He was of poor, lower samurai background when he moved to Tokyo in 1863 to learn the trade of a "moneychanger," soon becoming quite good at it and using political connections to expand his business.[99]

The Ōkura family fortune was started just before the Meiji Restoration through selling guns to all factions in the political conflicts of the time. It was with this money and government sponsorship that the founder of the Ōkura *zaibatsu*, Ōkura Kihachirō, from a poor peasant family, traveled through Europe after the Meiji Restoration to study business practices before setting up a successful trading company.

The founder of the Fujita *zaibatsu*, Fujita Denzaburō, came from a family who brewed sake and soy sauce, and in 1869 he started a company in Osaka selling goods to the new government. He was later able to use his government connections to win large contracts for civil engineering works.

The Mitsubishi *zaibatsu* was founded by Iwasaki Yatarō who came from lower samurai origins. His fortunes, and the root activities of his *zaibatsu*, came from a government-sponsored shipping line, and later shipbuilding.

Three of the other most powerful *zaibatsu* centered their economic activities in mining. The Sumitomo *zaibatsu* developed from one of the other very old merchant houses, but unlike Mitsui, their wealth was in copper mining long before the Meiji period. The founder of the Furukawa *zaibatsu*, Furukawa Ichibei, got his start as a manager of an Ono family store, and then used his connections and managerial skills to get into the copper business when the House of Ono collapsed after 1874. And in one of the most interesting cases, the Asano *zaibatsu* was started by a poor street vender, Asano Sōichirō, who began by selling coke for fuel, later expanding it into a coal and oil empire.

What was, in effect, made by political elites at first was not always firmly controlled by political elites, however. Later, it became a question of how much power the *zaibatsu* developed over the government. A key to the success of these huge *zaibatsu* corporations was gradual independence from the government: none of the first big corporate groups unable to shake off government dependency made it to large *zaibatsu* status.[100]

It is not exactly clear how much political power these *zaibatsu* families had, but it was no doubt extensive after the turn of the century. After the earliest years of the Meiji period there was a slow process of becoming *slightly* more democratic. After the constitution of 1890 was promulgated, early political elites (the *genrō*) began to die off, and political parties became increasingly important. These political parties, however, came to be dominated by the largest *zaibatsu* corporations after the turn of the century, with large *zaibatsu* often in control of "their own" political parties. Even with political policy and the administration of government programs dominated by bureaucrats, especially from the late 1920s, this new situation gave the *zaibatsu* extensive political influence.

There is an important point to be made with respect to the pre-war political influence of *zaibatsu* and later corporate elites from the post-war *keiretsu* groups: with greater division between major *zaibatsu* houses, with some dominating their own separate political parties, the *zaibatsu* were less united and likewise less able to take much coordinated political action toward their common class interests. Had this not been the case it is possible that World War II could have been avoided, or at least been quite different in its nature, as the major *zaibatsu* families and their corporate managers wanted to avoid war. The following chapters expand upon this point to consider how the new corporate elite in control of the new *keiretsu* are more politically influential, and the effects of this influence.

Zaibatsu Wealth and Corporate Control

Great wealth and stock ownership does not always mean control of corporations, and certainly not always the day-to-day management of corporations. It has commonly been assumed that because the old *zaibatsu* families were so wealthy and held the most stock in their corporations that they were comparable to first generations of Rockefellers, Mellons, and Morgans in the United States who took active control of their companies and guided them to their dominant positions in the world economy. But a curious thing happened to most of the biggest *zaibatsu* families about ten to twenty-five years into the new century: they lost much of their active control over the economy *and* their own corporations. In what has been called the "Buddenbrooks effect" in reference to the Buddenbrooks family decline in Thomas Mann's famous novel, the succeeding generations of the famous *zaibatsu* founders often lost drive, lost interest, or were less than competent business managers.

In many cases the *zaibatsu* realized what was happening and recruited specifically talented men to marry their daughters, in some cases then also officially adopting the young men as sons (*yōshi*). For example, there was Shiraishi Motojirō of the Asano *zaibatsu*: when Shiraishi graduated from the Tokyo University Faculty of Law in 1892 he was immediately hired by the head of the Asano *zaibatsu*, Asano Shōichirō, and made manager of the petroleum division. He was then married to the second daughter of Asano Sōichirō in 1895 and later moved to top management of the *zaibatsu* as a whole. There was also Iomi Teiichi who graduated from the Tokyo University Faculty of Law at the same time as Shiraishi in 1892. He was hired by the Yasuda Bank, and by 1897 was married to Yasuda Zenjirō's second daughter and became a *yōshi* when adopted as a son, taking the new name Yasuda Zenzaburō. And for a last example, there was Motoyama Hikoichi who left the Ministry of Finance to become a newspaper editor, later joining the Fujita *zaibatsu* in 1886. In only two years it was arranged that he become married to the eldest daughter of Kuhara Shozaburō, brother of founder Fujita Zenzaburō, and later top manager of the *zaibatsu*.[101] Few families, however, could continue this method of recruitment consistently, and more typically Western methods of recruiting top managers from outside the family became also common.

The Mitsui *zaibatsu* was perhaps extreme, but not completely untypical of the top *zaibatsu* families. As one biographer of the Mitsui dynasty put it, "In general . . . the Mitsuis were an average lot, and even at their best were hopelessly outclassed by their hired executives, carefully selected from among the most brilliant businessmen of the times."[102] Already by 1871, Minomura, the hired manager of the Mitsui *zaibatsu* brought in during economic difficulties, was telling the Mitsui family they must become better educated and start out at the bottom of company operations to learn their job if the family was going to keep the *zaibatsu* from falling. Then, in 1875, with more economic difficulties, one of the founding political leaders of Meiji Japan, Inoue, called the main Mitsui family heads to his office in Tokyo to demand that they give more authority to their competent managers.[103] From that time onward the Mitsui family became less and less active in running their *zaibatsu* corporations.

There were exceptions, and one of the biggest was the Mitsubishi *zaibatsu*, which continued to be actively run by members of the founding Iwasaki family up through World War II. The exception can be described by the case of the president of Mitsubishi, Ltd., from 1916 to 1945. Iwasaki Koyata was graduated from the Tokyo University Faculty of Law, after which he went on to England, where he took a graduate degree from Cambridge.

The exceptional case of Mitsubishi is indicated in recent research on the top ten *zaibatsu* by Morikawa Hidemasa.[104] Through extensive examination of corporate histories, board meetings, government interventions, and such, Morikawa found that the Mitsui family were the first to lose extensive control of their *zaibatsu* by a change in corporate organization in 1912. The other top *zaibatsu*, in varying degrees, and with Mitsubishi at the other extreme, lost most of their control soon afterward.

This process, then, opened up the top managerial circles in Japan to new talent. To be sure, the new managers did not move up from the bottom of the society. Two-thirds of the active managers of the top ten *zaibatsu* in the early 1900s were from samurai backgrounds, and three-fifths had come from beginning careers in the government ministries, with the same percentage having some experience in Europe. They were also a remarkably young group, half under forty years of age, which defies the current situation of a highly age-ranked corporate Japan.[105]

These were men such as Mitsui's Nakamigawa Hikojirō, who graduated from the elite Keiō University, then spent four years studying in London where he met the famous Inoue (the George Washington and Thomas Jefferson of modern Japan), who later asked Nakamigawa to join him at the ministries of industry and foreign affairs. When Mitsui got in trouble and the *genrō* political elite stepped in, it was Nakamigawa who took over Mitsui Bank.

Shōda Heigorō presents another typical case of a young man moving into the top. Born into the family of a Confucian scholar, he also graduated from Keiō University and studied in England before being promoted rapidly into a top executive position at Mitsubishi. Suzuki Masaya presents yet another case. Of samurai background, he graduated from Tokyo University, then moved to government service first in the Ministry of Foreign Affairs, then to the Bank of Japan before taking a top executive position with Sumitomo.

But it must be clear that none of this means the *zaibatsu* families at the time lost their wealth. On the contrary, the wealth of most of the *zaibatsu* families continued to grow. The Mitsui, for example, were far richer by the 1920s and 1930s than they ever had been. In fact, it was not until the late 1920s, with their corporations in control of hired managers, that the Mitsui family took over the top position of wealth in Japan, a position the family kept until the end of the war.

What these talented young men did was to take over management of the Japanese *zaibatsu* in the name of the rich families, protecting and expanding the profits of these families, while, of course, taking a substantial amount for themselves in salaries. The hired managers of the *zaibatsu* corporations allowed most of the *zaibatsu* rich to become a leisure class concerned with their art collections, their garden parties, and their place in the status pecking order, especially when it came to the marriage prospects of their sons and daughters.

A EUROPEAN-STYLE PEERAGE FOR JAPAN: THE STATUS ORDER LOST . . . AND REGAINED

The United States, of course, never established a formal system of titled nobility like the one American "founding fathers" had left behind in Europe, though some of the founding fathers were in favor of doing so.[106] As the Frenchman Alexis de Tocqueville observed to his surprise while visiting the United States in the 1830s, there was more equality of status and informality in social interaction than he had ever seen in Europe.[107] The mood of the American masses, and the pretense of greater democracy, would not allow a formal peerage of noble rankings to be transported to the "New World." American elites had to settle for an unofficial and even semi-hidden status order with "blue books," social clubs, and private school connections—which, in fact, turned out to serve many of the functions of a peerage system quite well.[108]

With the fall of the Tokugawa shogunate in 1868, the new Meiji government elites set about modernizing the country's institutions and discarding as much of the old feudal system as they could. Official feudal privileges and titles given to daimyo lords and samurai were among the first to go, by 1869.[109] Considering Japanese traditions of family ranking and cliques, however, it was perhaps inevitable that some type of status hierarchy would reemerge, informally if not formally. There has always been pressure in Japan to seek protection within an exclusive group, and the family has always been a central means of doing so. As we saw in the previous chapter, there also had been a long tradition of arranged marriages among the Japanese upper class, a tradition that would be most difficult to continue if the actual family status of potential marriage partners was ambiguous.

For the Japanese, therefore, the absence of a formal system of status ranking after 1869 seems to have created an intolerable void. Never mind that what existed before the end of the Tokugawa shogunate was a facade—at least everyone knew his or her place in the status order. In contrast to the American elite, with loss of their feudal titles the Japanese elites were not content to leave such an unofficial and ambiguous mess. They soon created a new, official, government-sanctioned system of ranking, complete with formal titles. Or rather than create a new one, we should say that after spending time studying what Europe had to offer a modernizing country, the new Japanese elites decided they were rather fond of the Prussian system of peerage. It seems the new elite liked the ring of "marquis, count, viscount, and baron."

The new German-style peerage, called *gōtōjo no gyōkeibun*, was formally instituted by the Japanese government in 1884.[110] The royal family, of course, was on top, followed by five major ranks (in descending order of importance): *koshaku* (duke), *kōshaku* (marquis), *hakushaku* (count), *shishaku* (viscount), and *danshaku* (baron). In all, there were about 500 family heads to receive a title, with most of these at the lower levels of viscount or baron, which had increased to about 900 by 1948. The pre-Meiji position of a family was considered when giving out these titles, but was not the determining factor. As it turned out, the new political elites who took power in the Meiji Restoration acquired many of the top ranks in the peerage system, which means they gave the titles to themselves, along with the former daimyo lords and samurai. The wealthy merchants who were developing the powerful *zaibatsu* corporations, such as the Mitsui and Sumitomo families, received the lowest titles, which did not make them exceptionally happy.[111] Over the years before World War II, however, these *zaibatsu* families were able to move up in the peerage through strategic marriage arrangements with those having higher rank but much less money.

The peerage system formalized in 1884 must not be seen as merely a boost to the egos of the rich and powerful, it had important functions for upper class organization in industrializing Japan. As depicted in personal biographies and novels about the period—such as the tetralogy describing the changing fortunes of Japan from 1912 to the 1960s, *The Sea of Fertility* by Mishima Yukio—these peerage titles were not just important forms of address, but also a means of organizing social interaction.[112] And, of course, when the new constitution of 1890 established a two-house system of representation based upon those of contemporary England and Germany, the peerage system was handy for filling the newly created equivalent of the House of Lords, again giving those in the upper classes a tremendous advantage.

Perhaps most important, however, the peerage system recreated a status hierarchy of interlocked families, a means of creating an in-group and out-group, defining who was acceptable for many types of social interaction, club membership, or private school attendance, as well as a means of forming alliances and unity among the most powerful families in the newly industrializing Japan. There was again a means of defining acceptable marriage partners for children of the elite through arranged marriages that could create new bonds among those with wealth and political, or economic, power. Less research has been done on this subject in Japan than in Europe and the United States, but it is quite likely that in Japan as well the upper-class status ranking system helped create a unity of purpose, a common worldview, and thus the ability to take some unified action on common interests, something which is often much more difficult to do in the lower classes.

Much like the informal upper-class family status circles in the United States during the same period, the more formal Japanese system was not a completely closed system. While it was difficult to do so, people could move into the higher status circles. Most importantly, the family trying to break into the higher circles through marriage needed to have the proper background, the right education, respectability, and of course, wealth and power might help. But as in the United States, new wealth was suspect: it took a second or third generation after the fortune was made before the family could break into the higher social circles, as it did, for example, with the subsequent generations of the Rockefellers and Kennedys. The first *zaibatsu* families in Japan—such as the Mitsui, Sumitomo, Iwasaki, and Yasuda—started out in the accepted higher status circles, though in the lower peerage. Later, in the next generations, through strategic marriages they tended to move into the higher peerage ranks.

By the 1920s and 1930s there were *shinkō-zaibatsu* or "new *zaibatsu*" corporate families emerging in Japan with wealth and power, in some cases with more wealth and power than the original *zaibatsu* families. However, these "new *zaibatsu*" families—such as Matsukata (Kawasaki corporations), Nomura (mostly financial firms), Iwai (steel and other heavy production), Suzuki (imports), and Aikawa (Nissan)—were much like their American counterparts among the new rich a few decades ago. They were not easily accepted in the old upper-class social circles. New money is somehow suspect, and the new rich were still like the "crude Texas millionaires" whom the old rich would like to keep at a distance, especially when it came to marriage.[113]

NOMURA: A NEW *ZAIBATSU*

Today, Nomura Securities is the biggest stockbrokerage in the world, accounting for about 20 percent of all stock traded in Japan. Among the many Nomura-affiliated companies is Nippon Life Insurance, whose chairman, Hirose Gen, appeared in Chapter 1. Nippon Life is also one of the world's biggest life insurance companies and with control of about 3 percent of all Japanese corporate stock, controls more stock in other Japanese corporations than any other firm or family.[114] But the house of Nomura was a relatively late developer, providing us with an example of the new *zaibatsu* becoming ever more important to Japan's economy in the 1920s and 1930s. Like Nomura, these new *zaibatsu* were often more acceptable to the new military government, were increasingly more wealthy than many of the old *zaibatsu*, and were involved in the newer industries and financial arrangements of the comparatively more mature Japanese economy.

The Nomura family fortune was started by Nomura Tokushichi, born in 1850 to a samurai father and servant girl. Tokushichi's father gave him to a wealthy landowner at an early age, who then assigned him as an apprentice to an Osaka money changer. This Osaka merchant family had been moderately wealthy since the 1600s through speculation in something similar to a futures market for rice, then later as a moneylender, much like some of the early Mitsui family members.

At the beginning of the Meiji period, Nomura Tokushichi inherited the money changer's business, but did little to take advantage of new opportunities opening in Japan at the time. As sake consumption became more of his aim in life, his wife took over operation of the business and saw to it that their oldest son acquired the knowledge and experience needed to run the business in future years.

Nomura Tokushichi II (earlier named Shinnosuki) took over his father's business in 1904, becoming more involved in the new Japanese stock market that had been established in 1878, the year of his birth. Especially at the turn of the century, and to some extent even today, Japanese people regarded the stock market as a form of gambling to be ignored by respectable merchants. But Nomura II had no such reservations, and during the 1905 war with Russia he expanded his investments in the stock market just in time for the great bull market in 1906. He then began speculating on a sharp decline in the market, which happened in 1907, allowing him to make $60 million at the age of 28.

After making an even greater fortune in the stock market during World War I, Nomura II began to copy the business expansion into many other types of industries made earlier by the original *zaibatsu* families. And by the 1930s, Nomura became one of the most important companies taking up the military government's offers to expand into new Japanese territories in Asia for Japanese expansion and to support military operations.

By this time Nomura II was as wealthy, and his corporate operations as big, as many of the established *zaibatsu*, but he was never fully accepted by them. "All his adult life he struggled to gain the social and commercial recognition he felt he deserved." It was never to be: he "was branded an 'arriviste' by the *zaibatsu* clans, a man who had climbed to wealth during World War I with blood money made through the stock market."[115] Nomura II died of a heart attack in 1945 as Japan was losing the war, and many of his employees were killed and his property destroyed. His son, Yoshitarō, died shortly afterward of a heart attack, on August 24, the day MacArthur landed in Japan.

AND THE MASSES GET POORER

While the old and new *zaibatsu* were becoming fabulously rich in the first half of the twentieth century, the majority of other Japanese were doing rather badly. Around 93 percent of Japanese households in the mid-1930s lived on an average of $166 a year. About 50 percent of the population lived on approximately $110 a year or less. Even in the most profitable of the *zaibatsu* corporations, the gap between the top management and new workers was something like 100 to one in the mid-1930s, compared to around seven to one today. As might be expected from all of this, in a country which today has the highest life expectancy in the world, during the mid-1930s life expectancy was less than 50 years.[116]

At the other end of the hierarchy, the top 100 families had incomes which accounted for some 16 percent of all corporate profits. About 10 percent of all annual income during the 1930s went to .001 percent of the Japanese population. After the emperor, the top income earner was Baron Sumitomo Kichizaemon, with about 20 million yen, or about $5.6 million given the exchange rate at the time. The heads of the eleven Mitsui families had a combined yearly income of 30 million yen per year.

It can accurately be said that rapid industrialization in Japan was in large measure achieved through labor and peasant exploitation.[117] For the urban working class, jobs were low-paying, dangerous, and certainly not "lifetime," as made famous in post-war Japan. In 1911, for example, investigations showed the average wage to be about twenty yen a month, which was also the official poverty line at the time. Japan's new factories had accident rates which were among the highest in the world. Average length of employment was only twenty-two months.[118] And in many urban industries most workers were young girls, in effect sold to the factory owners by their peasant parents who could not afford to care for them. But these were the lucky girls. Many thousands more were sold into prostitution by parents who preferred not to see them starve.[119]

In the countryside things were much worse. Already by the 1880s peasants were losing their land in the hundreds of thousands every year. In 1872, only 29 percent of agricultural land was worked by peasants who owned no land; by 1890 the figure had gone up to over 40 percent. The main problem was high taxes to help pay for the government expansion into new industries, which of course were soon sold off to the emerging *zaibatsu* families at below cost.[120]

Despite the image of passive Japanese accepting authority and adversity with restraint, the poor masses often rebelled in these early years of Japanese industrialization. In 1873, for example, 300,000 poor people rioted in Fukuoka, "incensed by the high prices they believed to be caused by wealthy merchants hoarding rice."[121] There were large rice riots in 1918, and the number of tenant disputes in the countryside stayed at around 100,000 or more per year from 1921 until 1935.

In the cities, however, repression was a bit more successful in preventing strikes and unionization. In the early years of industrialization, around the turn of the century until 1920, half or more of urban laborers were young women and children. Neither had much opportunity to rebel, strike, or join unions. Because many of the young women were "bought" from their parents in the countryside, they would simply be sent back, with payment returned by the parents, and replaced by other young girls.[122] By the 1920s and 1930s, however, with more heavy industry accounting for the nation's GNP, men began to make up more and more of the urban labor force: labor repression began in earnest. Any and all kinds of threats and violence against workers were employed by corporate managers, often with their own little private armies. In pre-war Japan, unionization never reached above 7 percent of the work force.[123]

DESTRUCTION, DEFEAT, AND . . . A LITTLE REFORM

The two U.S. Army trucks that stopped at the Mitsui headquarters on October 8, 1945, proceeded on to the Mitsubishi headquarters where they picked up securities worth another fifty million yen. Less than two months after the war's end, other trucks had visited more *zaibatsu* headquarters for the same purpose. As a biographer of the Mitsui clan put it, "The great American crusade against monopoly had begun with a bang."[124]

The United States had taken control of Japan under the Supreme Commander for the Allied Powers (SCAP), General Douglas MacArthur, who was to dominate the country until 1952. Almost everything of importance done by the new Japanese government until that time had to be approved by SCAP. In none of the other defeated countries after World War II was such extensive control exercised. And with the U.S. Occupation forces and MacArthur in control of Japan, it can accurately be said that dramatic changes occurred—but then again, little changed.

Some Key Changes . . .

Among the most dramatic changes was the collapse of the *zaibatsu* empires: the largest *zaibatsu* families lost the vast majority of their wealth, which was never to be regained. Specifically, action was initiated in September of 1945 to impound all corporate stock held by the five largest *zaibatsu* families: Mitsui, Mitsubishi, Sumitomo, Yasuda, and Fuji. In March of 1947, the assets of fifty-six people from the ten largest *zaibatsu* families were frozen and their corporate stock also taken. Then, in 1948, the "Law for the Termination of Zaibatsu" was forced through the new Diet which further formalized confiscation of corporate stock from these *zaibatsu* families, and provided relatively minor compensation in the form of government bonds. These bonds, however, could not be cashed for ten years, at which time they were worth almost nothing due to inflation.[125] The companies once controlled by these *zaibatsu* families were divided into smaller ones, and use of the old *zaibatsu* names was forbidden. The huge Mitsui Trading Company (Mitsui Bussan), for example, was cut into 170 companies by SCAP.

Also, rather dramatically, Japan's old constitution was thrown out, replaced by a totally new one, written in English by a small group of Americans selected by MacArthur. This new constitution allowed all adults to vote (no women could vote before), stated complete legal equality between the sexes (though did not enforce it), and included the famous Article 9 "forever denouncing war." Labor unions were encouraged, sparking an explosion of labor activism. The Socialist Party was the first to win a majority in the new Diet, and selected a socialist prime minister. Land redistribution was carried out to reverse the terrible conditions which had obtained for rural people since the beginning of industrialization, and it was strikingly effective. While only 54 percent of the land was worked by peasant owners in 1947, after land reform measures came into effect in 1950, 90 percent of all agricultural land was worked by peasants who owned their own land.[126]

Finally, on top of all of this humiliation for the Japanese upper class, they also lost their titles: the peerage system instituted during the Meiji period to replace old feudal status ranks was eliminated. No longer was it Baron Mitsui, or Prince Konoe, or Viscount Iwakura, it was all gone, and legally they were commoners once again.

. . . But More Continuities

Behind all of this change, however, there was much more that was not changed, or was soon reestablished. Among the most important, the government bureaucracy and top officials running this bureaucracy before the war actually carried on much as before.[127] The SCAP did not seem to realize the importance of the bureaucracy, and in fact inadvertently made the bureaucratic elites stronger by purging key pre-war politicians, thus weakening the legislative branch of government that might have acted as a counter bureaucratic elite power.

The major *zaibatsu* groups of corporations were dismantled, of course, and the major *zaibatsu* families lost almost all of their wealth. But the curious thing about it, and what was actually more important for the post-war Japanese economy, was that they soon re-formed into another system of corporate organization. A few years after the major *zaibatsu* corporations were broken up, the top managers of many of these old corporations re-emerged as top managers of companies that were more or less continuations of the old firms.[128] Since Morikawa's detailed research on the old *zaibatsu*, this reemergence of the old firms is not difficult to understand. The *zaibatsu* families who lost their wealth and stock control after 1945 had seldom been actively running these corporations anyway since as far back as the 1920s. Through great difficulty and effort many managers of these old *zaibatsu* firms were eventually able to put together enough capital to reestablish the companies in much the same way as before; the primary difference was that the rather unfunctional *zaibatsu* families were out of the picture. One of the best examples involves the old trading company, Mitsui Bussan. Niizeki Yasutarō, along with some other former managers, was able to put together $30,000 to restart the company. Mitsui Trading Company is now in competition with Itōchū Trading Company for the title of Japan's largest, with $147 billion in sales during 1993, and 200 foreign offices found in eighty-eight countries doing business for Japan.[129]

There was, however, more to the reemergence of these corporations which made it seem as if the *zaibatsu* had reappeared. As will be considered in more detail in Chapter 4, new groups of corporations called *keiretsu*, often following old *zaibatsu* lines, soon re-formed and became as important for the economy as were the old *zaibatsu* groups. And, to make it seem even more as if the major *zaibatsu* never went away, the law prohibiting the use of old *zaibatsu* corporate names—names such as Mitsui, Mitsubishi, Fuji, and Sumitomo—was changed so that once again we can refer to corporate groups using these names.

It must again be noted that this discussion refers only to the major or largest of the pre-war *zaibatsu*. Although it had been intended, the remainder of the *zaibatsu* were never broken up. Reasons for this lack of change were the coming of the Cold War and a new political administration in Washington. Also, conservative U.S. business interests began applying pressure to reverse many of the changes in Japan, and to prevent others from being carried out.[130] To put it simply and briefly, with the Communist takeover in China, and then the Korean War, the U.S. government reversed much of its thinking about the need for more democracy and less monopoly capitalism in Japan. Life was again made difficult for leftists, socialist politicians, and unions in Japan. In the end, only forty-two holding companies of the old *zaibatsu* were broken up, though future holding companies were prohibited, and the big *zaibatsu* banks which were central members of the old *zaibatsu* organization never were broken up.

Finally, we must mention again the loss of the peerage system and titles for the Japanese upper class. The peerage system was not simply a show of snobbery and status for the ego, it was a system which drew lines around the Japanese upper class, helped create some unity and class consciousness, and promoted alliances through intermarriage. The loss of the peerage system, combined with the loss of the *zaibatsu* family networks, would have clearly limited upper-class influence—that is, if nothing had been there to replace it. Chapter 7 will show in some detail how a system of upper-class family alliances called *keibatsu* grew and became very important as a replacement for the family alliances previously maintained through the *zaibatsu* organization and peerage system. The new *keibatsu* family groupings are in no way as visible as were the old family groupings, but in other ways they serve the function of uniting powerful families and creating powerful alliances even more efficiently. For example, the new *keibatsu* family system seems to be more flexible with respect to who may be brought into upper-class family circles, allowing bureaucratic, corporate, and political elite members all to be united in specific *keibatsu*.[131]

Zaibatsu Family Descendants

The end of the *zaibatsu* era was swift, and if not complete for their old corporations, it was rather complete for the old *zaibatsu* families. The wealthy plutocrats and their families woke one day to find their financial situations only a little above that of the masses of the middle class. There was even a fairly widespread feeling in post-war Japan, driven by a liberated left-wing population of intellectuals who for the first time in more than almost two decades could safely promulgate their point of view, that the *zaibatsu*, every bit as much as the military, were responsible for leading Japan into war and the ruin of defeat. Even Japanese who did not directly blame the *zaibatsu* for war and defeat, wrote and spoke little in their defense. There was little noticeable empathy from any Japanese we have ever talked to for those families who lived so differently from ordinary people and then lost virtually all of their wealth or had their great mansions fall out of family hands, as when the huge Iwasaki family compound in Yūjima was taken over as officers' quarters by the U.S. military.

None of this, however, should lead anyone to assume that *zaibatsu* families suffered a measure of disgrace which has left them outside the new economic system. If the former *zaibatsu* families suffered any significant disgrace, it did not last very long nor did it manifest itself in the core of the business world. The *zaibatsu* families did not just melt away. Despite some comments to the contrary about the Mitsui family,[132] descendants of nearly the entire former Japanese plutarchy are sprinkled liberally throughout the roster of Japanese big business, sometimes in companies stemming from former *zaibatsu* segments after the breakup of the cartels, and in other cases in completely unrelated businesses. The rise of *zaibatsu* descendants has either been missed by more recent writings about Japan, or the writings are based upon much older information—information which may have been more accurate not many years after the war but is no longer so accurate.

Real Japanese wealth today is essentially post-war wealth, new wealth so to speak. Members of the Iwasaki, Yasuda, and Mitsui families all live today under what could only be considered as quite ordinary circumstances compared to others in the Japanese upper middle class. On the other hand, an old *zaibatsu* family name can make a young man or woman an especially attractive marriage candidate for a rich family with an eye for sinking something like aristocratic roots. Even businesses which could not be pressured, as they were during *zaibatsu* days, to take a young plutocrat into the executive fast track seem to have more than their share of former *zaibatsu* names on the list of fast-moving young executives. In fact, in looking over the present generation of *zaibatsu* family descendants, one can see that having a *zaibatsu* family background does give at least some advantage. Still, even members of these families *must* graduate from the best Japanese universities, such as Tokyo University, or a top position is almost out of the question, as it is for anyone else. But once graduation from a top university has been achieved, there remains some glamor to a *zaibatsu* family name.

Through examination of current *zaibatsu* family genealogies and studies of *keibatsu* family groupings we can provide a few examples.[133] Yasuda Hiroshi, great-grandson of Yasuda Zenjirō, the founder of the Yasuda cartel, is today Vice President of Asia Minkan Securities. His half brother (from father Yasuda Zenjirō II's second marriage),Yasuda Arata, is Operations Director of Shōwa Transportation Company. Arata's brother Kusuo is Director General of Chiba Bank. Yet another brother, Ryōki, holds the title of General Counselor at a company called Kōsei Industries. The sons of two of these brothers, young men from the most recent generation of the Yasuda family, are rising executives in Fuji Bank, a direct descendant of the former Yasuda Bank, the financial wellspring of Yasuda enterprises.

When we look carefully at the family at the center of the Mitsubishi cartel we see that here too descendants of founder Iwasaki Yatarō are still employed, and several hold prominent positions in the business world. Mitsubishi Bank itself is even today headed by a family member, Iwasaki Kanya, Yatarō's great-grandson. Iwasaki Masao, who sits on the board of directors of Kirin Brewing Company, is the great-grandson of Iwasaki Yanosuke, Yatorō's younger brother, who took over as head of the cartel when Yatorō died at the turn of the century. Although they do not carry the Iwasaki family name, Nomura Masayoshi, Chairman of Sankō Trading Company, and Matsukata Ryōzō, President of Sanki Industries, are also both great-grandsons of Iwasaki Yanosuke. Another great-grandson of Iwasaki Yatarō, Kiuchi Shoin, heads the Asia desk of the Foreign Ministry.

While *zaibatsu* descendants do number among the elites, it must again be stressed that the economic influence of these families, as opposed to that of their former corporations, is far from great. Though these names still look nice on a company register or when extending a family tree, there is little other advantage for a young Mitsui, Yasuda, Iwasaki, or Fuji in trying to break into the corporate elite or bureaucratic elite in today's Japan.

THE REORGANIZATION OF JAPANESE ELITES

In his speech to the Japanese people asking them to stop the fighting soon after the destruction of Hiroshima and Nagasaki, the emperor began by saying, "The war has turned out not necessarily to Japan's advantage." Spoken at a time when Japan was soundly defeated and most of her cities and factories were in ruins, this sentence has been repeated again and again as an ironic understatement. But with fifty years of hindsight, the tentative nature of the statement can be reconsidered in a rather different light.

Following Solzhenitsyn's words—"in war not victories are blessed but defeats"—it can be argued that defeat served Japan quite well in some respects. Solzhenitsyn goes on, "A people needs defeat just as an individual needs suffering and misfortune: they compel the deepening of the inner life and generate a spiritual upsurge."[134] Well, maybe. But the upsurge in Japan in the aftermath of World War II was not so much "spiritual" as structural. Most simply, there were some important changes in corporate organization, politics, and elite networks which set the stage for huge economic growth a few years later. And while many forms of exploitation and inequalities exist in today's Japan, compared to the first half of the twentieth century, there has been economic growth in the second half of the century with *much* less inequality and exploitation of the average Japanese person.

Several major changes that took place due to the U.S. pressure were especially beneficial for Japanese corporate elites. First, the rather inactive *zaibatsu* families who often did little but took huge profits for themselves were gone. Second, when these families were out of the picture after the war, more systematic recruitment mechanisms were instituted to select corporate elite from among the best university graduates in Japan. Thus, the divided *zaibatsu* groups also gave way to a corporate elite now more unified through "old school ties" and more able to cooperate for common corporate interests than was ever before possible. Third, once again the Japanese upper class lost their formal system of status markers with loss of the peerage system. But once again their status markers were regained. Unlike the Meiji period, when the loss of feudal status and titles gave way to a new formalized system of peerage, however, after the war the status order for the upper classes became informal. Much like the American upper class at the end of the nineteenth century, a collection of national upper-class family networks became much more important. What are referred to as *keibatsu* had existed before the war, but were primarily for the elite corporate managers who were not *zaibatsu* family members.[135] With the peerage system and *zaibatsu* families no longer there, the *keibatsu* family network became a more general means for family and status alliances among all types of elites. And with the greater image of democracy and equality in post-war Japan, as in the United States, a more informal and relatively discrete system of family groupings and status markers was more practical for the upper class.

Finally, we have noted that some hired managers from the *zaibatsu* corporations were able to rebuild their corporations and become a part of the new Japanese corporate structure of *keiretsu*. However, it is important to recognize that after the war, the top was dramatically opened to new talent from many levels of Japanese society. There was a quite extensive circulation of elites in the government bureaucracy as well as in the corporate world. This infusion of new blood, with new ideas and backgrounds, had a positive impact on Japanese society in many ways in the few decades after the war.

Many other changes forced upon Japan were also beneficial to the masses in the long run, such as reduced inequality and some reforms helping to increase democracy. But even these changes have had positive effects for the upper classes in Japan through promoting more cooperation from below and improving legitimacy for those above.

CHAPTER 4

The Corporate Elite: A New Upper Class for "Japan, Inc."

The richest man in the world during 1991 and 1992 did not make it to the 1993 title: he died in February of 1993 at eighty-eight. Had he lived, it is still questionable whether he would have headed the 1993 list of most wealthy individuals in the world. Mōri Taikichirō's money, at least most of it, was made and is still tied up in Tokyo real estate—the most highly valued property in the world. Beginning in 1992, of course, the value of this real estate dropped considerably, as Governor Mieno of the Bank of Japan set interest rates to burst the "bubble economy," in part, he said, to help the less affluent in Japan afford homes. Still, there is no question that in 1993 and beyond, Mōri would have continued to be a very rich man.

Mōri Taikichirō started his adult life as a college teacher, with a position at Yokohama City University soon after the war. But he left academics in the mid-1950s to take over his father's comparatively small real estate business, Mōri Building, and the two buildings his family managed at the time. Gradually he came to own more and more real estate in downtown Tokyo, finally eighty-three buildings in the Toranomon area near the Imperial Palace. Mōri was known as a kind man—called *Ōya-san* (a friendly nickname for landlord)—with a simple lifestyle despite his estimated wealth of $15 billion.

Mōri, however, was *not* a member of the powerful corporate elites of Japan. He did not have the power or the high status granted top executives of Japan's biggest corporations, men who have much less wealth than Mōri. Unlike these top corporate elites in Japan, Mōri had little influence over the Japanese economy as a whole, or even over a single mighty corporation.

As one of the best commentators on the American power elite noted almost forty years ago, history has brought an "enlargement and centralization" of the means of power not possible in an earlier age.[136] Real power is now located in large institutions, in big corporations, and in government bureaucracies. A person with, say, $1 billion who puts this money in real estate or some interest-bearing financial paper holds very little power compared to a person who puts this money into a large corporation and gains a major shareholding. The person with a $1 billion stake in a particular corporation has considerable power within that corporation, and a voice in how the other billions of assets held by that corporations are to be used. However, even without $1 billion in a corporation, a high institutional position in that corporation brings considerable power. In addition to this, such a high institutional position will likely put a person in contact with similar individuals who then come together in order to form associations to enhance their individual powers.

Great wealth, power, and social status, in the long run, tend to correspond—but not always. As we have seen, wealth, power, and status were especially divergent in Tokugawa Japan (1600s to 1863). With rapid industrialization and modernization during the Meiji period which followed, all of this changed: merchants, capitalists, and businessmen had wealth and power. But at first they still had an image problem. As with several other countries in the region, "Confucian doctrine always did put the merchant at the bottom of the social hierarchy, inferior in usefulness to the peasant and the artisan."[137] In a typically practical fashion for the Japanese, however, the image problem was eventually rectified. The Meiji rulers simply reinvented the concept of businessman, giving it a new title which did not carry implications of selfishness and greed.[138] As industrialization progressed, the elite among these new businessmen, especially from the *zaibatsu* families, finally could have wealth, power, and high status.

The continuing high status of business leaders today is indicated in the current popularity of "business novels" in Japan.[139] These novels are written about and often by members of the corporate elite, utilizing fictional as well as actual characters deemed responsible for the Japanese "economic miracle." These men have been revered as the new samurai doing battle to protect Japan's interests around the world.[140]

THE NEW CORPORATE ELITE: THE TOYODAS

We have already encountered one of the new type of corporate elite in Japan—a corporate elite of talent, immense power, but relatively little wealth—when considering Hirose Gen of Nippon Life in Chapter 1. But surely, one would think, the Toyoda brothers who run Japan's biggest auto corporation, started by their father, would be closer to the traditional American capitalist families of wealth.[141]

In 1992, Toyoda Tatsurō took over as head of Toyota Motor Company from his older brother, Shoichiro, who became chairman of Toyota, and then later chairman of the powerful business organization Keidanren in 1994.[142] Toyoda Tatsurō and Toyoda Shoichiro are the grandsons of Toyota's founder, Toyoda Sakichi, who was born into a carpenter's family in a small village in 1867. The young Sakichi invented a type of power loom—so, he later said, people like his mother wouldn't have to sweat over the old-style loom all day—and with the help of Mitsui Company started the Toyota Automated Loom Company in 1882. The father of the current president of Toyota Motor Company, Toyoda Kiichirō, who graduated from Tokyo University in 1926, started the auto company as a branch of the loom company in 1933. As the size of the company and family wealth increased, Kiichirō's sons not only got into top universities, but also were able to marry into the higher circles of the upper-class elite—linked, for example, to the Mitsui and Yasuda families of old *zaibatsu* lineage still of high status, even if no longer so wealthy.

Despite the status and power of the Toyoda brothers today, and the fact that they run the biggest auto company in Japan, their lifestyles are relatively modest. The Toyoda brothers have no private offices at the company, and Toyoda Shoichiro's 1991 salary of $690,000 (with *no* stock options), while quite high by Japanese standards, was far below the $4.5 million, $1.2 million, and $1.6 million salaries of the top executives of the three major auto companies in the United States that same year. And perhaps most importantly, the Toyoda family is not wealthy compared to the pre-war *zaibatsu* upper class or the American upper class of today. The Toyoda family, for example, now owns less than 3 percent of the Toyota corporate stock and is far down the list of the most wealthy Japanese, not even close to the top fifty Japanese in wealth.

In post-war Japan, there is again some separation between status, power, and wealth. Many of the most powerful people, such as the Toyoda brothers, do not have a great deal of private wealth, though they enjoy a good measure of high status. The most wealthy, on the other hand, do not usually have much power or status.

THE NOUVEAU RICHE

There are some very wealthy people in Japan today. Like Mōri Taikichirō, they have most often made their millions or billions through real estate manipulations and are often looked down upon as *nari-agari*—"new rich status climbers."[143] Of the 100 top income-earners in Japan in 1991, for example, eighty-five made their income primarily in real estate speculation.[144] On the recent yearly lists of the fifty most wealthy Japanese compiled by *Forbes*, at least half of these people, and most likely many more, have their wealth based in real estate.[145]

how — must wealthy in Jpn → not much power

The most wealthy individual in Japan, and the world, since Mōri died in 1993, is only a slight exception to this separation of wealth, power, and status. Tsutsumi Yoshiaki was believed to hold assets of about $14 billion as of 1991, with his half brother Tsutsumi Seiji also on the list of the fifty most wealthy people in Japan in 1991, but with a mere $1 billion.

The fortune was started by their father, Tsutsumi "Pistol" Yasujirō, before World War II in railroads and real estate.[146] In typical robber baron style, Pistol would somehow find out where the construction of new railroads was being planned, then move in quickly to buy up the land at low cost. Pistol's assets were greatly expanded after the war when he saw a chance for easy money in Japan's destruction. As described in the then-popular novel *The Setting Sun* by Dazai Osamu the old Japanese upper class was in rapid decline, and their property could be had at a fraction of its true value by someone with the money to take it. Pistol had the money.

Tsutsumi Yoshiaki, like his father before him, continues to have most of his assets in real estate. And also much like his father, Yoshiaki's personal life is less than acceptable to those in high status circles. Yoshiaki's half brother, Tsutsumi Seiji, has focused his assets and empire building upon development of one of the biggest conglomerates in Japan, a country where such conglomerates are relatively rare. His Saison Group, with 124,000 employees and $31.8 billion in assets, includes Japan' biggest department store chain (Seibu Department Stores, along with one of the best professional baseball teams in the country, the Seibu Lions), as well as restaurant chains, food stores, an insurance company, and one of the biggest credit card companies, to name only a few. But Tsutsumi Seiji also has been unable to find much acceptance among the higher circles of status and power, and neither brother has married into an important *keibatsu* family grouping. Among other things, in the case of Seiji, it didn't help when he divorced his first wife to marry a geisha. In a half-hearted attempt to save status, the former geisha was adopted by Seiji's close friend, thus providing her with the appearance of acceptable family background. The tabloids caught on, and it didn't work.

Much like the crude Texas millionaire in the United States who may not have been socially acceptable to the old Eastern upper class earlier in this century, the Tsutsumi brothers have not gone to the right schools and universities, joined the right clubs, cultivated a proper lifestyle, or married into established upper-class families—in Japanese terms, they lack the proper *keibatsu*.

Unlike Mōri or Tsutsumi, the Toyoda brothers dominate one of the biggest corporations in Japan, which is also part of a bigger network of other corporations, all coming together to reinforce the power of each. The pinnacle of power on which the Toyoda brothers are located has been attained with only a relatively modest 3 percent of the shares of stock in Toyota Motor Company, but this is even rare among Japan's corporate elite: most own much less. One of the Tsutsumi brothers, Seiji, is something of an exception in Japan today—extremely rich and powerful—because he controls a huge corporate conglomerate. Still, as we will see, this conglomerate can not match the corporate network or *keiretsu* to which the Toyoda brothers are attached.

To fully understand the above we must turn to the nature of these corporate networks in modern Japan. And we must also contrast this Japanese corporate network with that in the United States. For while at first glance, and especially on paper, the Japanese corporation looks much like its counterpart in the United States, there are some very important differences.

THE JAPANESE ECONOMY

It is best to begin with a few basics. Japan has a modern industrial economy, as do the United States, Germany, Canada, England, Italy, and France. These countries all have minor differences. Japan, for example, continues to have a somewhat larger work force in agriculture, but a somewhat smaller blue-collar labor force, and a larger percentage of its work force in the wholesale and distribution sectors. However, it is more important to note that like the United States, and unlike much of Western Europe, Japan falls much further to the side of "private" ownership of capital, which is to say, closer to the traditional definition of a free-market capitalist economy. This means that in Japan there is very little government ownership or government control of stock in major corporations.[147] In Western Europe, by contrast, much, if not most or all, of the steelmaking, shipbuilding, auto production, banking, and commercial transportation is done by corporations controlled by central governments or at least partially owned by central governments. In fact, what little of this kind of government ownership existed in Japan's past has been dismantled: as of the late 1980s and early 1990s, the government no longer controls most of the railroads or telecommunications.

None of this is to suggest that the Japanese government has less influence over the economy than governments in Europe. Vice-Minister of Finance Ozaki has considerable power, and there are many more like him. For now, the important point is this: in contrast to most nations in Western Europe, private individuals *can* have more control over basic industries in Japan. But this statement leaves out many complicating factors, in particular who owns and/or controls the major Japanese corporations, and the Japanese tendency to form cliques or groups for mutual aid and protection.

Corporate Control

Back in the 1930s, with reference to the United States, Berle and Means started one of the longest-running debates in the social sciences over the question of ownership and control of corporations.[148] In what was called a "managerial revolution" they claimed that the true owners of corporations, those who own the corporation's stock, are no longer in control of these corporations. At that time stock ownership was becoming so dispersed that in many of the biggest corporations even the most wealthy families—such as the Rockefellers, Mellons, Morgans, and Carnegies—no longer owned enough stock to say they were in control.[149] By default, it was said, the managers of each corporation had become the controllers. The debate gravitated toward one central question: exactly how many of the biggest companies are still controlled by upper-class families and how many are under managerial control?

With respect to the very biggest U.S. corporations, we know there is little direct family control. For example, considering the 122 largest corporations in several industries (accounting for about 40 percent of all corporate assets in the United States), in only thirteen of these corporations do we find a family or individual with 10 percent or more of the stock.[150] Among the thirteen is the Ford Motor Company, where the Ford family continues to control about 40 percent of the stock. Other family-controlled firms include Du Pont and Coca-Cola. The most important stock controllers, however, are "institutional investors"—bank trust departments, investment firms, and some pension funds, who are not themselves controlled by family wealth. These institutional investors have stock control through managing billions of dollars in trust funds, most from private pension programs. For example, if we consider the top five stock voters in each of the large 122 corporations in this study (122 companies × top 5 stock holders in each company = 610 top five positions), we find that half of all of these top five positions are held by institutional investors.[151]

There are many reasons why Berle and Means' managerial control or managerial revolution thesis remains overly simple. It is difficult to say that the biggest American corporations are controlled by their individual managers, free of outside influence. And it can be argued that top executives of these institutional investors and banks help create an overarching "corporate class" that has replaced the old upper-class families in influence. But one thing is clear: among the biggest U.S. corporations the old upper-class family presence is almost gone.

Back to Japan: to what extent does this pattern of stock control by other than wealthy families fit Japan? And if major stock ownership is not in the hands of wealthy families in Japan, who or what has control of most stock in the major corporations? These questions are central to the existence of a new corporate class or new upper class, as well as the nature of the famous *keiretsu* corporate groups, and Japan's post-war economic performance.

One answer to the above questions is relatively simple: we have already seen how the major *zaibatsu* families had their stock control severely reduced soon after the war. Before the war, ten families in Japan controlled about 75 percent of all assets in industrial and financial corporations, and just four families had 25 percent of all corporate assets.[152] However, only the nine largest *zaibatsu* family groups were broken up at the time, and many Japanese question whether or not the old families have somehow regained their control. Thus, this question of ownership and control of corporations in Japan must be answered before we can proceed to other issues about Japanese elites.

In recent years, Japanese social scientists also have taken up the questions posed by the Berle and Means managerial revolution thesis, and many of their answers are similar to those found in the United States.[153] But there are some important differences that establish the Japanese economy and corporate elite as rather unique in the capitalist world.

One of the key differences is easy to explain; for in almost all of the biggest Japanese corporations, the old upper-class families are out, and continue to be out—at least in terms of major stock control. Many more than the nine largest *zaibatsu* family corporate groups, in time, lost most of their wealth in the post-war period. To a much greater extent than in the American pattern, we find few individuals owning much stock at all in the biggest corporations. In 1949, about 70 percent of the corporate stock in Japan was still family-owned. Today, after the breakup of the *zaibatsu* and other changes in the economy (such as very high taxes on the affluent), about 80 percent of corporate stock is self-owned—that is, *the corporations own each other*.[154] One of the most recent Japanese studies of the largest 300 corporations found only 6 percent which could be said to be under family or individual control through stock ownership.

This reality is reflected in relations between large Japanese corporations and their few remaining human stockholders. Annual stockholders' meetings in the United States tend to be rather unexciting; most decisions already have been made and the results of stock votes on various issues are known well in advance, and in fact highly organized behind the scenes. In Japan, stockholders' meetings are incredibly underwhelming.[155] In 1992, the average Japanese stockholders' meeting lasted just thirty minutes, with one dragging on for a record two minutes. This average of thirty minutes has remained stable for at least the past twenty years.[156] Most individuals who buy stock over the counter and who are otherwise outsiders to the corporation, it is safe to say, have little voice in Japanese companies.

If private individuals and families have little stock control in Japan, who or what, then, does control most corporate stock? In sharp contrast to the United States, where about 50 percent of all stock is owned by pension funds, the percentage is close to zero in Japan.[157] The biggest amount of corporate stock in Japan, 26 percent, is in fact owned by industrial corporations (not their own stock, but the stock of other corporations), with another 18 percent held by banks, and 17 percent held by insurance companies. And it must be said again; this stock in other companies is actually

Table 4.1
Stock Ownership Patterns in the Top 100 Japanese Industrial Corporations

	Number One Stockholder Positions
Held By	*Percent of Top Positions*
Banks	16
Insurance and other financial firms	47
Families/individuals	10
Industrial corporations	19
Foreign firms*	5
Private trust fund	1

*In one case this was a foreign individual.

owned by these corporations, not just held in managed trust funds which they do not actually own.

To assess the situation in the largest Japanese corporations, along with a Japanese colleague, we examined the stockholding patterns for 1987 in the largest 100 industrial corporations (Table 4.1) and the largest twenty-five banks in Japan (Table 4.2).[158] Focusing on the number one stockholder in each of the 100 largest industrial corporations, as indicated below, we found only ten of these companies to have a family or individual as the number one stockholder. Forty-seven companies had an insurance company or other financial firm as the number one stockholder, while in sixteen it was a bank, and in nineteen it was another industrial corporation. As for the top twenty-five banks, 84 percent of them had an insurance company or other financial institution as the number one stockholder, while in 12 percent of the cases it was another bank, in 4 percent an industrial corporation, and in no case was the number one stockholder an individual or family.[159] Further, we found only eight families or individuals among these 100 top industries and none among the top twenty-five banks who had 10 percent or more of the stock in a company.

In contrast to the situation in the United States, the absence of institutional investors using pension fund money to amass large amounts of stock control in Japan has very important implications for corporate elites and the overall economy. The huge amount of stock in the large 122 U.S. corporations (described earlier) held by institutional investors is rather fluid. While the overall amount of this institutional stock control remains over 50 percent from year to year, exactly who the top five stock voters are in *each corporation* is subject to change. The U.S. institutional investors are buying stock with their managed trusts and pension funds to make short-term profits— seldom for other reasons, such as to support or exert influence in another

Table 4.2
Stock Ownership Patterns in the Top 25 Japanese Banks

Number One Stockholder Positions

Held By	Percent of Top Positions Held
Banks	12
Insurance and other financial firms	84
Families/individuals	0
Industrial corporations	4
Foreign firms	0

Source: Japan Company Handbook (1987).

corporation. Thus, in contrast to Japan, institutional investors or stockholders from other corporations tend to have less influence over American corporate managers.

People and corporations in Japan, of course, buy and sell stock through the stock market all the time. But the largest blocs of stockholders in the biggest Japanese corporations remain relatively stable from year to year. For example, from 1980 to 1984 in Japan, 81 percent of the top ten stockholders in the largest 250 Japanese corporations remained the same. Among the top 250 American corporations only 23 percent of the top ten stockholders remained unchanged between 1980 and 1984.[160] This stock in Japan is held for the long term, and the other companies holding this stock are very interested in how the company is being managed and how it is performing.[161] Research on the biggest 250 corporations in Japan has indicated that this cross-stockholding among corporations comes mainly *after* they have established some other kind of business tie.[162] This also means that if the company is not performing well, not only is the value of stock held by an outside corporation threatened, but so are other types of long-term business relations. This is why a chief executive in Japan will receive extensive pressure from other corporate executives to clean up the situation, and if he does not, to resign.

To bring into focus the most salient features of the ownership and control of Japanese corporations: First, as in the United States, there is very little stock control by families or individuals in the biggest Japanese corporations. But second, unlike the situation in the United States, most stock control in Japan does not come from institutional investors who manage pension funds. The main stock controllers in Japan are banks, insurance companies, and other corporations who *own the stock in other corporations themselves.* This stock is not bought and sold simply to make money; rather, it is held over the long term for other business-related reasons. Third, if by managerial control or a managerial revolution is meant that the managers of each corporation are in control without much outside pressure, the managerial control thesis applies even less to Japan than to the United States. The old wealthy families in Japan are seldom major stock controllers any longer, but there are additional outside forces in the form of other corporate elites applying pressure on the typical Japanese executive to perform.[163]

These ownership and control patterns in Japan's major corporations interact with the Japanese propensity to form cliques in the production of what have come to be called *keiretsu*, highly significant groups for the formation of a powerful interlocked corporate elite in Japan.

Keiretsu and *Gurūpu*

Major corporations, in Japan or anywhere, would be much less influential if they remained isolated from other corporations with which they could share various kinds of business, information, personnel, and perhaps organize for political pressure. And relatively isolated corporations make for less powerful executives of these corporations. Thus, locating the real corporate elite and understanding their power requires us to consider the Japanese tendency to form groups, cliques, and coalitions as described in Chapter 2.

Cliques of Japanese corporations are most often referred to as *keiretsu* (translated simply as "economic groupings").[164] There are actually two types of *keiretsu*. First are the groups of very large corporations, from many different industries, who come together on a somewhat equal basis to buy each others' stock, exchange personnel and information, form a guiding presidents' council, and of course share many types of business dealings. The terms horizontal *keiretsu* or *gurūpu* can be used to distinguish this type of *keiretsu* from the other.[165] Originally, the term *keiretsu* referred only to vertical corporate groupings, the second most extensive major form of corporate groupings today. At the center of vertical *keiretsu* is always a major corporation with smaller companies dependent upon the big company as suppliers or providers of other important business resources tied to the central corporation.[166]

Both types of *keiretsu* began forming as the old family-controlled *zaibatsu* corporate groups broke up after the war.[167] When wealthy families were forced to dispose of their stock by the Occupation reforms, few individuals had the resources to buy this stock, and by default other companies stepped in as buyers. Later, when the Japanese economy became more open in 1961, there was fear among the Japanese corporate elites and government officials that foreigners would buy up Japanese corporate assets. Government ministry officials again encouraged other Japanese companies to buy corporate assets to keep out the foreign competition. And finally, with the greater importance of bank loans as apposed to new stock issues for corporate growth and development in Japan, the big Japanese banks helped promote *keiretsu* cross-shareholding ties, especially with themselves, to protect and oversee their loans to these corporations.

The Man behind Toshiba

It is time to consider another human example. The post-war corporate elite has been personified by men such as the late Ishizaka Taizō. Though from a humble rural background, he gained entry into the elite track at Tokyo University Faculty of Law before the war, and upon graduation landed a fast-track position in the postal ministry.[168] His position in the postal ministry brought high status, but little money or as yet economic power. However, in a career move to become more and more common among many of the bureaucratic elite after the war, Taizō left the government ministry at an early age for a high corporate position with a large insurance firm, Daiichi Insurance Company. He eventually became president of this company, and was successful in bringing it from thirteenth to second in ranking among Japanese insurance companies. Jumping from one company to another was not, and still is not, typical of Japanese executives, but Taizō did just that. He made the biggest move of his life in joining the young and growing Toshiba Electronic Company, ending up as its president. In the post-war climate allowing newer companies to compete more freely, Taizō was able to bring Toshiba to the first rank of Japanese corporations.

Ishizaka Taizō is among the inner group of the corporate elite not only because of Toshiba's size and assets, but also because Toshiba is in a central position within a powerful group of interlocked corporations, the Mitsui *keiretsu*, which is in fact the biggest and most powerful of the big six *keiretsu* today. Thus, as can be seen in Table 4.3, the president of Toshiba also sits on the Nikikai presidents' club, or presidents' association, with the presidents of the many other corporations in the main Mitsui *keiretsu*.

In addition, Toshiba is directly tied through stock ownership and/or a dominant business relationship to more than 200 smaller companies.[169] These companies make up the Toshiba vertical *keiretsu*, with the main company and its president, for example Ishizaka Taizō, in a commanding position. But in addition to all of this, Ishizaka was a central member of the corporate elite for another reason: from 1956 to 1968 he was chairman of the most powerful big business organization in Japan, Keidanren, the association of the largest corporations. Ishizaka was the second person to be chairman of Keidanren after it was founded in the post-war period, and is credited with establishing this organization as a major force in the coordination of industrial policy for the nation, as it continues to be today.

Table 4.3
Mitsui *Keiretsu*[170]

Main Companies	*Additional Members of Nikikai Presidents' Association*
Mitsui Manufacturing	Toshiba
Mitsui Real Estate	Toyota
Taiyō-Kobe\Mitsui Bank	Mitsukoshi Stores
Mitsui Tōatsu Chemicals	Mitsui Maritime Casualty
Mitsui Storage	Tore Industries
Mitsui Trust Bank	Ōji Paper Products
Mitsui Shipbuilding	Sanki Heavy Industries
Ōsaka Shipping\Mitsui Shipping	Japan Steel Co.
Mitsui Metals and Ore	Japan Flour Products
Mitsui Construction	Ōnoma Cement
Mitsui Mines	
Mitsui Life Insurance	
Mitsui Petrochemical Industries	
	Associate Companies
Mitsui Leasing Enterprises	Electrochemical Industries
Mitsui Information Development	Ishikawajima\Harima Heavy Industries
Mitsui Liquid Gas	
Mitsui Homes	Tōyō Engineering
Mitsui Aluminum	Tōmen Corporation
Mitsui Agricultural Products	General Petroleum

GURŪPU: THE BIG SIX

There is wide agreement in Japan on the six most powerful *gurūpu* or horizontal *keiretsu* today. Depending upon whose definition is followed, these big six together contain from 187 to 193 main corporations, accounting for about 15 percent of all corporate assets, including 40 percent of all banking assets, 53 percent of all insurance assets, and 53 percent of the real estate business.[171] On the average, each of the 187 to 193 corporations

Table 4.4
The Mitsubishi Group of Interlocked Corporations[172]

Company of Stock Issue	Percent of Stock Owned Within
Mitsubishi Bank	26.9
Mitsubishi Trust Bank	32.3
Tokyo Marine	21.7
Mitsubishi Heavy Industries	23.2
Mitsubishi Corporation	42.2
Mitsubishi Electric	16.3
Asahi Glass	29.3
Kirin Beer	12.7
Mitsubishi Chemical	24.5
N.Y.K. Shipping	27.5

within one of the big six is linked through stock ownership with 54 percent of the other companies within the group, with an average of 21.6 percent of the stock of each of these corporations held collectively by other corporations within the group. As an example of the cross-stockholdings among the big six, Table 4.4 includes ten of the biggest companies in the Mitsubishi Group and the percentage of their stock held by the other nineteen corporations within the group.

The following is a list of the six big groups, along with the number of main companies within each group, the number of affiliated companies which are less powerful but tied to the others, and the name of the "presidents' club" for each group, which coordinates each *gurūpu*'s economic and political activities.

Mitsubishi Group. Twenty-eight main companies and ninety-three affiliate companies.[173] Presidents' club—Kinyōkai (Friday Club).

Mitsui Group. Twenty-four main companies and ninety-two affiliate companies. Presidents' club—Nikikai (Two Pillars Club).

Sumitomo Group. Twenty-one main companies and ninety-five affiliate companies. Presidents' club—Hakusuikai (White Water Club).

Fuji Group. Twenty-nine main companies and seventy-four affiliate companies. Presidents' club—Fuyōkai (Lotus Club).

Daiichi Kangyo Group. Forty-seven main companies and forty-five affiliates. Presidents' club—Sankinkai (Three Gold Club).

Sanwa Group. Forty-four main companies and twenty-seven affiliates. Presidents' club—Sansuikai (Three Waters Club).

Four of these big six are remnants of the old *zaibatsu* broken up after the war, while two are newly-formed groups. The Matsushita Corporation, a member of the Sumitomo group, provides an example of how the *gurūpu* survived in altered form.[174] In 1950 Matsushita Kōnosuke still owned 43.25 percent of the stock in Matsushita Electronics. At that time no bank owned even 1 percent of Matsushita stock, while another family (Inoue) owned 3.9 percent, putting them in second place. By 1955 Matsushita Kōnosuke's share had fallen to 20.43 percent, with Sumitomo Insurance Co., the next stockholder, with 4.04 percent. In 1965 Nihon Kyōdō Securities was the biggest Matsushita stockholder with 5.58 percent, and Matsushita Kōnosuke's share had fallen the third place with 4.8 percent. By 1975 Matsushita Konosuke was in fourth place with only 3.7 percent of the stock, while the three top holders were Sumitomo Bank (5.5 percent), Sumitomo Insurance (4.4 percent), and Nippon Life (3.8 percent).

Zaibatsu Descendants

The dissolution of *zaibatsu* family wealth, however, does not mean these people or their descendants have all fallen into the middle class. While they are comparatively much less wealthy, and unable to control corporations like they once did, descendants of the old *zaibatsu* are still highly respected and often found within their old companies. This of course makes these family members still quite powerful, and one is tempted to suggest there is some form of stock control or other hidden means of control over the company by *zaibatsu* descendants. Japanese researchers, however, have not found any such hidden control, and they explain the continued presence of *zaibatsu* family descendants by noting how useful their status is to the company. There is still respect for these old families, and their continued presence lends a sense of continuity and prestige to the company. There is even a phrase for this in Japanese, *gisei dōzoku shinhai*, which means roughly "imitation family control."[175]

A good example of the continuing importance of *zaibatsu* descendants without major wealth or stock control is Mitsui.[176] In the 1920s and 1930s there were still extant several divisions of the old Mitsui clan going back to the original Osaka merchant family during the Tokugawa period (1600 to 1850s). But through intermarriage the name was close to being lost, so the descendants officially reestablished Mitsui as their legal name. Looking at the Mitsui family tree today, one can find ten men in top positions in major corporations, including the head of Mitsui Production, and two directors in Mitsui Heavy Industries and Mitsui Chemical. Among other famous old *zaibatsu* families, Yasuda has seven descendants in major corporate positions today, Sumitomo has six, and Iwazaki (from the original Mitsubishi) has four.

Shachō-kai

While the big six corporate *gurūpu* are tied by cross-stockholdings and many business ties, there is another, perhaps even more important, means by which these big six are held together. *Shachō-kai*, or "presidents' clubs," formally bring together presidents and chairmen of the major corporations in the *gurūpu*. Gerlach and Lincoln, for example, have found that a corporation's membership in the *shachō-kai* is the best predictor of the other ties, such as cross-stockholding.[177] And while levels of cross-stock ownership among *gurūpu* members may change and other business ties fluctuate over the years, membership in the *shachō-kai* has remained quite stable within the big six *gurūpu*.

Above all else, it is the coordination and organization provided by the *shachō-kai* that are most important. These are more or less secret organizations in that what goes on within them is not open to outside scrutiny, except for material released by them to the media. For example, in a brochure for the celebration of "one hundred years of Mitsubishi" it was stated flatly that, "The Presidents' Cooperative Society which was set up to further cooperation among the parent company and all the affiliates was banned in 1948. It was necessary then to immediately establish an organization to take its place, so it was decided to set up a Friday Noon Luncheon Society which would meet on Fridays at noon to coordinate relationships."[178] In other words, this society, which became the Mitsubishi *shachō-kai*, was established to subvert the Occupation forces order, and all four of the former *zaibatsu* big six *gurūpu* had established a *shachō-kai* by 1951.

Under the old system, associations of *zaibatsu* executives were important parts of the function of the networks. They were mainly for the purpose of communicating policy dictated from the top down. Modern presidents' clubs, however, are really of quite a different character, since the big six *gurūpu* have a completely different type of association. Unlike the old *zaibatsu* groups, the main corporations within each *gurūpu* today are more equal in influence. There are three primary functions of the new *shachō-kai*[179]:

1. To reach consensus about important decisions affecting the group as a whole, such as formulation of joint stock-owned companies. For example, the 1970 exposition and the opening of the Okinawa Maritime Pavilion, which required cooperation among several Mitsubishi companies, was decided by the Friday Club.

2. To coordinate dealings with outside groups and agencies such as the other big six members and *keiretsu*, foreign companies and governments, and Japanese political and government organizations.

3. To help member companies in trouble. For example, in 1954 the Sumitomo

Heavy Machine Company missed a dividend payment due to a sea of red ink and was on the verge of bankruptcy. The Hakusuikai, Sumitomo's Presidents' Club, "arranged" for the resignation of the president and for a new president to be brought in from another Sumitomo company during a period of restructuring. The Hakusuikai then sent other executives from Sumitomo Bank, Sumitomo Trading Company, and four other Sumitomo companies to help straighten things out.

At times these *shachō-kai* play the role of disciplinary agencies, even to the point of forcing out executives who have done something wrong. In 1972, Mitsubishi's Friday Club is reported to have arranged for the replacement of the president of Mitsubishi Petrochemical Company with the vice president after discovery of some underhanded dealings, a scandal involving the president's mistress with some business operations in Hong Kong. It is well known in business circles that it was the Mitsui group's *shachō-kai* that was responsible for the sudden announcement in 1982 by Okada Shigeru, president of an affiliate member company, Mitsukoshi Department Stores, that he had decided to retire after repeatedly stating to the press in the weeks preceding the event that he would not step down under any circumstances.[180]

Interlocking Corporate Directors

In the United States, of course, there are nothing like *shachō-kai*. But one of the major ways in which the inner group of the corporate elite and major corporations come together is through interlocking corporate directorates. Interlocking directorates are formed when a top executive or member of the board of directors of one corporation sits on the board of directors of another company at the same time. Thus, we can say that IBM and General Motors are interlocked if a board member or executive of IBM also sits on the board of directors at General Motors. Such interlocking directorates are very extensive in the United States, with an average of ten or more direct interlocks among the biggest corporations.[181]

There are several theories about why these direct interlocks exist in the United States, but little conclusive evidence.[182] It is clear, however, that these interlocks help the corporate elite exchange information and create some unity among the biggest corporations. *And* these interlocks help form the basis for a group of corporate elites, said to be the "inner group of the corporate class," which has several important functions.

Japanese corporations have little need for such interlocking directorates to bring them together and organize their activities: They already have extensive means to do so through their *shachō-kai*. There is also the unprecedented (in the United States) big-business organization in Japan,

Keidanren, which organizes and unites all of the major corporations (Keidanren will be considered in more detail in Chapter 7).

Interlocking corporate directorates do exist in Japan, though limited in type and number. Interlocking directorates are limited in number for the simple reason that few corporate board members in Japanese corporations are "outside directors"—meaning they come from outside the corporation's management.[183] In theory, members of the board of directors of a company are to oversee managers of the company for the owners of the corporation, the stockholders, who elect the board members. In the case of Japanese corporations, therefore, we would expect few outside board members from the stockholders because the stockholders, except other corporations within the *gurūpu* or *keiretsu*, are usually powerless. But neither do we find many outside directors in Japanese corporations from other corporations who are members of the *gurūpu* or *keiretsu*, most likely because the existence of a *shachō-kai* makes interlocking directorates unnecessary.

There are two major exceptions to the relative lack of interlocking directorates in Japan. As noted earlier, Japanese corporations, in contrast to American corporations, are much more likely to obtain capital from bank loans than from new stock issues. And 39 to 23 percent of all loans come from the central bank within each *gurūpu*. Interlocking directorates are often formed between the central bank in the *gurūpu* and other corporations when a corporation has a large debt owed to the bank, and when a corporation within the *gurūpu* has developed major economic problems. In the latter case, the central bank in the *gurūpu* is likely to send one of its executives to the board of the troubled company. All of this has been shown by one of the most extensive studies to date of the big six corporations, which has also shown that the central banks in these *gurūpu* are more likely to send interlocking directorates *to* the other corporations and have more stock ownership in the other corporations within the *gurūpu* than other types of corporations.[184] These findings support what has long been suspected and said by others: The big banks are most powerful in Japan, and can be considered as the central hub of the mass of *gurūpu* and *keiretsu* connections.

The big six corporate *gurūpu* are clearly formidable, commanding organizations in the Japanese economy. They account for much of Japanese economic activity and are the best organized participants in politics and in the economy. And equally important, it is within these giant corporations that we find most of the corporate elite within Japan today. There are few rich actors standing outside of the major corporations who can be truly influential in the economy given the changes in stock ownership we have outlined. And it is necessary to understand how these huge corporations are united and organized to see how this corporate elite can in many ways be more dominant than corporate elites in other countries, or in Japan's past. We will return to these points, after considering briefly the other type of corporate grouping in post-war Japan.

Vertical *Keiretsu*

Somewhat less important for corporate elite formation and influence in Japan, but very important in the conduct and success of the Japanese economy, are the vertical *keiretsu*. As the term vertical implies, in this case of corporate groups we are referring to corporations arranged as a hierarchy, with big corporations at the top and the smaller corporations dependent upon them below. Like the big six, there are presidents' organizations, shared stockholdings, and other ties. But the main purpose of the vertical *keiretsu* are business relations that remain favorable (mainly to the top company) and stable.

A major company such as Toyota, for example, has a vertical *keiretsu* made up of suppliers of parts and services needed to build cars. Much of the efficient practices of Japanese companies, such as *kanban*, or the just-in-time system, are made possible by these dependent companies within the vertical *keiretsu*.[185] And stable profits, lifetime employment, and higher wages, among other advantages held by the bigger corporations in Japan, are made possible in part because the smaller dependent companies bear the costs of problems and economic downturns.

It is understandable, then, that much of the criticism from other industrial nations directed toward Japan is related to the existence of these vertical *keiretsu*. Much business is done within the vertical *keiretsu*, making it difficult for an outsider, especially a foreign company, to do business with one of the companies in the group. And when major Japanese companies move operations to other countries (as "transplants") they are likely to bring some of their *keiretsu* suppliers with them, or create others in the new location.[186] It is the vertical *keiretsu* that has been one of the main targets of the U.S.-Japan trade agreement known as the Structural Impediments Initiative, which was an unprecedented agreement intended to change not just trade practices, but economic characteristics of another country.

THE INNER GROUP OF THE CORPORATE ELITE

There are in Japan, of course, the same sorts of small independent businesses found in all capitalist countries, mostly small retail stores, craft shops and so on. The most important sectors of the Japanese economy, however, can be visualized as overlapping groups of corporations formed by the vertical and horizontal *keiretsu* or *gurūpu*. Most important are the big six corporate groups, but most of the main 193 members of these big six have their own vertical *keiretsu* including dozens and sometimes hundreds of smaller corporations. The lines of power are then relatively clear: the central corporate elites are in the big Japanese banks and other financial institutions, as well as the other main companies of the big six *gurūpu*. Then the smaller corporations fall in line and are under the coordination of the central corporations in the vertical *keiretsu*. This form of corporate organization gives corporate elites at the center more power and ability to coordinate economic and political activities than elites in any other industrial nation.

The organization of corporate Japan provides the bases for an inner group of a corporate elite more powerful, more interconnected, and much more in control of the economy than can be found in any other capitalist nation. Even more than the American inner group of the corporate elite, members of this Japanese inner group are in a position to protect their corporate interests against both foreigners and other Japanese.[187]

There are, however, many more parts to this puzzle of corporate elite power. This Japanese inner group is unified and tied through an "old boy network" to a much greater extent than in other industrial nations, and it is tied more closely to important government ministries and political parties than would be possible in the United States. Big business organizations in Japan, such as Keidanren, unite and represent corporate interests in a way that would most likely be seen as illegal in the United States. The next step is to the bureaucratic elite. It is critical to understand how people such as Ishizaka from Toshiba, Hirose from Nippon Life, and Ozaki across town in the finance ministry are interconnected, understand each other, and are by no means the adversaries one might suppose them to be if using American assumptions to view the corporate and government sectors.

CHAPTER 5

The Bureaucratic Elite: The Guiding Hand and Training Ground for a New Upper Class

In today's world economy the state must provide at least some level of economic guidance, coordination, and a strong infrastructure if an industrial nation is to remain competitive. Japan is most definitely competitive, not some bungling Third World country run by an irresponsible dictator. How can this situation be explained given the political disarray of the late 1980s and early 1990s?

As indicated by the overwhelming vote against incumbents in November of 1994, Americans do not always hold politicans in high esteem. High esteem or not, however, it is this elected part of government that comes to mind first among Americans when their thoughts turn to government. For Americans, elected officials govern. In Japan this is not necessarily the case.

Political cartoons, always biting, have gotten even more acerbic in Japan recently. One we saw recently (and before the April 1995 gas attacks) had two policemen standing accross the street from the Diet building in front of another building most Japanese recognize as the Diet members' office quarters. Scurrying in the background are what appear to be civil disaster workers carrying stretchers with bodies on them. One policeman says, "What a tragedy that the gas leak caused all the Diet members to be found dead at their desks." The other policeman chimes in, "Yes, but great luck that the leak was confined to this one building so that no important functions of government are directly effected." In fact, the most important day-to-day decisions, even those with long-run implications for the lives of most Japanese, are made by an un-elected bureaucratic elite. If politicians have acted irresponsibly and illegally, the bureaucratic elite has quietly worked away, administering the laws, interpreting the laws, and, as we will see, even writing the vast majority of laws passed by politicians in the Diet. In post-war Japan, the bureaucratic elite has been generally trusted, and though often seen as arrogant, has been relatively well respected. There is a Japanese term, *kanryōdō*, which means "the way of the bureaucrat." *Kanryōdō* takes a cue from the word *bushidō*, "the way of the warrior," the idealized lifestyle and philosophy of the samurai. No one, it is worth noting, employs a similar term for "the way of the politician." And the term *amakudari*, "descent from heaven," is used to describe where the bureaucratic elite come from when they make a career move to the corporate world.

As the noted Japan scholar Chalmers Johnson put it in the early 1980s, "In general, the Japanese public places greater trust in the honesty of state officials than in the honesty of politicians or business leaders. Such petty corruption as does occur—gifts from businessmen, golf club fees, dinner parties, junkets—is more common among non-career officials than among the higher bureaucrats, and was more common in the period of shortages in the 1950s than in later years."[188] One large empirical study of corruption among Japanese government bureaucrats found only six cases of petty corruption per 10,000 officials in the 1960s. From the early 1970s until 1985 (the last year included) corruption fell to only two cases per 10,000 officials.[189]

The jokes contrasting corrupt politicians to responsible bureaucrats, however, were no longer funny as the scandals continued to unfold in the late 1980s and early 1990s; at that point they began to include even a few of the bureaucratic elite. The Recruit Cosmos scandal, for example, implicated a vice-minister of education. Following that, a former labor vice-minister received a two-year sentence for taking 3,000 shares of insider-traded stock while in office. The chairman and some senior executives of the quasi-government Nippon Telegraph and Telephone Corporation were also convicted. Japan's bureaucratic elite, once seen as the direct representatives of the god-like emperor, is no longer above suspicion. In fact, many of Japan's problems are now being attributed to the power of bureaucrats and their resistance to change.

Before further consideration of the growing mistrust of the bureaucratic elite, however, we must examine the model bureaucrats of past and present, who they are, their talents, training, interests, and influence. Only after doing so can we really appreciate the importance of Japan's bureaucratic elite in the post-war period. It will be helpful, as before, to begin with a couple of specific examples.

GOVERNOR, BANK OF JAPAN: A MAN OF THE PEOPLE?

Among the most respected bureaucratic elites today is certainly Mieno Yasushi, governor of the Bank of Japan from 1989 to 1994.[190] The Bank of Japan is government-owned and -controlled, much like those owned by central governments in Europe, with additional functions similar to those of the Federal Reserve System in the United States. The Bank of Japan has extensive influence over private Japanese banks, and is an important arm of the government's policies in coordinating and directing the overall economy. As head of this bank, Mieno is one of the career bureaucrats who have had considerable influence in Japan's economic success. It is always difficult to separate public images from real personalities, but if we are to believe what many Japanese think and say about Mieno Yasushi, he is also a man who has had the courage to face down powerful political and business interests in order to protect the welfare of ordinary middle-class consumers.

Mieno is one of those who achieved great personal success after living through what today is dimly remembered in Japan as the darkest days of poverty and hardship after the war. His father had been a minor civil servant in the Japanese puppet state of Manchukuo before the family was repatriated in 1945, penniless, to a Japan struggling to provide basic necessities to a beleaguered and defeated populace. While his father eked out a living as a street peddler, Mieno Yasushi helped out by selling soap from door to door. In spite of family circumstances, he was a bright and accomplished student, and he passed the examination which allowed him to enroll in Tokyo's Number One High School, a training ground for possible entry to the prize and the dream of all bright young Japanese men—Tokyo University. Finally, he did in fact make it into Tokyo University, in terms of traditional academic screening, surely the most difficult university to enter on the planet.

At Tokyo University, it is said, Mieno was a brilliant student, but when he graduated the family was still in financial need. He decided not to pursue a career in the Ministry of Finance or MITI as the top students so often do; rather, he began a career at the Bank of Japan. It paid a little better.

Mieno moved to the top of his professional career as a bureaucrat when he assumed the post of governor of the Bank of Japan in December of 1989. Almost immediately he did something which angered much of the Japanese corporate community in Japan and brought one Liberal Democratic Party member to denounce him on the Diet floor as the "Saddam Hussein of Japanese government."[191] He is credited with ending the Japanese "economic bubble."

The officially calculated inflation rate in Japan appeared quite low; but what Mieno called "invisible inflation" was rampant. For years there had been huge increases in the value of land which kept other prices artificially high, especially the price of stocks. Previous governors of the bank had bowed to pressure from the Finance Ministry to keep interest rates low, lower than for any other industrial nation, mainly in order to fuel economic growth. Mieno defied the Finance Ministry, and using the power he wielded as the person who officially sets rates, he raised the rates quite rapidly, given Japanese traditions. He was well aware that many people would be hurt by his decision, but most observers now agree that for Japan to have continued with its unrealistic interest rates eventually would have hurt the economy in a much more damaging way. And many of those who supported the change in interest rates interpreted the move as long-overdue aid to the average consumer. This view has enhanced Mieno's image as a man of the people, who in fact can be seen nearly every week shopping with his wife in the rather modest neighborhood where the Mienos live, purportedly to keep in touch with the prices of ordinary household consumer goods.

A HERO AT MITI

Another respected member of the bureaucratic elite was Sahashi Shigeru, vice-minister of the Ministry of International Trade and Industry (MITI) from 1964 to 1966, a man who is given credit for much of MITI's success in shaping the "economic miracle" of the 1950s and 1960s. His fame is such that three novels have been written with Sahashi as hero, like the samurai of old, fighting selfish big business interests, as well as other bureaucrats, to implement policies he believes are important for the good of the country.[192] Novels with a bureaucrat as hero, of course, tell us as much about the Japanese respect for the bureaucratic elite and *kanryōdō* as they do about particular individuals.[193]

Sahashi Shigeru was born in 1913 in a small city in Gifu Prefecture. Though his father was a small businessman with little wealth or influence in the community, Sahashi was able to get into the Tokyo University Faculty of Law, from which he graduated in 1937. Lacking the proper family connections, upon graduation he applied to several ministries for employment, assuming his chances for this type of job were not good. But he eventually found a position with the Ministry of Commerce and Industry (MCI), the pre-war predecessor of the Ministry of International Trade and Industry. Soon after attaining this position, however, he was drafted into military service in the China war, returning to MCI in 1941 to begin his ascent to the upper reaches of power in the post-war MITI.

Like all career bureaucrats, Sahashi had to work his way to the top by serving in many divisions of the ministry so as to learn as much as possible about the overall functions of the agency. By 1957, however, he was in an important position to guide and participate in policy-making within MITI, and he is held responsible for establishing the concept of "administrative guidance" which helped make MITI a key agency directing the Japanese "economic miracle."

THE AMERICAN CONTRAST

Parallels to individuals such as Mieno and Sahashi would be difficult to find in the United States; there are no comparable positions for them. Career bureaucrats in the United States are not necessarily any less talented, though in contrast to those in Japan they are much less likely to come from the very best universities, or receive Japanese-style on-the-job training (explained below) once their career positions are attained. The key difference, however, is that it is almost impossible to find a person in a policy-making position, or anywhere near a top position of authority in the government of the United States, who started as a career civil servant.

When a new president takes office in the United States he makes well over 1,000 political appointments. These people assume top government bureaucratic and executive positions similar to those held by the Japanese bureaucratic elite; even the sub-cabinet positions down through several layers of authority are selected anew by each incoming president of the United States. These Americans in the top executive and bureaucratic positions are almost always outsiders to the agencies they run, not career bureaucrats who have worked their way to the top through numerous positions within the agency to learn their jobs "inside-out." The United States, in fact, is most extreme among the democratic industrial nations in this respect, with England the only nation somewhat similar to the United States, and Germany most similar to Japan.[194]

In contrast to the Japanese bureaucratic elites, one observer insists, "the American president's power to make political appointments for the top positions in the departments of the American government renders them completely dependent on the president and robs the bureaucracy of its daring, autonomy, and in the long run, talent."[195] Compared to Japan, the U.S. method of selecting bureaucratic elites results in inexperience; the U.S. method also makes it easy for outside special interest groups to capture government agencies for their own agendas.[196] For example, from 1897 to 1973, over 75 percent of U.S. cabinet members have had direct links with major corporations, most coming directly from a top corporate position to the president's cabinet.[197] This characteristic of the American government is no doubt responsible for one conclusion from a Swiss study ranking the twenty largest industrial nations on 283 criteria: only one country was considered to have more outside special interest group influence on its government policy than the United States.[198]

THE NATURE OF THE JAPANESE BUREAUCRACY

In contrast to a new U.S. president, when a Japanese prime minister takes office he appoints individuals to twenty positions—that is it. The prime minister appoints the ministers and heads of the twenty main bureaucratic agencies in Japan. But it must also be pointed out that these ministers are not considered to be the most powerful individuals in these ministries. They are temporary, less experienced, and primarily dependent upon the vice-minister in the agency. The vice-minister, on the other hand, is a career bureaucrat who has spent all of his working life in the same government agency, moving up the career ladder to the top since graduation from a major university. These are the people considered most powerful individuals within each Japanese government agency.

The Japanese prime minister, it is said, has less power than any other top government executive from a leading industrial nation.[199] The constitutional structure of Japan, of course, helps account for this weak chief executive. Culture and traditions, however, should not be neglected as causal factors, though in our opinion these have been given too much consideration in the past. Lucian Pye is worth quoting on this point:

Indeed, the great paradox about power in Japan is that although the culture was profoundly shaped by a warrior-samurai tradition, and although the country has carried out imperial conquests and now, because of the ties between government and business, is considered to be a dynamic economic force, the Japanese have never embraced the idea of leadership as decisive executive power. To the Western mind it was inconceivable that Japan could have initiated the Pacific war without a decisive, ultimate leader, and hence it became necessary in the West to make Tōjō Hideki into a kind of dictator comparable to Hitler and Mussolini, when in fact Tōjō played a much more subtle and indirect role.[200]

It is in this context that we find a government with a tendency toward collective rule. This collective rule does not emanate primarily from the Diet or even the Liberal Democratic Party, though power is certainly found in these bodies: Rather, as most students of the Japanese government have argued, Japan has a "bureaucratocracy." Top bureaucratic officials have broad authority to govern, and studies of this bureaucratic elite have found they feel a personal obligation and right to govern the *makiminsha*—"the herd."[201]

It is largely the high status and sense of mission among the bureaucratic elite in Japan (at least during the post-war period) that has helped them attract a large share of the best and brightest young college graduates. The attraction has certainly not been high pay. In a study of what Japanese researchers defined as the top industrial elite (154 individuals) and the top national bureaucratic officials (113 individuals), the following annual income distribution was found (in 1984 American dollars)[202]:

	Industrial Elite	Bureaucratic Elite
Over $160,000	43%	0%
$80,000–160,000	34%	7%
$48,000–79,000	14%	70%
Under $48,000	9%	23%

Our description of the Japanese bureaucratic elite thus far may be difficult for Americans to accept. The best and brightest, from the most respected universities, devoting many years of their lives to serving the nation, working 60 hour weeks, for what in comparison to the corporate world amounts to very low pay! How is this possible? But it has been possible; at least until recently. To understand the situation better requires a closer examination of this bureaucracy.

A Brief History of the Bureaucratic Elite

A strong central government bureaucracy is not uncommon among late-developing nations such as Japan, especially in East Asia and Southeast Asia.[203] In fact, a strong central government bureaucracy, with talented people and relatively little corruption, seems to be a requirement for late development, ennabling a country to catch up with the already industrialized nations. But in some ways Japan's central bureaucracy is unique.

In contrast to China and Korea, Japan had no long tradition of bureaucratic officials selected through examinations to carry out extensive governmental functions. Japan, therefore, had to create a "tradition" of "national servants" in the process of modernization and industrialization. We have seen that the first ruling elites of the Meiji period (beginning in the 1860s) were members of the lower samurai who helped overthrow the Tokugawa shogunate. But with pressures for democracy from below the elite level, and a desire to copy at least some aspects of Western government, a new constitution allowing some democracy (1.5 percent of the population could vote) was created, taking effect in 1889.

During the 1870s and 1880s Japan sent its new leaders and intellectuals to the industrialized West to gather information on how to proceed with developing its own institutions and industries, from education to shipbuilding. With respect to governmental institutions, this Meiji elite found much to like in Bismarck's Germany, the "Prussian model."[204] After consulting with the German constitutional scholar von Stein, as well as with Bismarck himself, one of the founders of the new Japanese government, Itō Hirobumi, wrote home:

The trends in our country today erroneously lead to a belief in the works of the extreme liberals and radicals of England, America and France and to considering their theories as the supreme norm. In having found principles and means of reversing these trends, I believe I have rendered an important service to my country, and I feel that I can die a happy man.[205]

This Prussian model of government gave considerable powers to an independent bureaucracy that theoretically answered to the emperor, not to the elected Diet. But in reality, this bureaucracy, when it answered to anyone, answered to the *genrō*, or elder statesmen, former samurai who had helped overthrow the Tokugawa shogunate.[206]

With Japan's defeat in World War II came the new constitution written by the Occupation forces under MacArthur (not by the Japanese), and written originally in English, which still creates some problems in interpretation. The post-war constitution continued to allow for extensive bureaucratic power, though does not require it. The Occupation unwittingly made it almost certain that the bureaucratic elite would not only maintain but actually expand its power. First, because the Occupation forces did not fully understand the pre-war Japanese political system, they assumed that the military and politicians had most power before the war, and were therefore responsible for the war. These people were promptly purged. Over 79 percent of these purges involved military officers, and 16 percent involved politicians—less than 1 percent involved the bureaucratic elite.[207] Second, the remaining, untainted politicians placed into positions of power by the Occupation were inexperienced and mostly incompetent.[208] The resulting power vacuum was filled by the bureaucratic elite.

STAFFING THE ELITE POSITIONS

Two basic points must be made about the bureaucratic elite, especially since World War II: (1) the bureaucratic elite is selected based upon merit, and (2) it is exceptionally well trained. These bureaucrats are not people who attain their positions only because of family background or connections, nor are they individuals who can relax and sit back while others do the work once they have attained positions in the higher levels of the ministry. We will note some elements of change in recent years, but it is not unreasonable to say that these elite individuals in the powerful ministries deserve the high respect given them by the nation, and most other nations would be better off if they had such individuals running their governments.

From the beginning, which is to say, from the Meiji period when the government bureaucracy was established, the ministry elite have come up through the most respected universities in Japan. For example, "Of the ninety-seven men who were appointed as higher-civil-service trainees . . . in the 1888–1891 period, all but nine were Tōdai graduates" (Tokyo Imperial University).[209] This pattern of selection from the top universities, especially from Tokyo University, has continued up to the present.[210] Since World War II it has been even more difficult to pass the entrance exams for these top universities, with Tokyo University the most difficult in the nation. Thus, because graduation from one of the top universities is almost without exception required for bureaucratic elite selection, a strong element of meritocracy is created.

Beyond the requirement of a top university degree for bureaucratic elite selection, however, are other exams. Each ministry has its own exams every year to determine which graduates enter the ministry. There are in fact four types of exams for each ministry, corresponding to four tracks of career placement. The truly elite track (we can say the "fast track") requires a recent college graduate to pass the Type 1 exam.[211] Only after an exam for the ministry track has been passed is there some discretion on the part of the ministry as to who is selected. Factors such as personality and connections can enter at this point. For example, Owada Masako, the woman who finally gave up a promising career and agreed to marry the crown prince after an embarrassingly long search for a bride ending in 1993, was in a fast-track position in the Foreign Ministry. She attended Oxford University and graduated from Harvard University, speaks several languages, and passed the tough exam at the Foreign Ministry to become a candidate for the fast-track position. After that, and only after that, it no doubt helped a great deal that her father was the vice-minister.[212]

As with major corporations in Japan, once accepted into the fast track, the person becomes a member of the "freshman class," made up of all individuals entering a ministry that year. All the people who join a formal organization—private or public—are part of the same *doki*, which has something of the feeling of "class" in traditional Western academic life. These are the people that members feel are their true peers, even though eventually it is with the *doki*, and only with the *doki*, that competition for high-level advancement will take place. The members of the *doki* are promoted together through the first several years of the careers of members and they all receive similar training. The training process at the Ministry of Finance is rather typical.[213] In the first year new employees on the elite track receive extensive orientation and each is assigned to a person one year senior to "learn the ropes." In the second year they are sent to work in the field, at a local tax office, for example. The third year is mostly devoted to further study, with professors invited into the ministry, or at a university. There is then a couple of years or so in other positions in various divisions of the ministry, followed by a few more years as chief of a local office, before moving into higher, policy-making positions. In other ministries with more international responsibilities (such as MITI or the Foreign Ministry) the first ten years will include foreign assignments as well.

By the time these men reach their late 40s and early 50s, as is also typical in the Japanese corporate world, their career mobility options begin to narrow.[214] All of the members of the *doki* on the fast track can no longer be promoted together. At this point selections for truly elite positions are made, and the conflicts and infighting between factions and sections of the ministries begin.

Those who are not promoted at this time are expected to retire. This is one reason for *amakudari* (the "descent from heaven" into the corporate world), but only one reason, especially in recent years. Younger members of the fast tracks in recent years are showing evidence of altering this pattern with even earlier self-determined retirements for moves to the corporate sector. This alteration creates a new individualistic strategy for career advancement to greater income for the ambitious who have entered the ministry less intent on service to the ministry and society.

THE SOURCES OF BUREAUCRATIC ELITE POWER

There has been debate within Japan over the extent to which some Diet members are gaining more influence in relation to the bureaucratic elite. While clearly overstated, a new phrase appeared in the Japanese media, *tōkō kantei* ("party predominant-bureaucracy subordinate"), which would have been unthinkable a couple of decades ago.[215]

A major part of the argument for expanded Diet power was that a few new groups of LDP politicians in the Diet, called *zoku*, had gained sufficient expertise on particular policy issues (such as education policy) to enable them to counter the ministry elite, actually making important decisions themselves, and dictating these decisions to the ministry.[216] There are still questions such as how often this happens, with how many policy issues, and who the *zoku* are really serving, the LDP or the bureaucratic elite.[217] Many of these *zoku* members in the Diet are, in fact, retired bureaucratic officials.

The loss of power by the LDP in 1993, and the general disarray among politicians before and since the fall of the LDP, brings this notion of *"zoku* power" into serious question today. However, to understand how the postwar bureaucratic elite has normally dominated the Diet and its policies, and how future politicians may or may not gain more power, one must consider the sources of bureaucratic elite influence.

There are twelve main ministries in the Japanese government, and several less important agencies.[218] The most important ministries, which is to say the ministries said to have most power in the Japanese government, are the ministries of Justice, Foreign Affairs, Finance, and International Trade and Industry.[219] The prime minister selects the minister for each of the twelve ministries, as well as the heads of eight other agencies. These people then make up the prime minister's cabinet, much as in the United States. However, as noted earlier, it is the vice-minister in each of these ministries who is considered most knowledgeable and powerful. As political appointees, compared to the vice-ministers, who are career civil servants, the ministers of these bureaucracies are inexperienced, outsiders to the agencies, and to a large extent at the mercy of the vice-ministers. The vice-minister of each agency has spent his whole career in the ministry, working his way to the top since college graduation thirty to forty years previous. The vice-minister, therefore, has wide experience and training in the agency, extensive knowledge of the particular aspects of the Japanese society the agency is to regulate, and the loyalty of thousands of other ministry officials in the agency. Politicians and temporary outsiders coming in as a minister of the agency are at a disadvantage.

Beyond these means of influence, however, the vice-ministers and their assistants have several others that are outcomes of the resources described above. One of the most important is their ability to write legislation. Like the U.S. Congress, the Diet is the legislative branch of government. But in reality, most Japanese laws are written by ministry officials and handed to the Diet for passage. The ministry officials' ability to do this is partially related to the fact that Diet members are given very few staff members to help with their work (in vast contrast to members of the U.S. Congress), while there are thousands of ministry officials directed by the vice-ministers. And not only are most bills which go through the Diet written by ministry officials, about 80 percent of the ministry-sponsored bills pass the Diet, compared to 30 percent or less of the Diet-sponsored bills. Between 1955 and 1970, for example, the ministry-sponsored bills had a 75 percent passage rate, compared to about 14 percent for Diet-sponsored bills.[220] But it is not only that most legislation is written by ministry officials, it is also how those laws are written. In Japan laws are often vague and leave wide gaps of interpretation. The ministries, of course, administer the laws, and in the process they also have the luxury of interpreting the laws because of how they have written the laws.

The most famous source of ministry influence is "administrative guidance." The basis of administrative guidance comes from Japanese law giving the ministries the authority to issue directives, requests, warnings, and to offer suggestions and encouragement to private organizations and individuals. "Administrative guidance is constrained only by the requirement that the 'guidees' must come under a given governmental organ's jurisdiction. . . ."[221]

Finally, among all other means of bureaucratic elite influence, the important influence held by the economically related agencies, the Ministry of Finance and MITI, over the Japanese economy and corporations must be mentioned. A key ingredient in this "economic guidance" is the control these ministries have over commercial loans. In contrast to the United States, corporations in Japan are more likely to expand through bank loans rather than new stock issues.[222] These ministries can target industries for development and carry out their plans by influencing which corporations and industries are able to secure the capital for their growth or survival through administrative guidance to private banks, and their control over the Japan Development Bank and the Bank of Japan (both government agencies).[223]

A typical example of Japanese bureaucratic power has been noted in earlier pages: the stock market "crash" of the early 1990s was, as suggested earlier, in fact stimulated by Mieno at the Bank of Japan, but then managed by the Ministry of Finance. The Ministry of Finance realized that the "economic bubble" had deflated too far when the Japanese stock market fell by 60 percent through 1992. The Ministry of Finance then went into action. To stop the slide in stock values they first ordered many big companies to suspend stock sales temporarily. Secondly, they gave administrative guidance (read, "leaned on") institutional investors to buy stock in big quantities. Finally, the ministry itself started buying large sums of stock with public funds, including $22 billion in public pensions funds. The only debate in the Ministry of Finance was over the timing of the intervention.[224]

The impression given, however, should not be that the Japanese ministries are all-powerful and always successful in what they attempt. As Johnson points out with many examples in the post-war period, there is not always simple compliance to these ministry directives under administrative guidance. From time to time there is successful resistance. The ministries contribute to some of this due to internal conflicts, and there are also conflicts between ministries. The ministries on occasion have also turned out to be dead wrong.

In one of the most famous cases of non-compliance, and a spectacular example of a bad call by a ministry, back in the 1970s MITI "ordered" Honda (the motorcycle maker) not to get into the car business. MITI reasoned that there were already enough auto makers in Japan, and more competition would be harmful to the industry. MITI was convinced that Honda could never catch up to the other big auto makers to the point of staying in the game and showing a profit. Honda Sōichirō, "Papa" Honda as he was called by many Japanese, the founder and still controller of the company at the time, didn't agree. He defied MITI and was able to begin building cars anyway. The rest, as the saying goes, is history.

The successes of MITI and the other ministries, however, are numerous, including Japan's success in overtaking the United States in consumer electronics, in auto quality, and computer chips, among many others.[225] There is Japan's huge reduction in energy consumption in the 1970s after the first big world-wide "oil shock," together with the way the economy was managed to minimize the disruption from big price increases in oil at this time; all of this has been attributed to the ministries. And it can be noted that Japan had one of the world's biggest rates of industrial pollution and industrial accidents in the 1960s. Today, these rates in Japan are among the lowest of all industrial nations. Responsibility, again, has been given to Japan's ministries for their action and concern for long-term national interests over the short-term interests of particular corporations.

AMAKUDARI: THE UNIFYING DESCENT FROM HEAVEN

In his historical study of Japan's elite, Okumura Hiroshi argues that since World War II the bureaucratic elite and corporate elite have been more united than has ever been the case, perhaps more united than in any other capitalist nation in history. Before the war, the old *zaibatsu* corporate groups found it difficult to cooperate on broad issues, and political factions in government were associated with particular *zaibatsu*.[226] The Kenseikai political faction was tied to the Mitsubishi *zaibatsu*, for example, while the Seiyūkai political faction was tied to the Mitsui *zaibatsu*. These groups were always fighting for advantage, which usually blocked any unified action for their common interests.

Since World War II, however, cooperation, coordination, and unity have become more common. Japanese corporations compete with each other ferociously for market share and profits. But at the same time, they have remarkable cooperation on common interests. The organization of Japanese elites is in large part responsible for this ability to cooperate on many issues. Some of this was considered in the previous chapter, and other factors promoting unity will be considered in later chapters. But much of this unity can be attributed to *amakudari*. The heaven referred to in this case is the lofty heights of influence held by the bureaucratic elite in post-war Japan, while the descent is retirement from a government ministry to a corporate position. Before we consider the importance of *amakudari* in more detail, let's consider how it all worked in the case of one of Japan's famous elite.

The "King of Tokyo"

"Rags to riches" stories do exist in Japan, as suggested in the tradition of *kontaikō*, the self-made men of Japan. How quickly some men can achieve their success through first securing a fast-track ministry position as a means of later acceptance into elite corporate circles is demonstrated by the story of Gōtō Keitarō (1883–1959).[227] Keitarō was called variously "King of Tokyo," or "Robber Keitarō," depending on the speaker's point of view. Gōtō was the first to see the potential for residential development in the way that concept was used in the United States. His idea was to buy up land outside of a city which was certain to grow in size in the future, build a rail line to the land, and later build houses on the land. The residents would then have to use his rail line to commute back and forth from their homes to work. This was long before automobile ownership was extensive in Japan, but even now the system works quite well. Specifically, Gōtō developed huge areas to the southwest of Tokyo around two commuter rail lines including the famous Denenchōfu, home to many of Tokyo's wealthiest residents. By the end of his career, Gōtō was most closely associated in Japanese business circles with the Tōkyū Railways and Tōkyū department stores which he created in the process.

Gōtō Keitarō was born in a mountain village near the town of Ueda in Nagano Prefecture, into a family so poor that he had to delay going to school. Keitarō finally managed to finish high school two years late, and was still able to get into Tokyo University Faculty of Law. While attending Tōdai he worked as tutor for some wealthy students preparing for the ministry examinations. One of them was Katō Takaaki, a scion of the Mitsui family and a man who eventually became prime minister in the 1920s. After graduation Keitarō served in the Ministry of Agriculture, and later moved to the Ministry of Railroads.

In 1921 Keitarō was recommended as a sort of pre-war version of *amakudari* by one of his former tutees to take the position of operations director at the recently formed Musashi Railroad Company. He gradually became the company's president and kept buying more and more of its stock. He eventually became a one-man ruler of the company as if he had founded it. The name of the company was changed in the 1930s to Tokyo Express Lines (abbreviated as Tōkyū), and he began buying up development land as well as other companies such as retail stores, hotels, and so forth. Since the company was not big enough to be treated like a *zaibatsu* corporation by the Occupation authorities after World War II, the organization was able to stay relatively intact, and continued to grow. Today the *keiretsu* to which Tōkyū belongs is one of the biggest, with 626 affiliated companies organized around fifteen main companies, employing over 86,000 people.

It is also important to note that back in 1910, while still with the Ministry of Railroads, Keitarō became *yōshi* (son-in-law and then adopted son) into the family of a famous architect who had helped remodel the old imperial palace to its present form. Their family name was Kume, but they gave Keitarō the surname Gōtō to revive the name of the main branch of their family. This adoption was instrumental in bringing him acceptance in the corporate elite world and opening doors. Thus, in the life of Gōtō Keitarō, we find a talented but very poor young man who was able to use his ministry status, along with old school ties, to gain acceptance into an elite family (actually becoming a legal member of this elite family) and later into the corporate world, where he applied his ambitions and talents to become one of the most powerful men in post-war Japan. This career-hopping with *amakudari* and the institution of *yōshi* has become more common since World War II, with Keitarō later taking *yōshi* for his own daughters to build an even stronger position in the top circles of the Japanese elite.

While Gōtō Keitarō's rise from poverty to extensive power and wealth may not be quite so typical today, his move from the ministry to corporate elite status, with an arranged marriage and adoption into an elite family along the way, is *not* untypical. During 1991 alone, 218 individuals who were members of the bureaucratic elite left their government positions for new corporate positions in companies which were regulated by the very ministry these individuals moved from. Research shows that the cases of *amakudari* increased greatly from the early 1960s through most of the 1980s. In 1963, for example, there were 165 cases, while by 1985 there was a high of 320.[228] Along with this trend has been the growing importance, along with the power, of the Ministry of Finance. Of the 218 indi-viduals involved in *amakudari* in 1991, fifty-four came from the Ministry of Finance.[229]

Before the war, and soon after, the typical *amakudari* involved a bureau-cratic official who had almost reached the top of a ministry or in fact had reached the top, retiring at age fifty or so to a corporate position. This form of *amakudari* is even more common today. The new trend in recent years, however, is for a bureaucratic official on a ministry fast track to "retire" to a corporate position in his 40s, or even earlier.[230] Gōtō Keitarō was rather unusual in doing this during the pre-war years; it is not so unusual today. To understand these trends it is important to see what corporations get out of *amakudari*, then see what motivates the bureaucratic officials involved in the move.

As in the cases of personnel from U.S. government agencies who move to corporate positions from the Defense Department or regulatory agencies, it can be said that the former government officials knew they would be rewarded later for being "soft" on the corporation; thus, they get a delayed bribe, so to speak. *Amakudari* can also work in this manner, but it is even more complicated.[231]

One important reason that former bureaucratic officials are so attractive to big business has to do with the role played by MITI and other govern-ment regulative agencies in recent decades. For a capitalist economy, as we have said, Japan has an unusually close relationship between the administra-tive arm of the government and large corporations. Administrative guidance is carried out through meetings and then reams of regulations are based on decisions made at these meetings. These regulations are constantly changing both in their wording, and most importantly, in the way they are inter-preted. *Amakudari* employees are not hired randomly; they enter companies regulated by the ministry for whom they were employed before. These in-coming officials from the ministry "speak the language" of those doing the regulating and are very important links to the ministry, allowing corpora-tions to anticipate future ministry actions, as well as to understand better the complex rules which are handed down.

The age-based promotion system in Japan creates another logic for *amak-udari* in that the top bureaucratic officials who leave for corporate positions will always be seen as seniors deserving of respect and consideration by the bureaucratic officials replacing them from the younger age rank. But there is another logic to this system, and in this case a logic for taking younger men from the ministries. In government ministries as well as in corporations, young college graduates start out in the company or ministry at the same time. They are in the "freshman class" of the company or ministry together. They are all hired on the same day, go through orientation and training together, and become close associates in the experience. They are then pro-moted up the ladder together, until at the top ranges (at around ages fifty

Table 5.1
***Amakudari* Employees in the Top 100 Corporations[232]**

From Ministry of Finance	151
From MITI	118
From Ministry of Development	74
From Ministry of Transportation	65
From Bureau of the Environment	40
From Postal Service	34
From Bureau of Defense	33
Other	55

to fifty-five) some are promoted over others, with those not promoted nor-mally retiring. A corporation who takes an *amakudari* at age thirty-five or so is making an investment. This employee will be of help in the present for explaining the new rules of the agency, and perhaps in suggesting what the company can anticipate from the employee's inside knowledge of the min-istry. However, in another fifteen years or so, some of the *amakudari* em-ployee's "freshman class" friends from the ministry will begin moving in positions of power in the ministry. Then the old boy ties will become more valuable.

We can now take a closer look at evidence on the extent of *amakudari* in Japan in recent years. Table 5.1 lists the number of *amakudari* employees in only the largest 100 corporations in Japan (as of 1978) and some of the ministries from which they came.

Another way to indicate the importance and extent of *amakudari* is to consider one of the top ministries and the most important official within the ministry, the vice-minister. Listed in Table 5.2 are all of the former vice-ministers of MITI since World War II and the corporate positions they obtained upon *amakudari*.

From the point of view of the bureaucratic officials making their moves through *amakudari* we can understand their motivations, and what keeps the system in operation. To begin with, of course, there is more money. As we pointed out before, the salaries of bureaucrats, even in the top positions, is quite low compared to corporate salaries. But there is more than just higher salaries, or most of the graduates from Tokyo University, for exam-ple, would take their first position in the corporate world rather than in a ministry.

One way to put *amakudari* as a career path in perspective is to reflect upon the restructuring of Japan after the war. For half a century there were

Table 5.2
Former Vice-Ministers of MITI and Their Later Top Corporate Positions, Since World War II[233]

Name	*Corporate Position*
Yamanoto Takayuki	Vice-President, Fuji Iron and Steel
Tamaki Keizō	President and Chairman, Toshiba Electric Co.
Hirai Tomisaburō	President, New Japan Steel Corp.
Ishihara Takeo	Vice-President, Tokyo Electric Power
Ueno Koshichi	Vice-President, Kansai Electric Power
Tokunaga Hisatsugo	Vice-President, New Japan Steel Corp.
Matsuo Kinzō	Chairman, Nippon Kōkan Steel Corp.
Imai Zen'ei	President, Japan Petrochemical Corp.
Sahashi Shigeru	Chairman, Japan Leisure Development Center
Yamanoto Shigenobu	Executive Director, Toyota Motor Co.
Kumagai Yoshifumi	President, Sumitomo Metals Corp.
Ojimi Yoshihisa	President, Arabian Oil Co.
Morozumi Yoshihiko	President, Electric Power Development Co.
Yamashita Eimei	Managing Director, Mitsui Trading Co.
Komatsu Yūgorō	Director, Kobe Steel Corp.

two avenues open to bright and ambitious young men who wanted low-risk advancement opportunities in return for devotion to service or study. One was Japan's large military world, a giant bureaucracy with highly specific and dependable criteria for upward mobility. The other was the bureaucracy, rooted mainly in scholarship. Suddenly one was completely eliminated, but the other remained almost completely intact. The world of public administration had always attracted bright people, but especially in the era of great uncertainty of business ventures up until the late 1950s, the life of a ministry official was for a time more attractive than ever for Japan's brightest. The idea that people who get into and move up the ladder within major ministries are the smartest people in Japan became an accepted fact after the war and is likely to persist for a long time, thus making these people highly attractive for corporations.

Besides the status of having been a ministry official, however, is the variety of career patterns it opens up, especially for a young man who is not well connected to a wealthy family already. If one starts with a corporation after graduation, moving to another corporation, not to mention to a totally different career, is not very likely. And in recent years moving to the very top of the corporate world has become more difficult without family connections. But if one begins with a ministry career, several options are open. First, of course, is the option of staying with the ministry throughout a career, ending up in a top position of the ministry. Second is the option of *amakudari*, though it is difficult to move to the very top reaches of the corporate world in this manner. Third is the option of courting favor with the LDP or another political party to be sponsored for election to the Diet. The fourth option is to become a *yōshi* through marriage and then legal adoption into a wife's family, giving the husband a claim to his wife's family fortunes in later life.

A wealthy corporate family without a male heir is a sad thing in male-dominated Japan. But given Japanese tradition it is perfectly acceptable for the wealthy family to arrange a marriage for their daughter to a promising and talented young man who can be adopted to run family affairs in later years. Today, young fast-track ministry officials make for attractive prospects. To begin with, they have the status of the ministry position. But also, they have proven their talent to a large extent by getting into a top university and passing the ministry exam to get into the fast track. And finally, what better future son to have for a corporate executive than one already possessing connections in MITI or the Ministry of Finance? To bring such a young man into the family can do wonders for the corporation's future. And, in fact, even if the executive already has a son or two of his own at home, it would not hurt to have another one through taking a *yōshi* who has such ministry connections.

In order to continue this discussion of elite convergance, the last of the "iron triangle," the political elite, must be considered.

CHAPTER 6

The Political Elite: Junior Partner and Protectorate

There were big changes in Japan during the middle 1990s. The Liberal Democratic Party (LDP) which had ruled Japan since 1955 was briefly out of power; several of the old LDP elite were in jail or awaiting trial; a group of new political parties took power with a coalition government in 1993; and under Prime Minister Hosokawa new election reform laws were passed by the Diet. But perhaps most shocking of all, old archenemies, the Socialists and the conservative LDP, formed a coalition government, in effect allowing the LDP to regain power. Decades-old political principles were thrown out the window by the Socialists almost overnight so both they and the LDP could keep their jobs, threatened by reform-minded politicians in new parties. For their policy reversals, Socialists were allowed by the LDP to take the prime minister position in a coalition government clearly dominated by the LDP.

Behind many of these events was a new "kingmaker," Ozawa Ichirō, who led the break from the LDP and helped form the coalition of new parties which briefly took power in 1993. In his book, *Blueprints for Building a New Japan*, which sold over 500,000 copies in just a few months during 1993, Ozawa wrote that Japan must become a "normal nation" which takes care of international responsibilities, and it must become more democratic, which primarily means extensive campaign reform and capping the power of the increasingly hated bureaucratic elite. Indeed, Ozawa argues in this book that the whole nature of the Japanese society must change: Japanese people work too hard, and they have a much lower standard of living than they deserve considering the world-wide success of their economy. Even the "groupism mentality" of the Japanese society must be changed. For Japan, this was heavy stuff.

There is, however, a saying about Japan, popular among those who know the country well: "There are big changes going on in Japan, but Japan as usual is not changing very much." The changes outlined above, put simply, are more apparent than real. Many of the election law changes are likely to be ignored, avoided through a bewildering maze of loopholes, or simply not fully implemented. To the extent that some of the new election laws are finally implemented, such as the single-seat districts to be discussed below, they are almost certain to end up favoring conservative politicians who came up under old party elites in the LDP, while reducing the influence of liberal and leftist parties. In effect, Japan will likely end up with two LDP clones vying for power, with other political parties who are less pro-big business becoming extinct. But in the next few years, if not for much longer, the old bureaucratic elite considered in the previous chapter, in cooperation with the corporate elite, are likely to remain firmly in place, with their hands on the helm of Japanese society.

The apparent political turmoil in Japan during the 1990s is related to adjustments which must be made by conservative politicians and other elites in Japan in order to prop up the status quo. The old LDP elite by the late 1980s had become an embarrassment to everyone: $50 million stashed in Kanemaru's home safe, and another $35 million in a son's home, was a bit much. The Japanese people, who normally did not think much of the political elite anyway, were becoming increasingly angry while the rest of the world was laughing at the Japanese political scene, wondering how Japan could be such an economic power in light of all the misadventures of those believed to be running things.

Before we get to these subjects, however, we have some basics to cover. Compared to Japan's corporate system—with *keiretsu* ties, presidents' clubs, and stock control primarily in the hands of corporations themselves—and compared to Japan's governmental system which gives unelected bureaucratic elites so much power, Japan's political system looks much more familiar to people in Western democratic nations. Japan has national and local elections with politicians shouting many of the same slogans heard elsewhere; there is a national parliament (Diet) with an upper and lower house that debates and passes legislation, and there are political parties who elect their leader as prime minister when the party (or coalition) obtains a majority of the seats in the lower house. There are even the inevitable bribery scandals here and there, perhaps in greater numbers than in some other countries, but fewer compared to countries such as Italy. Yet these similarities are often misleading. As an example, the reform-oriented Prime Minister Hosokawa was forced out of office in April of 1994 with a popular approval rating of 65 percent, the highest for any post-war prime minister. Something doesn't seem quite right.

POLITICS IN JAPAN: BASIC FEATURES

What preceded the fall of the Liberal Democratic Party in 1993 was a growing number of scandals involving money illegally obtained and primarily used to hang on to political power. The first big wave of scandal culminated in 1989 when Prime Minister Takeshita finally resigned because of connections to the insider trading scandal involving the Recruit Cosmos corporation. A previous prime minister, Nakasone, was also connected to this scandal through key political supporters. The prime minister put up to replace Takeshita, Uno Sōsuke, lasted less than one year before an embarrassing scandal involving his kept geisha brought him down in 1990. The next LDP prime minister had a squeaky clean image, but again lasted only about one year because he actually tried to press for political reforms the party elite would not support. Then came Miyazawa Kiichi and an even bigger bribery scandal. While major politicians were condemning those involved in the Recruit Cosmos scandal of 1989, many of these same people were soon found to be taking much more money from the big Sagawa Express company, and this time the scandal involved a company with ties to the *yakuza* (organized crime). As we have seen, Prime Minister Miyazawa and the whole LDP party finally came down in 1993, to be replaced temporarily by a coalition of new parties and old opposition parties.

The image presented in most of the world's press at the time was of mass political revolt by voters in the July 1993 national election. There was certainly popular discontent. National opinion polls just a few months before the 1993 election found 70 percent of Japanese voters did not think the popular will of the people was reflected in government, 65 percent favored a complete ban on corporate campaign contributions, and only 10 percent of voters approved of Prime Minister Miyazawa and his government—close to Takeshita's all-time low of 8 percent in 1989.[234]

The revolt by voters, however, was quite tame by international standards. The LDP were forced into the July national election to begin with because they lost their majority in the Diet when thirty-six LDP politicians deserted the party to join newly formed parties.[235]

When elections finally occurred in July of 1993, most old politicians were reelected. Going into the July election, and after the earlier desertion by some key LDP politicians, the LDP had 227 members out of 511 in the more powerful lower house of the Diet. After the election they had lost only four members, leaving the LDP with 223.[236] In the end, what brought down the LDP was an internal revolt by some younger Diet members who bolted the party before July, seeking power by getting around the old party leadership.

While all of this was going on in Japan there were also national elections in scandal-ridden Italy. With criticisms of Italian politicians similar to those made in Japan, the Italians certainly did "throw the rascals out": approximately two-thirds of those elected in 1994 were running for office the first time. Why was there no popular revolt in Japan? Why did they not also "throw the rascals out"?

When Japanese voters went to the polls in 1993, national issues and big new scandals seemed to matter much less than in Italy. Shortly before the Japanese vote, polls indicated the number one issue for voters was concern about pensions and medical funds, with the high prices of consumer goods second, and political scandals only a distant third. What must be recognized is that the LDP's hold on power since 1955, and the continuing influence of the LDP and related politicians even after the 1993 elections, is based upon a political system that operates differently than most in the West. Japanese politics are based more upon the old style of "pork-barrel" local politics that used to exist in big American city governments such as Chicago, rather than upon national elections based upon political principles or national issues.

THE 1947 CONSTITUTION

Soon after the Tokugawa shogunate fell and the Meiji Restoration of 1868 began, the new leaders of Japan set about planning for a modern, Western-style constitution. The new Meiji Constitution, finally in place in 1889, was modeled on that of Germany more than of Britain because of the power it gave to the bureaucracy and other unelected political elites. Japan's first prime minister, and the man most responsible for writing the Constitution of 1889, Itō Hirobumi, visited Europe in the 1880s to study political systems. He was told by the conservative British social Darwinist Herbert Spencer that Japan should retain "traditional obligations to superiors."[237] The Japanese constitution was hardly the model of democracy. Few people in Japan at the time even understood the concept, which really mattered little because for several decades only slightly more than 1 percent of the people were allowed to vote under the new constitution anyway.[238]

With Japan's defeat and then occupation after World War II, the Meiji Constitution was abolished. And in a curious turn of events, after the Occupation forces under General MacArthur rejected attempt after attempt by the Japanese to write a new constitution, MacArthur ordered a small staff of rather inexperienced Americans to write the new constitution for the Japanese, in English, and then forced it upon Japanese politicians.[239]

This is the constitution Japan retains to this day, and it is a constitution which, in fact, grants more freedoms and provisions to promote democracy than most Western democratic constitutions.[240] All adults can now vote for representatives to both houses of the Diet, and in fact over 70 percent of the people usually do vote, in contrast to half or less of those eligible who vote in national elections in the United States. There are several parties which win at least some seats, including a Communist Party holding fifteen seats after the 1993 national elections.

As with any other parliamentary system, the party with a majority of seats, or one that can form a coalition with other parties giving the coalition enough seats, forms a government and appoints cabinet ministers. To repeat, the Liberal Democratic Party (LDP) had held such a majority since 1955, but lost its majority in the more powerful lower house of the Diet in 1993. As a means of judging party diversity in Japan, as well as the success of the coalition which replaced the LDP in 1993, we can consider results of the 1993 election.

The lower house of the Diet had 511 seats at the time of the 1993 election, with 256 therefore needed for a majority. In 1990 the LDP held 275 seats, but only 227 after the defections shortly before the 1993 election, and only 223 after the election.[241] The next largest party was the Social Democratic Party of Japan (formerly simply the Socialist Party) with 136 seats in 1990, but only 70 after the 1993 election. One of the main parties formed by politicians breaking away from the LDP, Shinsetō, gained 55 seats in 1993, and another breakaway party, Shintō Sakigake, gained 13 seats, while the new party formed by Hosokawa Morihiro, the Japan New Party, won 35 seats. Other parties and their standing after the 1993 election include Kōmeitō (51), Japanese Communist Party (15), Social Democratic Party (15), and Shaminren (4), with the remaining 30 seats held by independents.

While the Diet organization and party system may seem rather familiar when compared to parliamentary systems of Western nations, there are several features of the Japanese political system that create a political game which is played quite differently in Japan. Two of these features deserve our attention. The first has to do with party loyalty and party factions, while the second has to do with the local focus of "national" politicians.

One key difference is that party leaders have much more influence over party members in Japan, even though this has been weakened in recent years.[242] When the LDP leadership decides how the party will vote, for example, with very few exceptions that is how the party members will vote. Devotion to the group, and respect for leaders play a part in this, but quite simply, party elites have more control over such things as campaign funds, endorsements, and choice positions in the Diet than party leaders in other countries. This is to say, most issues are decided by party elites in the legendary smoke-filled rooms (literally smoke-filled with so many heavy smokers) or expensive restaurants, and once decided, that is how the party will vote. There is seldom much drama in the Diet while votes are tallied, and if there is much drama it has all been carefully planned well beforehand.

Another different feature of Japanese political parties has to do with the important relationship between a *sempai* and *kōhai*—or the senior-junior bond.[243] A junior person usually seeks a "big brother" in every group, a person who will help protect and sponsor the junior person in return for the person's loyalty. As a result, organizations in Japan are often structured by inverted "Vs" of one person who has one or more junior sponsors (*kō-hai*), with the "Vs" running from bottom to top of the organization. Thus, people of approximately equal rank represent potential fracture lines in the organization: they may take their juniors, and the juniors of their juniors, out of the group, forming factions that are in competition within the larger group.

Because of this, the Liberal Democratic Party and other major parties have in some ways been several parties in one, each with their leader (or king-maker) competing with others for power and favor.[244] At times, as in the early 1990s within the LDP, these factions may in fact result in complete breaks to form new parties. Within the party power is obtained by getting more members in your faction, and to get more members you must have rewards worth handing out, such as campaign money (legally or illegally obtained) and positions (present or future potential for giving positions). The kingmakers with such rewards under their control may not be so obvious to outsiders, and may seem to defy the laws of political gravity, which brings us to the remarkable case of former Prime Minister Tanaka.

Tanaka Kakuei, Prime Minister from 1972 to 1974, and one of the most powerful political figures in Japan until shortly before his death in 1994, was something of an anomaly in Japan. For one thing, he became perhaps the most powerful prime minister in this century, but did so with no elite college background (in fact, with no college background at all) or elite family ties.[245] Many argue that Tanaka was one of the few prime ministers to give orders successfully to ministry bureaucrats, rather than the other way around, which temporarily at least had the effect of creating a more democratic climate in government.[246]

Tanaka was also the first prime minister in Japanese history to be convicted of a crime—the famous $2 million Lockheed bribery scandal, which led to his loss of the position of prime minister in 1974. But despite this conviction, Tanaka continued to be elected to the Diet time and again, and he continued to be the most powerful politician in the LDP for many years. It was Tanaka and his faction in the LDP which put in place prime ministers Nakasone and Takeshita, as well as the next famous kingmakers, Kanemaru and Ozawa—the man who finally broke the power of the LDP by taking his faction out of the party.

The other major feature of Japanese politics worth extended discussion, that is, the primacy of local politics, can also help us understand the staying power of the LDP, and particular politicians like Tanaka, despite one scandal after another. Local governments themselves are rather weak, heavily dependant upon national bureaucrats for approval of most projects, and the national Diet for most of their operating funds. National political representation also contains a huge bias toward small towns and rural areas due to population shifts since World War II that have not been adjusted for through redistricting. In some rural districts the vote advantage is as much as one to four compared to people in urban areas.

Because of all this, when time comes for national elections, most voters, especially the voters who count the most, think of what politicians can do for their local needs. Conversely, when most politicians are running for election or reelection, they too think of what they can do and have done for local development. Herein lies the root of what Americans call "pork barrel" politics—politicians are rated by how many bridges, roads, libraries, civic centers, etc., etc., have been forthcoming, not on ideology, and not on pressing national or world issues. This is why powerful politicians are not much affected by their involvement in scandals. Tanaka, Takeshita, and all of the others were reelected again and again, even after their implication in financial scandals, because they could deliver the goods to local voters.

The 1947 Constitution, as noted above, allows for more individual rights and principles of democracy than most others in the world today. There is also an elementary form of ward level or street level democracy in Japan much like that of the old Chicago political machines in the nature of pork barrel politics. Much of this democracy in Japan, however, is only paper democracy. There are many ways in which democracy is subverted.

SOME LIMITS TO JAPANESE DEMOCRACY

As in all democratic societies today, it takes money to get elected and reelected in Japan—lots of money. With the possible exception of Italy, it can be said that money has corrupted democracy in Japan more than in any other major industrial nation.[247]

Officially, the Communist Party in Japan brings in the largest amount of money for campaigning, though all agree these figures are grossly misleading because the Communist Party obtains comparatively little money "unofficially." As we have seen, some 90 percent of LDP campaign funds come from large corporations, and until 1994 the powerful big business organization, Keidanren, gave exclusively to the LDP.[248] Still, to most politicians, especially in the LDP, this is not enough.

Two overlapping sources of campaign funds have helped fuel money politics in recent years. One has to do with the extensive ties among the inner group of elites in Japan. Lacking advantages as outsiders it is most difficult for corporations and corporate elites *just below* the inner circle to expand and prosper. This is why corporations behind the biggest political scandals since the late 1980s, such as Recruit Cosmos and Sagawa Express, have used bribes, insider stock trading, and illegal loans to politicians in order to overcome the disadvantages of being locked out of the elite inner circle.[249] Toyota, for example, needs none of this illegal influence.

   A second source of political corruption involves the construction industry. Because, as noted above, much of Japanese politics involves local pork barrel projects for votes, there is big money to be made for construction firms, and consequently for politicians as well. During investigation of the Kanemaru bribery case, for example, Japanese prosecutors found lists in construction company files ranking politicians on their effectiveness in securing construction projects for the industry, with the amount of bribe money going to each politician determined by his rank on this list.[250] Kanemaru, as might be expected, headed the list, with former Prime Minister Takeshita close behind, while Prime Minister Miyazawa held a middle position, and former Prime Minister Kaifu (the short-term reform-minded prime minister) was placed toward the bottom.

   Another major limitation to democracy in Japan is found with ministry elite influence. Much of what is done by government in Japan is done by these unelected officials, who have few restraints over them from the elected side of government. As noted in the previous chapter, politicians lack sufficient staff to gather information and write legislation, and in most cases have far less knowledge and experience about important issues than the ministry elite. Most legislation that passes the Diet every year is written by, and promoted by, these unelected ministry officials. Further, the way these laws are written gives ministry bureaucrats extensive leeway in interpreting laws through administrative guidance. In any case, the ministry officials issue ordinances which outnumber laws from the Diet by nine to one.[251]

   There are other limits to democracy in Japan. Extensive democracy requires that citizens have accurate information about what is happening in their country or the world, what are the most important issues, and what is being done by politicians, corporations, and the government ministries. Extensive democracy also requires interest group organization and the freedom of social movements or protest groups to push for the rights and needs of non-elites. And among other things, democracy requires equal access to a court system for non-elites so they may press for protection or change. These subjects are all severely limited in Japan.

   None of this is to say there is no democracy in Japan—democracy is a matter of relative comparison and never an either/or category. Neither is the above to say that politicians are completely powerless compared to corporate elites and ministry elites in Japan—again it is a matter of degree, with the politicians coming out on the weaker side in most respects. Today there is the possibility of effective political reform which could increase the level of democracy in Japan, making politicians more influential over the ministry and corporate elite, and making voters more important in who is elected and what these elected officials do. Although there is this potential for reform, the chances of meaningful political reform in coming years seem slim. This subject is closely connected to such factors as who makes up the political elite, where they come from, how they were chosen, and how they are tied to other elites.

THE POLITICAL ELITE

Who is considered among the political elite in Japan is to some degree a matter of definition. In contrast to party systems in Western nations, however, top party officials in Japan are in more control of the Diet. Especially in comparison to the U.S. House and Senate, seldom do party members break ranks and vote in a way not authorized by the party elite. Unlike American presidents, a Japanese prime minister does not get on the telephone to members of his own party minutes before a big vote, "twisting arms" for votes. For this reason, it used to be a quite easy matter to locate political elites in Japan. The LDP was in control of the Diet, and those in control of the LDP—politicians such as Kanemaru, Tanaka, and Takeshita— were the party elites. Shifting party alliances have made it more difficult to identify elites though even in these new parties it is primarily defectors from the LDP who dominate. Even though a Socialist became prime minister in 1994, everyone knows LDP elites continue to call the shots.

In what follows we will provide figures on LDP members and their leaders up to the mid-1990s, along with some other politicians who must be considered among the elite.

Where Do the Political Elites Come From?

A few Diet members in Japan are *tarento*, famous people such as baseball players, movies stars, or news commentators. Former movie stars, of course, have the advantage of name recognition, especially when voters do not really understand important issues and thus vote on the basis of fame alone. But because candidates who win election, and certainly reelection, in Japan are primarily selected, trained, and financed by the major parties, these *tarento* are few and they last for only brief periods of time. Most importantly, in fact, the political elite are often former members of the *bureaucratic elite*— the people considered in the previous chapter.

Over all, only about 25 percent of Diet members have been career politicians, working their way up the ladder by beginning in local politics as is common in Western democratic societies. Most Japanese politicians came to politics late, from other careers, such as the approximately half of the members of the Democratic Socialist Party of Japan who came from labor unions. But another25 percent of Diet members, almost all from the LDP, came from positions among the bureaucratic elite—a sort of political *amakudari*.

Post-war prime ministers, much more than other politicians, have been former members of the bureaucratic elite. As noted below, to the end of the 1980s, twelve of sixteen prime ministers were from the bureaucratic elite. More importantly, of the forty-four years during this period, thirty-seven years found a former ministry bureaucrat in the position of prime minister[252]:

Shidehara Kijurō, 1945–1946, former Foreign Ministry bureaucrat.

Yoshida Shigeru, 1946–1947, former Foreign Ministry bureaucrat.

Katayama Tetsu, 1947–1948, lawyer (the only Socialist prime minister before Murayama in 1994).

Ashida Hitoshi, 1948, former foreign Ministry bureaucrat.

Yoshida Shigeru (again), 1948–1954.

Hatoyama Ichirō, 1954–1956, lawyer.

Ishibashi Tanzan, 1956–1957, former corporate president.

Kishi Nobosuke, 1957–1960, former MITI bureaucrat.

Ikeda Hayato, 1960–1964, former Finance Ministry bureaucrat.

Satō Eisaku, 1964–1972, former Ministry of Transportation bureaucrat.

Tanaka Kakuei, 1972–1974, former corporate president.

Miki Takeo, 1974–1976, career politician.

Fukuda Takeo, 1976–1978, former Finance Ministry bureaucrat.

Ōhira Masayoshi, 1978–1980, former Finance Ministry bureaucrat.

Suzuki Zenkō, 1980–1982, former official of the Fisheries Training Institute.

Nakasone Yasuhiro, 1982–1987, former Interior Ministry bureaucrat.

Takeshita Noboru, 1987–1989, career politician.

Implications of the ties formed when the bureaucratic elite move to corporate positions through the common practice of *amakudari* have already been noted. There are further implications for these ties between the political elite and their old colleagues back in the ministry, such as the power these ties provide for the political elite. At present, however, there are other questions about where these politicians "come from."

Second Generation

Term limits, discussed so intensely in recent years in the United States, have not exactly caught on in Japan. In fact, it is not simply that after election to the Diet politicians (especially from the LDP) seldom lose their seats until death or retirement (or more recently, imprisonment), but that there is an increasing tendency to pass these seats on to their offspring, in almost every case their sons.

Prime Minister Hata Tsutomu, who took over the coalition government in 1994 after Prime Minister Hosokawa was forced out, provides a typical example. Prime Minister Hata's credentials are otherwise atypical: born in 1935 and raised in Tokyo, Mr. Hata was unable to get into one of the universities which provide elite ties and training, such as Tokyo University.[253] After graduation from Seijo University, he failed the examination to become a newspaper reporter, then failed another examination to work for Sapporo Beer company. Through family connections, however, he got a job as a tour bus driver in 1960. In the meantime, his father, who had been purged briefly from politics by General MacArthur soon after the war, returned to the Diet in 1952. When his father became seriously ill in 1969, it was commonly assumed by the LDP and the people in his legislative district that Hata Tsutomu would run for his father's seat in the Diet. This he did in 1969, and like his father, immediately joined the Tanaka faction of the LDP when he won.

The Socialist prime minister (a front for LDP power) who followed Hata, Murayama Tomiichi, was more typical of the Socialists. He did not inherit his position or any significant wealth. He is the son of a fisherman of humble means who had eleven children—Murayama Tomiichi was the seventh. Before entering politics he was an activist and leader of a fishermen's union. He was elected as a city and then a prefectural assemblyman before being elected to the lower house of the Diet in 1972, to become chairman of the Socialist Party in September of 1993.

In 1987, of 511 Diet members of the lower house, 305 were from the LDP. Over one-third of these LDP politicians (118) were second- or third-generation Diet members! If we include the second- or third-generation Diet members from the other parties in the Diet, the number goes to 130, which is also to say that the LDP, as usual, dominates in this category.[254] Also, of nineteen post-war prime ministers, up to Miyazawa who became prime minister in 1991, twelve currently have family members serving in the Diet.[255]

Wealth and Income

The Japanese acceptance of family connections and the widely held assumption that the mantle of leadership can and should be passed on to one's son has helped allow the LDP to exploit the situation. The party used it to win new seats by running the sons of Diet members, and to keep seats in the party when one member retires or dies. There are many reasons why sons of Diet members would want to keep political positions in the family: power and fame, perhaps even service to the country, come to mind. But money is no doubt a primary factor.

As noted earlier, the pay of top ministry elites is very low, and compared to their counterparts in other parts of the capitalist world (especially in the United States), the pay and accumulated wealth of corporate executives in Japan is surprisingly low. Yet such is not the case for politicians in Japan.

These people get rich. To begin with, the pay of Diet members is not so low, about $160,000 per year in the mid-1980s.[256] But, politicians in Japan are not required to suspend as much of their previous (legal) economic activity once in office. Most of their money, however, comes from other sources, legal and illegal, after they attain office, and this is especially true for those who reach high positions in the Diet.

A revealing survey of the wealth of Diet members, required for the first time by a law which went into effect in 1993, provides a rough estimate of their assets. (Beginning in 1984 only cabinet members were required to make this disclosure.) But we must keep in mind that this is only a rough assessment, certainly an underestimate of assets because there is no penalty for incorrect reporting by politicians, and the survey does not even include "such items as demand deposits, jewelry and gold bars, or assets held under the names of Diet members' families or fund-raising organizations."[257] In other words, Kanemaru's $50 million in gold bars and securities back home in his safe, plus the other $35 million held by his son, were missed, and it is likely that there is more held by other politicians. Even with these limitations, though, the survey is quite interesting.

The 1992 assets of the 749 Diet members, including both upper and lower houses, averaged $843,800 per member. For LDP members alone the average was $1.25 million per member, with LDP politicians accounting for three-quarters of all assets of Diet members, and eighty-seven of the richest members. The top twenty LDP members alone accounted for 40 percent of all assets held by Diet members. Also, the 171 Diet members from both houses who were either married to daughters of Diet members or had fathers or grandfathers in the Diet had assets much higher than average, and accounted for about half of all assets held by Diet members.

The 1993 survey was even more interesting in many ways. It showed the cabinet put together by the Socialist Prime Minister Murayama, and dominated by the LDP, averaged more than $10 million in personal assets. Prime Minister Murayama himself had under $1 million in assets (mostly made by his wife in her legitimate business, we are told), while the LDP leader, Kōno Yōhei, was the most wealthy at $87.6 million in self-declared wealth.[258]

Corporate Support Groups

Finally, some of the most significant links between politicians and the corporate elite must be considered at this point, however briefly, because the subject will be taken up from other vantage points in the next chapter. One of these links is the direct ties gained by politicians through what can be generally called support groups.

Former Prime Minister Miyazawa explained that his political support group (Kōchikai, or "Broad Pond Society") began soon before he became prime minister.[259] Kōchikai eventually contained 613 business executives from 515 different corporations as members, and according to Miyazawa, met over 330 times on his behalf in the past thirty years.

Political support groups of this kind, generally called *suehirokai* (*suehiro* meaning "fan-shaped," or "fanning out"), were started originally by Prime Minister Ikeda in the early 1960s and have now been formed by most of the political elite. Typically, the corporate members of such groups are recruited from executives below the top level in leading corporations so as to have supporters who will remain active corporate members for a longer period of time, and thus will be in better position to help their chosen politicians. As the term "support group" implies, these corporate executives are recruited to give politicians help in various forms, from campaign contributions to advice, with the underlying assumption that in return these executives and their corporations will be taken care of in various ways.

Since World War II, as one might expect from the preceding discussion, many other means have been developed to bring leading politicians and top corporate executives together in settings where they may share information and provide mutual support. And there are groups formed by corporate and political elites to merge and protect broader elite interests, instead of focusing on one or a few particular politicians.

In the 1970s, for example, a group of then fairly young LDP up-and-comers formed the Shin Jiyū Kurabu, or New Freedom Club, which purportedly was to break away from the old ideas of the LDP and infuse Japanese politics with a fresh perspective. In effect, it really turned out to be a fusing of a new generation of top business and political elites. It had its birth in something called the Free Social Research Society made up of business and political people. From the LDP came people like Ishihara Shintarō, Nakakawa Ichirō, Watanabe Michio, and of course, Nakasone Yasuhiro. And the Society could operate most effectively with Sony's Morita Akio, its first chairman, on board. Other prominent members from the business community included Ishihashi Kanichirō of Bridgestone Tires, Inamori Kazuo, president of Kyōcera, Kawai Ryōichi, president of Komatsu Manufacturing Company (now the world's largest maker of heavy machinery), Toyoda Shoichirō, then vice president (now president) of Toyota, Tsutsumi Yoshiaki (later reported by the American press to be the richest man in the world), president of Seibu Railways (among other titles), and several more impressive names.[260]

Another such example of how the corporate elite and political elite come together is the "breakfast club" which meets once a month. On the political elite side, this breakfast club has always included the LDP party secretary, the party general manager, the coordinator of government committees, and the speaker of the lower house. On the business side the regular participants are the heads of the four main business groups in Japan (to be considered in some detail in the next chapter)—Keidanren, Nikkeiren, Keiza Dōyūkai and the Nihon Shōkō Kaigisho (Nissho).[261]

A major point of all the above is that ties between big business and core politicians in today's Japan have been far more pervasive and far more stable than in the pre-war situation.[262] There is said to be a greater tendency to take a situation and arrange for all factions of top business to benefit mutually with representatives of supposed competitors working with leading politicians to arrive at unified strategy. Thus, internal conflicts are reduced and there is more cooperation, which also means that political and corporate elites have been much more unified, and therefore have become stronger than ever before in Japan. Shifts in these corporate and political elite ties are no doubt occuring behind the scenes along with party realignment. But they are likely to be even stronger when all is sorted out in a few years.

POLITICAL CHANGE IN JAPAN?

As political corruption mounted in the late 1980s, discussion of political reform in Japan became ever more heated and serious. Certainly, the general population was becoming more angry, but other groups, including the corporate elite, were increasingly embarrassed and worried that popular revolt could bring more change than they were willing to tolerate. What are the prospects for political reform? What are the prospects in coming years for increased democracy in Japan? Which is also to ask, what are the prospects for breaking the grip over Japan's political process held by the "iron triangle" of elites, or at least weakening that grip so that other interest groups in Japan have a greater voice in the political system?

With the fall of the LDP and the Miyazawa government in July of 1993, and especially with the new Hosokawa government formed shortly thereafter, there were great expectations. Things did seem to be looking up. For example, some of the incredibly expensive restaurants called *ryōtei* around the Diet offices, used by politicians and business leaders to strike deals behind closed doors, sometimes charging nearly $1,000 per meal, were beginning to close down by December of 1993 due to a lack of well-heeled customers. One political survey found that the faction of seventy politicians led by Prime Minister Miyazawa spent nearly $638,800 at *ryōtei* on 197 occasions during 1992, about $3,240 for each dinner.[263] It is said in the Diet that "more secret deals and important policy matters were decided in Tokyo's Akasaka district, where many of the first-class *ryōtei* are located, than in the Diet." Upon assuming office in the summer of 1993, however, Prime Minister Hosokawa ordered his party colleagues and government officials not to use *ryōtei*, and many top ministry officials told their staff the same. In the same spirit, Prime Minister Hosokawa began having more regular and informative press conferences. Beyond all of this, the new prime minister simply seemed more open and honest.

Legislation for political reform finally passed in the more powerful lower house of the Diet in late 1993, and things began to look even more promising. There were even government commissions and business groups calling for reforms stemming the power of bureaucratic elites.

But, alas, the reform bill was held up in the upper house of the Diet until late January of 1994, and when finally passed, was greatly weakened and so full of loopholes that real reform remains questionable. Further, to the extent political changes are brought about by legislation, most predictions are they will result in a new two-party system in Japan—both parties clones of the old LDP. In effect, therefore, Prime Minister Hosokawa lost big, along with everyone else seeking real reform, and it was only a matter of time before Hosokawa would be forced out of office, as he was by April of 1994. But ironically, despite his reform image and the limited reform he did favor, Prime Minister Hosokawa was sponsored by very conservative political elements, and is extensively linked to elite families of today's corporate and Japan's aristocratic past. A bit more explanation is in order.

To begin with, there is little in the 1994 political reforms to effectively stop corruption by politicians, or to reduce the power of corporations over politicians through campaign contributions. There remains no broad disclosure requirement on campaign contributions, and though the threshold for reporting donations was lowered to a bit under $5,000 from the earlier $14,000, any political donor can simply split the campaign contribution into smaller amounts for multiple donations under $5,000 each. And there is nothing such as the United States Federal Election Commission to regulate and monitor all of this. On top of it all, the Japanese Supreme Court has ruled that politicians are not required to disclose publicly how they spent campaign money. The court ruled that a politician's right to privacy is more important than the right of the public to obtain this information.[264]

The other major issue for political reform is the potential change to single-seat districts for national elections. As it stood before 1994, there were 129 districts with multiple-seat elections, resulting in 511 elected Diet members.[265] What this meant was that the top one, two, and even up to five top vote-getters in some districts all received seats in the Diet. One effect of this, it is argued, is increased corruption as more and more money flows into the political race, with more candidates, many from the same party, competing for votes. But another major effect, less often discussed by political elites, is that the multiple-seat districts increase the chances for smaller political parties, those with less money and less favored by powerful interest groups, to achieve representation in the Diet.

The reform package passed by the Diet in January of 1994 reduces the number of seats in the lower house of the Diet to 500 from 511, and creates 300 new single-seat districts. The other 200 seats would be selected from votes in eleven proportional representation districts. But there is still a catch: to get the compromise bill passed, Hosokawa had to delay legislation which will create the districts and actually establish the single seats. Now that Hosokawa is out, a proposal expected to pass the Diet in late 1994 or 1995 would redistrict for lower house elections in a manner that will possibably give the LDP as many as fifty additional seats in the next national election.[266] Nor does this proposed redistricting do much to overcome the big bias toward rural voters which has always helped the LDP elite win elections.

In effect, the core of the LDP and Socialists formed their coalition government in 1994 to make sure political reform would not hurt them, or at least to minimize any damage that might be done. The Japanese people were shocked by the 1994 coalition between old ideological enemies, and especially so when the Socialist leaders openly rejected their old political principles. But when political careers were at stake, not to mention all of the money which could be made from them, the true nature of the old political game became more visible.

There has been much discussion of government deregulation in Japan, which means stemming the power of the bureaucrats, and deregulation bills were introduced by the Hosokawa government.[267] Some symbolic political actions were taken to rein in the power of bureaucrats, such as the firing of a MITI vice-minister who promoted one of his top officials just before he "retired" in order to run for the Diet under the LDP, thus improving his chances of election. Bureaucrats were rather shocked at the firing because such promotions were a common practice no one had tried to stop before.[268] Even corporate elites have gotten into the act. Various business advisory panels and even the powerful Keidanren have come out in favor of "deregulation" and reducing the power of bureaucrats.[269]

But alas, again there has been scant success. With Hosokawa out of office and the Diet in even more disarray, bureaucratic elites are only becoming stronger. As noted earlier, some have made the argument that the *zoku* of politicians—Diet members who are experts in certain areas of government policy—were slowly taking some power away from the ministry elite. With the LDP and Diet dramatically weakened since 1993, such talk of *zoku* power within the Diet has disappeared for now.

One of the most interesting things about all of this talk of political reform in the early 1990s was Hosokawa himself, and his elite background. One must question how far reform would have ever gone had he held on to the position of prime minister (a position which he almost regained in the summer of 1994), and achieved all he claimed to seek in the way of political reform.

ARISTOCRATIC PRESTIGE AND ELITE SPONSORSHIP: THE CASE OF HOSOKAWA

Several prime ministers of post-war Japan have had some kind of aristocratic family connections. In fact, for men who have succeeded to that office to have no ties either by blood or marriage to some sort of peripheral aristocratic claim is the exception. Not until recently, however, has any prime minister been of such direct blue-blood descent. It is most likely this fact that helped make Hosokawa the most popular prime minister in post-war history, with an unheard of 65 percent approval rating when he was forced out of office in the spring of 1994.

Hosokawa Morihito was in his late forties when he became prime minister in 1993, quite young in terms of the evolution of power careers in Japan. He had the image among most of the Japanese public as a naive outsider drafted by a new reform party to cleanse the tarnished image of Japanese national politics. For many Japanese, it was Hosokawa's aristocratic background that put him above the fray of dirty politics. These aristocratic credentials are indeed impressive. But in contrast to his image, Hosokawa Morihito was carefully nurtured for a top leadership position by a famous kingmaker for several years.

Before selection by the new reform party alliance to be the prime minister in 1993, Morihito was serving as a member of the upper house from his native central Kyushu. For several years his political career had been under the guidance of one Yotsumoto Yoshitaka, a character who pushed the career of Nakasone and whose story itself is fascinating if a little off the subject. Yotsumoto started out in politics as a student before the war as a member of a terrorist gang called the Blood Alliance. He was arrested for a plot to assassinate a political figure and was sentenced to jail in 1937. During the war, Prime Minister Konoe Fumimarō pardoned him. To this date he has been active behind the scenes in right-wing politics and has been an unofficial promoter of the careers of several people, although Tanaka, Takeshita, Uno, Kaifu, and Miyazawa made a public point of rejecting any connection with him.

The aristocratic credentials of Hosokawa come by way of the success his family had throughout history in backing winners. Technically the family can trace its heritage all the way back to the time, during the twelfth century, when the Minamoto and Ashikaga families split apart. These were the families of the first two shogunates, the secular center of power in medieval Japan. The surname Hosokawa was first used by a branch member of the Ashikaga in the second decade of the thirteenth century, and since that time it appears over and over again in the complicated narrative of the feudal history of the nation. The elite status of the Hosokawa family in modern times emanates more than anything from the family's alliance first with Oda Nobunaga, the warlord who finally unified most of Japan after centuries of civil war, and then after the death of Oda, with Hideyoshi Toyotomi, and finally with the Tokugawa family as each of these houses in turn became the center of power.

For its support of the Tokugawa clan in its struggle for supremacy, the shogun granted the head of the Hosokawa family the status of daimyo, or lord of a large fief, in northwest Kyushu. The fiefdom was later transferred to Kumamoto, an even larger holding in central Kyushu. Although thus favored by the Tokugawa shogunate, the Hosokawa family did not miss later opportunities to back winners again by supporting the rebels who overthrew the shogunate in 1868 to form the basis for the modern state. Again the head of the Hosokawa family was rewarded, this time by the leaders of the new Japan. Hosokawa Moritatsu, Prime Minister Hosokawa Morihito's grandfather, was given the rank of marquis, the second highest of five ranks in the new peerage system established in the early 1870s. This was a very high rank indeed: of 511 original peers in the official system, there were only twenty-four marquises and only eleven peers were ranked higher (as dukes).

The family fortunes were turned upward even further when Hosokawa Moritatsu's son, Hosokawa Morisada, and the father of former Prime Minister Hosokawa Morihito, become personal secretary to Konoe Fumimaro, then married Konoe's daughter Atsuko. Konoe Fumimaro was a man of such blue blood that only members of the inner Imperial family could be considered to outrank him. He was directly descended from the Fujiwara family, which provided the regents for emperors for more than a thousand years. There have been literally dozens of marriages between Fujiwara women and imperial crown princes throughout the centuries. Prince Konoe, as he was usually styled, served as prime minister three times from 1937 until 1941, later committing suicide, allegedly in contrition for his role in Japan's entry into and defeat in World War II. Hosokawa Morisada did not become a *yōshi* (an adopted son-in-law), but he kept his Hosokawa surname. Prince Konoe had one son, Fumitaka, whose marriage produced no children. In order to continue the family name, Konoe Fumitaka and his wife Masako adopted their own nephew, the younger brother of Hosokawa Morihito, Hosokawa Tadaki, who of course then became Konoe Tadaki.

Even if Hosokawa Morihito had not decided to become a politician, his family name would have continued to have wide exposure in Japan. Unlike other daimyo, the Hosokawa throughout the generations have had a keen interest in their own place in history, manifest in the way they preserved the artifacts of their ancestors. The Hosokawa historical artifact collection is by far the largest of any private collection in Japan. There is hardly a prominent museum in the country that does not carry pieces on loan from the family collection.

Before becoming prime minister, Hosokawa Morihito was groomed for the office of governor of Kumamoto Prefecture by his handlers, who included, in addition to Yotsumoto Yoshitaka, a group of Tokyo business leaders with ties to Kyushu. A periodical article published in 1992 suggested that Prime Minister Hosokawa had two major problems in creating and maintaining the image of squeaky clean reform politician.[270] One was the need to hide or play down his ties to a few businessmen who in turn are known to have ties to ultra-right-wing elements. Another problem has been converting the considerable family resources to his own political use. It seems that his father, Hosokawa Morisada, dislikes politics and has been critical of his son's using any part of the family inheritance to support a political career. And in spite of devaluation after the war, inheritance laws, and other pressures, the family has been able to maintain an unusual amount of inherited wealth for postwar Japan. The magazine estimates that Hosokawa Morisada has about 108 billion yen in personal real estate holdings, worth just over $100 million at current exchange rates, and Hosokawa Morihito has another $10 million worth in his own name. If he sold any of this the government would take about half the value, but of course half of several million is still a lot of money. The Hosokawa family retreat in Karuizawa was one of the largest in the area, covering hundreds of hectares, and Hosokawa Morisada still has a comparatively large *bessō* (second home) there. The father apparently did not want any of this used for his son's political career, although it appears that the son did quite well without it.

Former Prime Minister Hosokawa is a personal friend of Tsutsumi Seiji, and even has had some relationship with his half-brother Tsutsumi Yoshiaki, a man with real estate holdings worth about $14 billion, and by some accounts (including *Fortune* magazine) the richest man in the world. According to the magazine *Shūkan Bunshun*, there is strong evidence that development of southern Kyushu tourist facilities by Tsutsumi Yoshiaki was aided by favorable decisions in getting permits in exchange for financial support for future campaigns. But the charge that finally brought down Hosokawa was a political loan of almost $1 million he received from Sagawa Express, the same company said to have *yakuza* (organized crime) ties, and the same company that in the early 1990s brought down other leading political figures, such as the kingmaker Kanemaru who was caught with $50 million worth of gold in his home safe. But former Prime Minister Hosokawa's aristocratic lineage and bearing, along with his reformist image, were respected by the Japanese people. He remains a popular figure in politics today and will likely be heard from again.

CONCLUSION

In the end, the major conclusion about the period of seemingly important political change during the first half of the 1990s in Japan must be this: not much of significance has yet really changed. Results and details of changes will take years to sort themselves out, but when we look at who and what really rules Japan, little has been altered. The major elite groupings are still in place, even if under new party names, with relatively the same magnitude of power over what happens in Japan. The changes which occurred have been mostly window dressing, reforms to make it look like something dramatic and new is happening—but little more.

There are other parts to the puzzle of who and what rules Japan, and how it is done. So far we have examined the three major elite groupings, the "iron triangle" as some call it, but in a rather isolated manner. The three groups are not so isolated: they are, in fact, more unified than elites from any other industrial nation. The example of family connections held and forged by Hosokawa are only to some degree atypical, due to the extent of Hosokawa's aristocratic lineage, not in the extent of the connections themselves. It is useful to consider in more detail just how such interlocking and unification is possible.

CHAPTER 7

Uniting for Power: Intermarriage, *Keibatsu*, Business Groups, and Social Clubs

In every country, and in every generation, there is an inclination for people who have risen to the top, or were born there, to come together in numerous ways. In Japan it is not simply an inclination; Japanese elites are the experts. Many people in Japan are vaguely aware of various types of interlocks among elites in their country, but the extent of this convergence, and its importance for elite power and influence have become well documented only recently.

Among the most important members of the post-war Japanese political elite are certainly former prime ministers Yoshida Shigeru, Hamaguchi Osachi, Kishi Nobosuke, Satō Eisaku, Miki Takeo, and Ōhira Masayoshi. Included also in this political elite category must be former foreign ministers Yoshida Hiroshi and Abe Shintarō, who would likely have been a prime minister if not for his untimely death in 1990. Among the post-war corporate elite we can include presidents or former presidents of major corporations such as Uehara Masayoshi, Uehara Shōji, Hamaguchi Masahiko, Hamaguchi Genkon, Anzai Masao, Anzai Hiroshi, and Aso Takayoshi. Along with several other individuals unquestionably among the Japanese post-war elite—not to mention a brother of the late Emperor Hirohito and a brother and sister of the former Empress—all of these people are *members of the same family, directly related through marriage ties with brothers, sisters, or their own children.* In all, this sort of super-*keibatsu* (family group) has included six of twenty-one former post-war prime ministers, more than a dozen major industrialists, and through close relatives, the emperor himself. If we expand the definition of family to make it a bit more extended, say by including the next level of relatives, we find a super-*keibatsu* which in-cludes eleven of twenty-one post-war prime ministers of Japan, and of course, many, many more of the top corporate elite.[271]

From the vantage point of a typical elite family—say, the Ishihashi family behind the large Bridgestone Tire company—we can see how these elite *keibatsu* are established. We could, of course, go back a few generations, and include several degrees of family relations, but to keep it simple and brief, let us consider only Ishihashi Kanichirō, the president of Bridgestone Tire in the mid-1980s. To begin with, Ishihashi Kanichirō's sister is married to a member of the upper house of the Diet, who happens to be the son of Hatoyama Ichirō, a prime minister of Japan in the mid-1950s. Ishihashi Kanichirō's cousin, the son of his father's brother, Ishihashi Keiichi, happens to be married to the daughter of former Prime Minister (1960–1964) Ikeda Hayato. Ishihashi Kanichirō's sister Keiko is married to a head counselor for a central corporation in the Mitsui *keiretsu* corporate group (Mitsui Liquid Petroleum). Ishihashi's other sister, Tamako, is married to Ishii Kōichirō, president of a Bridgestone affiliate company, who is the son of Ishii Kōjirō, a former speaker of the lower house of the Diet.[272] In all, the Ishihashi family has a rather useful little group of political and corporate connections to be relied upon for all sorts of useful things elites might want to accom-plish, and we have simply looked at a fragment of these connections in this particular case.

As one Japanese source has put it, "As we approach a half-century of post-war existence, alongside the obvious elevation of circumstances for or-dinary people, we find that a further development has been the gradual formation of a new establishment based once again on family ties, and in some cases on relationship to the imperial institution." Further, "Like a great spreading cloud, this tight-knit power elite is bound together by a common point of value and an overall common purpose."[273]

Well, maybe "a great spreading cloud," but the key point is that the Japanese post-war elite are *more unified than their pre-war predecessors were,* at least since the early Meiji Period.[274] And as we will see, this unity is not only attained through the rather remarkable *keibatsu* family ties such as those described above, but also through business organizations, social clubs, and old school ties found to such a degree nowhere else in the industrialized world today.

Studies of the upper-class, corporate, and political elite in Western indus-trial societies, especially the United States, have devoted considerable effort in trying to show how these elite families and individuals are tied together. There are literally hundreds of research articles and many dozens of books exploring elite or upper-class convergence through such means as intermar-riage, social clubs, business organizations, interlocking corporate board memberships, and old school ties at the prep school and university levels.[275]

This subject of elite convergence is important because almost by definition a unified elite is much more powerful than one divided among itself. Such unity provides elites with the ability to coordinate activities in protecting common interests, and even promotes better understand of their common interests when the masses often find this almost impossible. Needless to say, there is evidence that a more unified elite comes to share a common psychology, or a common way of perceiving the world, which sets them apart from others in the society and also contributes to their unity and greater power.[276]

These issues of elite unity and convergence are the focus of the present chapter: but unlike investigations of elites and the upper classes in Western industrial nations, our job at this point is rather easy. Elite unity and interlock in Japan are so extensive and so obvious they require examination of only a few of their primary bases, such as business elite unity maintained through the *keiretsu* corporate structure and business organizations, and *keibatsu* family alliances, along with exclusive social and sports clubs.

SOME SOURCES AND FUNCTIONS OF ELITE UNITY

A rather long tradition of elite studies in Western industrial societies has identified some key *elite institutions* which function to maintain elite unity, class consciousness, and intermarriage.[277] Some of the most important of these elite institutions are worth noting at this point to establish benchmark comparisons for the higher degree of elite convergence in Japan.

At the beginning of the life cycle, all over the world, children of the elite tend to be separated from non-elites. They spend their first years in different surroundings, in different preschools, in summer resorts, and other social activities. But educating the future elite really begins in institutions such as exclusive prep schools like the British "public schools."[278] From these schools it is on to elite universities, and even further separation within exclusive clubs or fraternities within such universities. All along the way these young members of the elite receive educational experiences which signal to them that they are special, different, and superior to others in the society. And whether or not these educational experiences create superior values or morality, they certainly create a feeling of belonging and preference for the company of people with the same background and outlook on life, which is to say, they understand one another and work better together. Finally, not least in importance, these young people are forming friendship ties which will serve them the rest of their lives.

As for the next important matter in life, all over the world there are elite institutions which promote intermarriage among the elite. In the American society the promotion of upper-class intermarriage is something of a problem because of a greater sense of independence among young people, the ideal of romantic love behind marriage, and fewer barriers to cross-class interaction. Upper-class intermarriage is, in fact, happening less often than

in the past in the United States.[279] The old debutante balls did help en-
courage intermarriage, though it is more often encouraged today through
exclusive fraternities and sororities restricting "the marriage market," and
interaction at exclusive resorts and vacation spots.

In adult life, there are other important upper-class institutions designed
to maintain elite unity and solidarity, while keeping the non-elite at a distance. Much has been written, for example, about exclusive social clubs in
the United States, with about thirty of these clubs considered most important in serving this function—such as the Bohemian Club in San Francisco,
the Knickerbocker and Links clubs in New York, Somerset in Boston, and
the New Haven Lawn Club.[280] These clubs provide a social setting within
which their typically upper-class members can share their ideas about common political and economic concerns and maintain social and business ties.
Becoming a member of one of these clubs is no easy task: they pride themselves on being exclusive, and to a large degree view their job as gatekeepers
of the upper class.

Finally, of course, there are more specific business organizations and associations designed to forge common activities and compromises among the
upper classes and major corporate interests. Since World War II in the
United States, for example, among the most important of these have been
the Council of Foreign Relations, the Trilateral Commission, and Committee for Economic Development, though some others have become equally
important since the 1970s.

Japan, as we will see, has many of the same sorts of elite institutions—
but with various unique twists. To begin with, the Japanese educational
system is quite different and does not really allow the prep school option
since World War II. And getting into Japanese universities is substantially
different compared to the United States and Europe. Thus, elite education,
and even entrance to elite status through education in Japan, is different
today.

As for elite unity through business organizations in Japan, compared to
North America and Europe, the differences are less of kind than of degree.
Japanese corporate elites come together to an extent and by means that
would be clearly illegal in the United States. But the *keibatsu* family alliances
previewed above have no counterparts elsewhere in the industrial world. Yes,
the rich and powerful everywhere have tended to marry the sons and daughters to others among the rich and powerful. But nowhere is this done so
extensively and systematically as in Japan.

Finally, there are the exclusive social clubs of various kinds in every industrial nation which help define elite status and promote unity. Since World
War II in Japan, however, these clubs have been less important. As indicated
in Chapter 3, Japan's elite today is much less of a leisure class than before—
and never so leisurely as in England, where the "gentlemen's clubs" were
perfected, so to speak. For the most part, the Japanese elite have much less

time for such socializing and parties, and besides, with all the other means of unity, *keibatsu* and business organizations such as Keidanren, for instance, there is less need. Still, we refer only to matters of degree: social clubs are of continuing importance for many among the Japanese elite.

These contrasts and comparisons should help illuminate some details of the most important means of elite unity in Japan, beginning with the corporate world.

JAPANESE CORPORATE ELITE UNITY

We have already seen how the current organization and mutual ties among Japanese corporations create means to promote corporate elite unity unlike those found in any other industrial nation. The inner group of the Japanese corporate elite is generally referred to as the *zaikai*, or "higher business circles." Sometimes the term *zaikai* is used to refer to the organizations through which the inner group of the corporate elite achieve such status, while other times *zaikai* refers to the inner group of the business elite individuals themselves. In both cases, however, it is the interlocked nature of corporate organization in Japan which creates the foundation for the *zaikai*. This *keiretsu* corporate structure consists of groups of corporations tied through reciprocal stock ownership and presidents' clubs to coordinate economic and political activities. The cross-corporate business associations have membership cutting across separate *keiretsu* groups, as well as across all kinds of corporations and industries to bind Japan's corporate elite more tightly than any other.

There are four major business associations in Japan today: Keidanren (the Federation of Economic Organizations), Nikkeiren (Japan Federation of Employer's Association, which coordinates relations with Japan's labor unions and federations), Nihon Shōkō Kaigisho (Japan Chamber of Commerce and Industry), and Keizai Dōyūkai (Japan Committee for Economic Development). Of these four, however, the association of greatest importance is Keidanren.

Keidanren

The inner group of the corporate elite of Japan are found in Keidanren, with the top executives of virtually all of the most powerful corporations as members. By some accounts Keidanren is the single most powerful organization in Japan today, a kind of super-business establishment, or the parliament of big business, with the Keidanren chairman as the prime minister of it all. While there are of course disagreements among the corporate elite, it is through Keidanren that these elites come together to iron out their differences, to set common policy toward economic development and political action, and to decide how to deal with problems from troublesome countries, such as the United States pressuring Japan to open its markets. It is only a slight overstatement to say that the Liberal Democratic Party owes its existence to members of Keidanren. By way of example, it was in 1993, when the LDP became an embarrassment to the business elite, that a decision by Keidanren sealed their doom. It was at this time that Keidanren decided to withdraw its tradition of exclusive funding to the LDP, which had been running around $115 million per year.[281]

It is important to know that much of what is done by Keidanren would be clearly illegal if done by corporate executives in the United States, as it even may be in Japan despite weak anti-monopoly laws. It is understandable, therefore, that most of Keidanren's activities are not on the public record. And it is equally understandable that the organization has resisted attempts by researchers to obtain much detailed information.[282] But enough information has been put together by Japanese investigators to provide a general idea of Keidanren and its importance as the core organization of Japan's business elite.

Keidanren was founded in 1946, but not until around 1956 did it become so important. Shortly after World War II the Occupation prohibited the old business elite from forming organizations, especially the old *zaibatsu* elite. But many new business organizations were inaugurated in secret, some even under the same roof where U.S. officials were attempting to regulate and sort out the Japanese economy after the war.[283] One of the first to gain importance was the Industrial Club, out of which formed the more elite groups such as Mikka-Kai (Third-of-the-Month Club), Shigure-Kai, and Banchō-Kai. The central members of this last-named club are given responsibility for selecting two prime ministers and merging two political parties in 1955 to form the Liberal Democratic Party which was to rule the Japanese political system uninterrupted for the next thirty-eight years.

The real reemergence of Japanese corporate power, it is said, can be traced to May of 1956, when Ishizaka Taizō assumed the chairmanship of Keidanren.[284] Until then Keidanren had functioned mainly as a petitioner body, without much actual influence in economic policy or in organizing the most important among the corporate elite. Ishizaka, as we have seen, was then president of the emerging giant Toshiba Corporation, and under him Keidanren began to develop its present political character and play the dominant leadership role for the dominant business community in Japan.

There was an attempt to form a counter, anti-*zaibatsu* big-business organization with the Industrial Problems Research Committee in 1966, when some among the corporate elite felt the reemergence of old *zaibatsu* managers into the inner group of the corporate elite was harmful to Japan, but this attempt failed. Then slowly, there came a shift in dominance among members of Keidanren away from the old industrial corporations to new ones focused on such industries as electronics and auto manufacturing, as suggested by Morita Akio of Sony moving into the governing board of

Keidanren in the 1980s, and Toyoda Eiji of Toyota Motor Corporation taking over as president of Keidanren in 1994.

Estimates of the number of Keidanren members today range from 800 to 950.[285] And while less than 1 percent of Japan's corporations are said to have executives in the membership of Keidanren, this 1 percent of corporations represents some 40 percent of all sales and 50 percent of total corporate assets in Japan.[286] There is no official policy for selecting the chairman of Keidanren, and in reality, as is common among the Japanese elite, the chairman is selected through "negotiation" (read back room deals) among the active vice chairmen of Keidanren. The former chairmen of Keidanren who have held that position since 1956 and their corporate positions, however, are well known, and reflect the elite status of the organization:

Ishizaka Taizō, chairman 1956 to 1968, president of Toshiba.

Uemura Kangorō, chairman 1968 to 1974, president of NHK (the dominant, semi-government television network), and former top official in the Ministry of Agriculture.

Dokō Toshio, chairman 1974 to 1980, president of Toshiba.

Inayama Yoshihiro, chairman 1980 to 1986, president of Shin Nihon Steel.

Saitō Eijirō, chairman 1986 to 1990, president of Shin Nihon Steel.

Hiraiwa Gaishi, chairman 1990 to 1994, president of Tokyo Electric Power.

Toyoda Eiji, chairman 1994 to present, president of Toyota Motor Company.

The members of Keidanren and their corporations support a huge budget for Keidanren, with about 200 full-time staff members who help organize the many standing committees focused on differing problems and policy questions. The meetings of these committees and other gatherings of Keidanren are commonly attended by leading politicians and ministry bureaucrats, and it is in this way that Keidanren is able to quietly pass the word to their elite counterparts in government and the ministries. In addition to all of this, Keidanren sponsors other policy discussion gatherings, sends delegations abroad to maintain contacts with elites of other industrial nations, and even officially receives foreign dignitaries, including visiting heads of state from around the world.

There are other business organizations, of course, and three others of considerable importance.[287] In a fundamental way these four, including Keidanren, have divided up the tasks which must be done to protect the interests of Japan's corporate elite. For example, Nihon Keieisha Dantai Renmei, or Nikkeiren, deals with labor issues and confronts the big national labor confederation, Rengō. Nihon Shōkō Kaigisho deals with important legal issues, and Keizai Dōyūkai brings corporate leaders together from specific corporations rather than as representatives of industries in general. However, Keidanren is recognized as certainly the most important of these business organizations, and the description of Keidanren as the parliament of big business, and its chairman as the prime minister of big business, is by no means inaccurate.

KEIBATSU-BUILDING FOR ELITE POWER

Marriage is an important event in every society—though, of course, it is more important in some than in others. In Japan, it is not just an important matter, it is a deadly serious affair. Even among the middle class, young people and their parents can spend many hours each week for two, three, or more years in evaluating potential marriage partners. There are match-makers who specialize in aiding this process, often for a fee. Overall, the formal *omiai* process, where possible mates are evaluated along with the standing of their families, is found less often than previously among the middle class today. Still, as many as 30 percent of Japanese young people experience this process, sometimes many times before they finally marry.

Once the selection process is completed, the big money comes for the wedding ceremony itself: about $50,000 is a rough average for just a middle-class wedding in recent years. To begin it all, there is a private family ceremony officiated by a Shinto priest, the bride in a formal wedding kimono typically costing thousands of dollars; then comes a picture-taking ritual with all women of the family in formal wedding kimono (though these are less expensive—maybe only a few hundred dollars each), and the bride still in her formal kimono, but now with the white hood removed "to show her real horns for the first time"; next, it is on to the huge reception with perhaps hundreds of invited guests (the more the better), all provided with an expensive meal in a sufficiently exclusive hotel ballroom, with several gifts for each guest at the table, where they sit and wait for the bride and groom to make a grand entry—she in another expensive (now Western-style) wedding dress; finally, after many glasses of champagne and wine, speeches, cake-cutting, and perhaps a candle-lighting ceremony at the table of each guest, conducted by the bride and groom, the couple is sent off on a proper honeymoon, preferably to some exotic (and expensive) place, with the bride and groom changing into other expensive Western-style clothing (for the third time) to make their grand exit from the banquet hall. This typical marriage ritual is for the middle class—the elites put more into it.

But the big event, even for the middle class, is not just a personal matter of showing commitment to each other, and a ceremony incorporating a display of conspicuous consumption by the couple, it is a family matter. It is a time of assessing the status and importance of the extended family through the status and importance of the family of the chosen spouse. Have they married their son or daughter upward in the status scale—indicating the status of the whole family has been elevated—or downward—in which case there is disappointment and reflection on what has gone wrong.

At the top of the social and economic hierarchy, however, the importance of it all is magnified. Not only is the rank and status of the *ie* (extended family, literally "house") important for elite families, but alliance coalitions, sponsorship, and the proper connections to achieve almost anything in the Japanese society are equally important. A well-placed marriage, or even better, several, can create *keibatsu* ties which will do wonders for the wealth, power, and status of a family. And even more importantly for elites, the already existing coalition of families of which they are a part is further unified.

As you might imagine, with matters of such importance for elites, decisions are not usually left for the young couple involved. In pre-war years the old Mitsui *zaibatsu* established a formal family council to search for and approve marriage ties among family members. This was one of the ways in which they became and stayed so rich and powerful. During the 1920s, for instance, a key marriage alliance between the Mitsui and Sumitomo families helped bring down a challenge from a chief economic rival, the Mitsubishi *zaibatsu*.[288] In a more contemporary case, it is said that the political power broker of the 1990s, and potential prime minister, Ozawa Ichirō, married his wife, sight unseen, when requested to do so by his political mentor, then Prime Minister Tanaka Kakuei.

There is a quite long history of what today is called *keibatsu*-building in Japan, even as far back as prehistoric or mythological ages. "For example, Prince Minaki, later known as Emperor Sujin, who supposedly emerged as the first ruler of the Yamato region in the early fourth century A.D., allied himself with the chieftains of several distant regions through multiple marriages."[289] Since then, of course, such *keibatsu*-building, even one which is a mythical reconstruction of the past to "show" important ancestors, was common among the daimyo and samurai elites of feudal Japan.[290] And as we have already seen, such *keibatsu*-building was very important for the *zaibatsu* families of the late 1800s and pre-war Japan, as they merged wealth and power through promoting marriages among their sons and daughters, even commonly adopting sons-in-law into the family to consolidate power.[291]

The nobility of Europe, of course, were also active in building alliances through marriage ties. But compared to Europe, in Japan the practice has been, and continues to be, much more extensive, as well as qualitatively different because it is done in a more organized, planned, and systematic manner.

Keibatsu-Building Today

To outsiders the status order that is so important among elite Japanese families is usually a mystery. An example of this status order and outside ignorance of it involves the Yasuda family line—one of the original *zaibatsu*

families, and one with important ranks in the former peerage system. Before
the end of the war, the daughter of the famous Yasuda Zenjirō, Tei, took
as a *yōshi* a man who later was a member of the house of peers. The couple
had two sons and a daughter. The daughter, Isoko, married Ōno Eisuke,
who eventually became governor of the Bank of Japan—one of the most
powerful and respected positions in the Japanese bureaucracy. The Ōno
family had two children, a son Keisuke, recently a division manager for Mitsubishi Trading Co., and a daughter, Yoko Ōno. The daughter, a well-
known artist in her own right, married an obscure foreign musician by the
name of John Lennon. In light of that kind of family background it is
interesting to remember a comment made by one of the British tabloids
when John married Yoko back in the late 1960s: "So John married a Jap!
Well at least now he'll have clean laundry."

With respect to the significance and magnitude of *keibatsu* family alliances
today, one Japanese investigator writes, "When we examine this kind of
keibatsu-building, we see that with a nucleus centering ultimately on the
imperial household, the five big *keibatsu* of Kajima, Sanzai, Nagano, Ishi-
kawa and Asō have been woven together with the newer families Toyoda,
Masuda, and Saitō to form what could be called the eight great family charts
of interwoven ties." With their links to political elites since World War II,
"we see that with the exception of Katayama Tetsuo and Tanaka Kakuei,
the post-war prime ministers have all had family ties to the pre-war *zaibatsu*
families and to the post-war holders of great business power, forming one
great conservative phalanx at the center of the Japanese economic and government life."[292]

The exact number of important elite *keibatsu* today, and which ones are
more important, as one might expect, are in dispute. But there is no doubt
that the links are truly massive among the political, corporate, and to a lesser
extent the bureaucratic elite—primarily because when brought into a *keibatsu* they usually shift into the corporate or political elite positions. Also,
where one *keibatsu* stops and another begins is to some degree a matter of
judgment. A result is that some Japanese writers claim there are forty current
keibatsu of great importance, while others suggest lesser numbers.[293] Which-
ever is the case, however, the key point is that virtually all among the elite
in Japan today are linked through these *keibatsu*, and the unity and coordination among elites is extensive for it.

This brings us to some noteworthy differences among today's *keibatsu*
which make elite unity even more extensive. First, the present powerful *keibatsu* among elites are less defined or segregated, in contrast to the pre-war
zaibatsu family alliances. This is why it is more difficult now to tell where
one *keibatsu* stops and another begins. Second, Japanese *keibatsu* today are
less specialized by type of elite. The pre-war *keibatsu* were separated into
those for each of the wealthy *zaibatsu* families, others for less wealthy managers, and others for those among political and bureaucratic elites.[294] Finally,

in contrast to the pre-war years, there are the less rigid boundaries of elite *keibatsu* today. It is easier than before to combine or link separate elite *keibatsu*, as well as for non-elites to break into a *keibatsu* if they have something to offer members of the elite. Which now brings us to the issue of the primary goals of *keibatsu*-building.

There are three primary, and rather understandable, goals in *keibatsu*-building: the *keibatsu* builders seek power, wealth, and status (or prestige).[295] The lust for power needs little explanation, as we have seen in several contexts. *Keibatsu*-building has its practical side for the Japanese corporate elite who want to make family ties to other powerful corporate families, politicians, and key bureaucratic personnel. These people can be very good for business, as when a politician or especially a bureaucratic elite member is then able to influence government decisions that can mean millions, if not billions, of dollars to the corporate family.

Keibatsu-building for wealth, however, is less of a popular and worthwhile pursuit today: there is simply less significant private wealth in post-war Japan, and when there is significant private wealth, it is not always held by the kind of people with whom the true elite would like to be associated. Mergers with these wealthy families could even hurt a family's corporate power and certainly their respect and status.

Keibatsu-building for prestige, however, is an ongoing preoccupation of the elite in Japan, and perhaps even on the increase.[296] There has been something of a resurgence among Japanese in the old preoccupation with ancestors and their possible links to the pre-war peerage system or pre-Meiji feudal nobility. But even without this resurgence, it has always been common for the elite to claim peerage or nobility lineage in their past, or better still, to marry into the last remaining nobility category today—the extended imperial family. In a society which has always considered the status order terribly important, ties to royalty, or near-royalty, or even pretend royalty, can be quite useful, as we saw in the previous chapter with the case of former Prime Minister Hosokawa.

The Functions of Upper-Class Women and Methods of *Keibatsu*-Building

The position of Japanese women is highly misunderstood outside of Japan. Yes, Japanese women are heavily discriminated against in the workplace, in education, in professions, etc. For example, only Korean women hold a smaller percentage of managerial and professional positions among industrial or industrializing societies.[297] Until quite recently there was even much more discrimination by the Japanese legal system against women, making it difficult for them to own property, have custody of their children in the rare cases of divorce, and of course, women could not vote until the post-war constitution put in place by the Occupation.

Having said all of this, however, it must be noted that middle-class Japanese women are much more powerful than their Western sisters inside the home. For instance, it is typical that a Japanese woman take the husband's paycheck as soon as it is received, for it is her job to decide upon expenditures and control the money. Men are literally given an allowance by their wives, while it is the women who, often on their own, decide what to buy for the household and how to invest the money. This is why there was a rash of articles during 1992 in Japanese newspapers and magazines about the trouble created when thousands of Japanese women had to tell their husbands that they had lost the family savings in the stock market plunge. While most Japanese stock, over 80 percent, is owned by other corporations, a large percentage of the remainder is invested by and controlled by Japanese women. This is why stockbrokers in Japan commonly go from door to door promoting stocks, or set up booths in department stores, much like cosmetics salespeople.[298]

This is not to imply that women of the corporate, political, and bureaucratic elite in Japan operate just as middle-class Japanese women do, but it is certainly to say that upper-class Japanese women do not function only to have children and wear expensive furs and jewelry to make their husbands look good, as economist Thorstein Veblen described American upper-class women at the turn of the century in *The Theory of the Leisure Class*. In fact, the description was not even accurate for women of the American upper class. In one of the best analyses of the American upper class, G. William Domhoff describes three primary functions of upper-class women for overall upper-class interests: "First, they are the mistresses of the social institutions that keep this collection of rich families an intermarrying social class." Secondly, upper-class women set "social and cultural standards for the rest of the population." And third, an important function of upper-class women is their involvement in social welfare activities to improve conditions in the society, and "take some of the roughest edges off a profit-oriented business system that has cared little for specific human needs."[299]

Again we find remarkable similarities between elite circles in Western industrial nations and Japan. With only some changes in the details of exactly how these things are done, analyses of American upper-class women sound as though they were written for Japan. For example, one description of the women of the Japanese upper class written (with some overstatement) by an American woman who spent time among them sounds as if it was taken from an analysis of American upper-class women: "Within the elite, none have more power than the Old Guard ladies, the elders of the tribe of wives and widows who run the charity balls, fundraisers for socially correct high-minded causes. . . . With their bloodlines and big money, this constellation of tough-minded, pinched-lipped society queens hold themselves up as arbiters of who's who, and what's what, in the top ranks of Japanese society."[300]

One hundred years ago, when the Mitsui *zaibatsu* family council had a special committee for arranging marriage alliances it was all much easier. Children had very little or no choice in who they were to marry, and while they might not have been happy about it, they generally accepted their families' decisions. For the Japanese middle class today, marriage choices are primarily in the hands of the young people themselves. Parents are certainly involved in the decision-making much more than in Western countries, but still, the decisions are usually the childrens'. The *omiai* system of finding mates described earlier is currently used by perhaps 30 percent or less of young people, and even when it is used, the couple involved usually makes the final choice. With respect to families of Japanese elite circles, however, Baltzell's description of the American upper-class still applies: "the democratic whims of romantic love often play havoc with class solidarity. . . ."[301] This is where women of the Japanese upper class step in.

While not as restricted as pre-war Japanese upper-class offspring, these young people today have much less control over marriage decisions than their middle-class counterparts: quite simply, too much is at stake. As described in a perceptive study by Hamabata using participant observation techniques, Japanese women of the elite play key functions in uniting corporate, political, and bureaucratic interests through working to join families through marriage, and then they maintain strong ties with their daughters who have married into other elite families for use in gathering information and exerting influence in these other families.[302]

These women of the corporate elite told Hamabata that it is common for various upper-class women's clubs and organizations to get directly involved in matchmaking to promote ties and favorable matches for their corporate circles. This also includes women's groups associated with their husbands' membership in the powerful Keidanren, discussed above, who see themselves as well placed to arrange marriages within the corporate elite. In these gatherings of elite women Hamabata describes "an undercurrent of serious worrying, as each woman realized that she, her children, and her household were being inspected by the other women in the fluid process of judging household status. Status, affirmed by alliances created through marriage, made marriage a consistent topic of conversation. Marriage also defined one of the major realms of responsibility for the wives."[303]

The matches they attempt to make for their elite daughters, however, are not restricted to young men from families already within their elite circles. There is a tendency to use as a guide in their efforts the *Shinshiroku* (The Gentlemen's Directory) which lists the top "commoner" graduates of Tokyo University. With this *Shinshiroku* for advice these women attempt to marry their daughters to the most prominent "up and coming" young men, and often, as we have seen, later adopt these men into the family as *yōshi*, or *muko-yōshi*. And finally, we should note that there are more professional match-makers, *nakōdo*, who specialize in arranging marriages for the elite, often working within upper-class women's clubs and organizations.[304]

None of the above is meant to imply that women of Japanese elite families are working almost like employees of the corporation or corporate *keiretsu* to help form business alliances on the behalf of these corporations; more understandable, personal interests of these women are involved. Discriminated against in the business and professional world, these women know that they must rely upon family position for their lifestyles and protection. As some of them told Hamabata during his participant observations, "A women has only her family. For her sake, and for the sake of her daughters, a mother must see to its continuance, protect its 'meisei' (reputation), and since marriage affects the reputation and continuance of the family, it is only natural that she be the most concerned."[305] And once the links are made from one elite family to another through these strategic marriage placements, the links are maintained and used over the years not just for corporate business deals—though they are clearly used for these reasons as well. Again, these ties can be used for the protection and interests of these women. As Hamabata learned from his informants, "If your husband's household, as family and enterprise, is heavily indebted to a bank of which your older brother is president, then you have power in your husband's household. . . . Given her position as the link between two households and her powerlessness, the pursuit of aid from her natal household for her husband's household makes complete sense."[306]

Social Clubs, Golf Clubs, and Tennis: The Lighter Side of Building Unity

In Western industrial nations, especially England and the United States, the exclusive "gentlemen's clubs" have always provided an important means through which the upper classes draw status lines around themselves, keeping "commoner" and the new rich alike at a distance. This has been especially so in the United States with its lack of aristocratic traditions or a peerage. Investigations have shown that approximately thirty such "gentlemen's clubs" in the United States are considered most exclusive, with extensive restrictions on membership to keep them that way.[307]

But there is *much* more to these clubs and similar organizations than status snobbery: they are important mechanisms for promoting elite unity, maintaining specific business deals and creating new ones, as well as for selecting individuals for political positions and forming political policies. To cite only one of the many examples of this, in recent years top executives from 637 of the largest 797 corporations in the United States all had members in at least one (but usually more) of just fifteen such exclusive clubs or similar organizations.[308]

With a long history of exclusive clans and a highly ranked society where status distinctions were by law clearly displayed, Japan did not have a tradition of exclusive social clubs. But when the Japanese were forced to open to the West, and old aristocratic *ranks* were removed and a new European-

style peerage system was instituted, the Japanese elite also set about establishing some of their own exclusive social clubs. One of the first and most
famous, Rokumeikan ("Hall of the Baying Stag"), was established in 1883.
The hall, designed by a British architect in the style of an eighteenth-century
German palace, "was the scene of balls, soirees, and charitable events at
which ladies and gentlemen of international society could mingle with members of Japan's elite."[309]

Since World War II, however, these upper-class clubs in Japan have been
less numerous, and rather less important, though still certainly in evidence
among the very top elite. They are less numerous, in part, due to the demise
of the old *zaibatsu* wealth and leisure time. Japan's elite of today seldom
have the independent wealth and free time for such activities compared to
elites in the United States and Europe. There are certainly big parties, ban-
quets, and other types of elite social events. Japanese corporations spend
more money on such activities each year than the whole country pays on
national defense! But they are, well, more business-like: as one of the Japanese elite more familiar with European "high society" put it, "You know,
they're really unsophisticated country bumpkins. . . . The Japanese don't
have the true breeding, the style. . . ." And further, "It's all company money
anyway. Once they retire, they're nothing."[310] While a put-down of fellow
Japanese elites who lack European connections, there is at least some accuracy in the statement, especially the final part.

There are two further differences: it must be noted that the more egalitarian values of post-war Japan have many diverse effects.[311] Extensive dis-
plays of wealth, even though somewhat tolerated in the boom years of the
1980s, continue to be looked down upon. As one informant put it, "The
rich in Japan don't live like the rich in Europe and America. . . . If they did
they'd be laughed at."[312] And, quite simply, with *keibatsu* family ties, organizations such as Keidanren, and the many other means of tying the elite
together already described, Japanese elites have much less need for such
unifying clubs and organizations compared to their American and European
counterparts.

Still, the longing for status indicators, even if less pretentious, and the
exclusive company of other elites remain powerful. Along with memberships
in exclusive social clubs, "The possession of membership in golf and tennis
clubs is often considered to be a status attribute because such membership
is not only very expensive but also provides access to facilities which are
reserved exclusively for the inner circle of wealthy people."[313] Most common
are the exclusive and expensive golf clubs: there are hundreds of these which
bring varying degrees of status to their members, as well as connections for
business and political deals.

Those who know the Japanese elite, however, agree that one of the most
important clubs for status and connections is the Tokyo Lawn Tennis
Club.[314] Only fifty members a year are admitted, and as of 1990 there were

over 2,000 people on a waiting list for consideration, and many of them had been on the waiting list for over ten years. One member is quoted as saying, "We don't allow people to join who just make a lot of money in speculation or real estate or in the entertainment business."[315]

The Tokyo Lawn Tennis Club was originally established through the encouragement of Itō Hirobumi, a *genrō* and major author of the Meiji Constitution. He was also one of the architects of Japan's entry into the modern world who believed that mixing Japanese elite with foreign elite in such a Western setting was good for Japan's image and business contacts. The club was originally located on grounds where the Diet building stands today, then later moved about two kilometers east to Kōjimachi. In 1970 it was relocated again to its present location on land donated by the Imperial household in the exclusive area of Azabu, south of downtown Tokyo.

Today selected foreigners are still among the ranks of members of the Tokyo Lawn Tennis Club. Including family members, currently there are about 900 people listed as officially able to use the courts and other facilities. The emperor and empress are members, along with others of the imperial household and such members of former nobility as the Shimazu and Saionji families. Former *zaibatsu* names such as Mitsui and Mitsubishi are on the list of family groups. Post-war business tycoons like Ishibashi Kan'ichirō of Bridgestone Tire, Kobayashi Yōtarō of Fuji Xerox, Asō Yasuo of Asō Cement, distinguished professor of Tokyo University and former Chief Justice of the Supreme Court Yokata Kisaburō, are all on the membership list.

There are some other exclusive clubs which can be called holdovers from the pre-war era, such as the Tokyo Riding Club. Founded in 1922, the Tokyo Riding Club moved to its present location next to Meiji Shrine in the Yoyogi section of Shibuya Ward. The club is somewhat hidden from view, and few Tokyoites even know of its existence. Both the present emperor and his two sons learned to ride at the club. New candidates for membership must be recommended by at least two current members, with a membership committee making the final decisions. Considering its history of elite status, the Tokyo Riding Club is not all that expensive: new members pay 800,000 yen, and then 60,000 yen annually. But, alas, it is not as exclusive as it once was. There are about 500 members today, including some scions of the old aristocracy (a Tokugawa family member belongs), but members also include entertainers and recently wealthy land speculators. The imperial family rarely rides there anymore.

Among the hundreds noted above, there are several most exclusive golf clubs in Japan, with probably the most select being the Tokyo Golf Club. This golf club was founded in 1913, and is now located in Saitama Prefecture, about thirty miles from the center of Tokyo. Members include Prince Chichibunomiya, uncle of the present emperor, and the emperor's cousins, Prince Takamamado and Prince Mikasa. Non-royal members are carefully screened to keep out all but the most prestigious members of the business and political world. The initiation fee is surprisingly low at 85,000 yen, or about $850, with the low value of the dollar in the mid-1990s.

There are even a few clubs exclusively for the former nobility, such as the Kasumi Kaikan, located at the top of the thirty-one-story Kamusigaseki building near the Diet in downtown Tokyo. To be a member one must usually be a direct descendent of the old peerage, though there are today some "new aristocrats" making up the roughly 950 members of the Kasumi Kaikan, including the emperor.

Another club, which is said to have a somewhat intellectual bent to it, is reported to be the best place in Japan for informal contacts between businessmen and politicians. It is known as the Kōjunsha, a club started by the famous founder of Keiō University, Fukuzawa Yukichi. It was originally a gathering place for purposes of informal discussion among leaders of the Meiji regime, "for men of distinction both in and out of government," as the charter reads. Members were mostly nobility with a few rich or exceptionally accomplished commoners.

Most members of the Kōjunsha (by invitation only) are men of power in business and politics, but there are some writers and even a few fairly well-known academics among the membership. The initiation fee is the somewhat standard 600,000 yen ($6,000), with a smaller annual fee, although people who reside away from Tokyo get a slight break. As of 1990 there were 3,386 members. The average age of members is 76, and more than 400 are over 80. The club owns its own building close the center of Tokyo and rents out part of it. In the style of the old British gentlemen's club, there is a discussion room, a library (containing some of Fukuzawa's original writings), a *shōgi* and *gō* room, a golf practice range, three dining rooms and a large Japanese-style banquet room, a bar, and a barber shop.

Despite the large membership it has remained quite an exclusive club. For example, Prime Ministers Yoshida, Hatoyama, Kishi, Satō, and Fukuda are or were members. Some very powerful LDP members such as Sakurauchi Yoshio, Sasaki Ryōsaku and others are current members. Business leader members tend to be graduates of Keiō University, but also have included the likes of Matsushita Kōnosuke, head counselor for Mitsui Real Estate, Edō Hideo, and president of Asahi Chemicals, Miyasaki Teruo.[316]

ELITE UNITY: AN ASSESSMENT AND CONCLUSION

It is important to restate a key point: the Japanese elite are today more unified in many overlapping circles than any other elite in the industrial world. This chapter has conveyed only a part of this, but a big part: there are many direct links in the corporate world of Japan that bring these people together. On the lower levels there are the specific *keiretsu* ties of mutual stock ownership, interlocking boards of directors, and the presidents' clubs. On a level above the major *keiretsu* groupings there are major business or-

ganizations such as Keidanren which unite the corporate elite overall and
work for their common interests.

There are *keibatsu* family alliances which create a dense network of family
ties among all three types of ruling elites in Japan. These *keibatsu* family
groups are centered around the corporate elite, but the bureaucratic elite
are increasingly brought in, as are politicians.

In previous chapters we have described the ties created through *amaku-*
dari, the descent by top government ministry officials to major corporations
and politics. A recent survey by Tōyō Keizai, Inc., of 2,175 companies in
Japan, for example, found that 498 of these companies had 1,068 former
bureaucrats as corporate directors as of July 1993. Other information indicates that the extent of *amakudari* has been increasing in the post-war
period: during 1963 there were 165 cases of *amakudari*, while there were
176 during 1973; 267 during 1983; and 218 in 1992.[317]

Then there are clubs, today often centered around some type of sporting
activity, which bring the elite together in more informal circumstances where
they can meet and talk and socialize, not just for the fun of it, but for the
personal relationships which are necessary and useful in maintaining individual elite interests and the collective interests of what can be called the Japanese upper class today. But there are other ties that bind, ties that can be
even more important at times.

For now, former Prime Minister Nakasone Yasuhiro, one half of the "Ron
and Yasu" pair during the booming 80s for Japan and the United States,
provides us with a concluding typical example of elite unity and interlock in
post-war Japan. Nakasone's *keibatsu*-building actually started with his sister,
Yaesu, who was married to the son of a paper magnate, Saitō Ryōhei. Ryōhei's brother was a member of the Diet, and later governor of Shizuoka
Prefecture (state). Ryōhei's other brother is married to the daughter of Toyoda Kiichirō, past president of Toyota, and now chairman of the very powerful business organization, Keidanren. Nakasone Yasuhiro's own marriage
did not link him to powerful families, but those of his children did. Former
Prime Minister Nakasone is directly linked, through his children, to more
than a dozen major private and public organizations, including NHK (Japan's most important television network), Daiichi Kangyō Bank (biggest in
the world), Japan IBM, C. Itoh Trading Co., Mitsui Electronics, Mitsubishi
Bank, the Finance Ministry, and the list goes on and on. Not bad family
connections for a young man who hoped to one day be prime minister.

The wedding of Nakasone's daughter Mieko to Atsumi Naoki provides a
nice symbol of all this, and was an elaborate affair even by the standards of
influential Japanese. The reception took place in the famous Akebono room
of the Hotel Okura, with a list of over 300 in attendance which read like a
"Who's Who" of Japan. Morita Akio, chairman of Sony at the time, offi-
ciated as *nakōdo*, a kind of matchmaker and master of ceremonies at the
wedding. Those who gave the traditional speeches at the wedding included

Inayama Yoshihiro, then Keidanren chairman, and the wife of former prime minister Satō Eisaku.[318]

Prime Minister Nakasone is also a member of some of the most important sports clubs for the elite in Japan, which brings him together with others among the Japanese elite in other settings.[319] But there are many other means to bring Nakasone into repeated close contact with most of the other major elites in Japan. For example, as a top official of the Liberal Democratic Party, and certainly as Prime Minister, Nakasone attended the monthly "breakfast club" meetings which always include the LDP Party Secretary, the party's general manager, the coordinator of government committees, and the speaker of the lower house of the Diet to meet with the business side, which regularly includes the heads of the four major business organizations—Keidanren, Nikkeiren, Keizai Dōyūkai, and the Nihon Shoku Kaigishō.[320] Also, in his position as a top LDP official, Nakasone had much involvement with the government councils. There are twenty such councils, which allow business leaders to advise the government and promote cooperation between business and government. In 1986, of 404 seats on the government councils, 199 were held by executives from the major *keiretsu* corporate groupings.[321]

Before all of this, however, Nakasone was a "career" bureaucrat, who, like many others with whom he began his working life, later left the government ministry through the system of *amakudari* we have discussed earlier. But the ties among elites such as these in the bureaucracy, corporations, and upper positions in the Diet go even deeper, and much further back. To understand this additional source of elite unity, consideration of the extensive system of "old school ties" in post-war Japan is in order.

CHAPTER 8

The *Tōdai* Connection: Elite Recruitment and Reproduction

In one of his many stories about the rich, "Six of One—," F. Scott Fitzgerald begins by reflecting upon the advantages of six rich boys, and then
describes a disagreement between two characters over the relative potential
of people from more humble origins. A wager is made, and the main character selects six young men of modest means, and provides their support
through college. After several years, the rich boys have generally made a
mess of things, while the other six, for the most part, have done reasonably
well. Describing the thoughts of the main character with respect to the
meaning of it all, Fitzgerald writes that "it was too bad . . . that there
should be all that waste at the top; and he felt that he would not live long
enough to see it end, to see great seriousness in the same skin with great
opportunity. . . ."

Such views of the rich have been commonly held for centuries, with history providing at least some support for these beliefs. Grand theories of the
rise and fall of whole civilizations have even been built around such ideas.
But there is more than the danger of laziness or incompetence in the offspring of the rich and powerful who inherit positions at the top, there are
matters of stale ideas, arrogance, and a focus on narrow self-interest.

None of this is to suggest that a lack of elite circulation based upon merit
means a society will fall. Neither does it mean that elite circulation or in-
telligent elites will assure a society's survival: too many other factors are also
at work, such as the nature and degree of competition from other societies.
In a world where all elites are selected in roughly the same manner, in a
world where countries have little contact with each other, incompetent, even

cruel elites may muddle along for generations. But in a world that is rapidly changing, with competition on all sides, elite competency and legitimacy certainly do matter. This is the world Japan discovered when it was forced to open up to a larger world in the mid-nineteenth century, a world that is ever more competitive today.

Before the mid-nineteenth century, the top was almost completely closed in Japan. As we have seen, during the 1600s and until 1863, Japan had something quite similar to the Indian caste system. Almost from the beginning of rule by the Tokugawa shogunate, a rigid system of social stratification was instituted which prohibited movement from the rank in which one was born. Before the 1600s there was some mobility up and down the social hierarchy, and even into the top, but it was mainly the result of violent conflict and destruction of segments of the old order. Prior to Japan's industrialization, there was no tradition of upward movement through merit selection such as existed for Mandarins in China and *yangban* in Korea.[322] And during the Tokugawa period, the two and a half centuries of stability took away even the option of elite circulation through violent conflict.

Dramatic change, however slowly it began, was dictated by Japan's forced opening to the outside world. With the need for rapid industrialization, feudal lords and their samurai lost formal positions of status and wealth. And while it is true that many of these former elites were given titles when the peerage system was copied from Europe, the architects of the new Japanese social order also realized that modernization and industrialization required a more educated elite, one selected through at least some system based upon merit. With this in mind, the new Japanese educational system was modeled on that of France and Germany, with the university system eventually coming to resemble the German model most closely.[323] The tough high school and college entrance examinations that are well known in Japan today also got their start in the late 1800s with this restructuring of education for modernization.[324]

For selection and training of a modern elite, which at the same time primarily meant staffing the government ministries, the Imperial University, now known as Tokyo University, or Tōdai for short, was selected. There was no masking of intention, no apologies for what the leadership was doing: they wanted an Oxford, Cambridge, Harvard, Princeton, Yale all in one, and they got it—if not in quality, at least in its importance for elite selection. The Meiji Emperor himself appeared each year to hand out gifts to stress the importance of the graduates' new status as products of this most elite of universities.[325]

What began as a training ground for the government ministry elite, however, eventually ended up as a training ground for all elite positions. Corporate elites were slow to come by the Tōdai route; few individuals running the top corporations at the turn of the century had college training. But once *zaibatsu* family control of the economy was stabilized, their sons would attempt to go on to Tōdai to legitimate their positions. The ministry elite, however, were Tōdai grads from the start, with almost three fourths Tōdai grads by 1939. And so were prefectural (state) governors: one study of eight prefectures between 1905 and 1925 showed that fifty-eight of seventy-one governors were Tōdai graduates.[326]

Equality of educational opportunity, however, does not come automatically with the introduction of objective entrance examinations. From 1882 to the turn of the century, for example, around 90 percent of the Tōdai students had samurai family backgrounds. It was only those from privileged backgrounds who had the time for study needed to pass the entrance exams.[327]

In all industrial societies, education is the primary means of occupational attainment and movement up the social latter. And in contrast to the American myth of "the land of opportunity," there is surprisingly little difference among industrial nations in the amount of movement up and down the stratification system, or in the level of equality of opportunity through education in these societies.[328] This is no less the case for Japan, despite its reputation as a society where education is much more important.[329] However, when the subject is restricted to elites and elite positions, these statements do not necessarily apply.

With respect to elite selection, Japan is different: in no other industrial society is elite selection centered upon so few educational institutions, and so extensively based, at least initially, upon formal objective criteria. This does not necessarily mean there is, or has always been, more equality of opportunity to the top in modern Japan, or that Japanese institutions of higher education are the best in the world. The latter statement is definitely false, while the former involves complex themes and will require more explanation. The problem is that objective examinations for selection of college students can easily create an illusion of fairness that masks unequal advantages held by the children of the upper classes. But for now we must consider the institutional arrangements for elite selection in Japan and the resulting elite unity and old boy networks they help to erect.

JAPANESE UNIVERSITIES AND OLD SCHOOL TIES

As in all important matters in Japanese life, there is a rather definite and well known rank order of universities in Japan. This rank order is based not upon quality of university programs or faculty, but upon the reputation of the university. For Japan, therefore, the attainment of elite positions is based upon the perceived status of the institution and not necessarily the quality of an education received.

With few exceptions, and in contrast to the United States, the most respected universities in Japan are national, which is to say, government-funded and -operated universities. These top universities are therefore relatively inexpensive and financially accessible to the vast majority of Japanese. The top three national universities with respect to status are Tokyo University, Kyoto University, and Hitotsubashi University. Keiō and Waseda universities head the list of the most respected private universities. However, it is difficult to overstate the fact that Tokyo University, or Tōdai, is by far the most prestigious university, and thus most important in obtaining an elite position. In combination with the importance of age ranking in Japan, it is a degree from Tokyo University that largely accounts for an old boy network and elite unity unequalled in any other industrial society. The most important Japanese elites, in all sectors of the society, are very likely to have attended Tōdai, or at least one of the few other top universities, and because age ranking requires that they move into elite positions at about the same age, *most Japanese elites at one point in time were university classmates who knew each other*, lived together around campus, got drunk together, and created bonds which normally last a lifetime. The evidence for this is overwhelming.

The Ministry Elite

The old school ties are most centralized among the government ministry elite, as designed from the very beginning, when Tokyo Imperial University was made the training ground for the nation's elite. There are several ways of describing these "old school ties" today. For example, of all recent college graduates entering higher civil service positions in 1980 (1,344 individuals), 38.6 percent graduated from Tōdai. In 1991, of those entering the "fast track" to top ministry positions (306 individuals), 59 percent were Tōdai graduates.[330] As of 1976, of 1,600 persons in government ministries promoted beyond the rank of *kachō*, "department head," 1,001 were Tōdai graduates. And in 1981, all seven heads of the largest and most important ministries were Tōdai graduates except for one Kyoto University graduate (Imezawa Setsuo, chief of the Bureau of Taxation).[331]

The concentration within the "old boy network," however, is even greater than the figures above indicate. If we look to the most important and most powerful ministries, we find the Tōdai connections even greater: again considering those with the rank of *kachō* and above, in the late 1970s the percentage of Tōdai graduates at the Ministry of Finance, for example, was about 89 percent.[332]

But it is not *just* Tōdai; the question is from what academic department at Tōdai did the elite graduate? Considering the most powerful people of the main ministries from 1981 to 1987—that is, the vice-ministers—over 73 percent graduated with undergraduate law degrees from Tokyo University, with 13.5 percent graduating from some other department in Tōdai.[333] So extensive is this selection from a single department from a single university that more recently it has come under extensive criticism from the general population. In response to this criticism, in 1992, then Prime Minister Miyazawa pledged that in five years selections for top positions will be reduced from the current 59 percent to *only* 50 percent![334]

Political Elite

Overall, politicians in Japan are not as well-connected as the ministry elite, nor are they so important and powerful. But, of course, no one can deny the importance of prime ministers as the elite among politicians. In this case, we can simply list all of the post-war prime ministers in Japan and their educational backgrounds: the list speaks for itself.[335]

Shidehara Kijurō, prime minister 1945–1946, Tōdai, Law.

Yoshida Shigeru, various times 1946–1954, Tōdai, Law.

Katayama Tetsu, 1947–1948, Tōdai, Law.

Ashida Hitoshi, 1948, Tōdai, Law.

Hatoyama Ichirō, 1954–1956, Tōdai, Law.

Ishibashi Tanzan, 1956–1957, Waseda, Law.

Kishi Nobosuke, 1957–1960, Tōdai, Law.

Ikeda Hayato, 1960–1964, Kyoto University, Law.

Satō Eisaku, 1964–1972, Tōdai, Law.

Tanaka Kakuei, 1972–1974, high school only.

Miki Takeo, 1974–1976, Meiji University, Law.

Fukuda Takeo, 1976–1978, Tōdai, Law.

Ōhira Masayoshi, 1978–1980, Hitotsubashi University, Literature.

Suzuki Zenkō, 1980–1982, Fisheries Training Institute.

Nakasone Yasuhiro, 1982–1987, Tōdai Law.

Takeshita Noboru, 1987–1989, Waseda University, Law.

Uno Sōsuke, 1989–1990, high school only.

Kaifu Toshiki, 1990–1991, Waseda University, Law.

Miyazawa Kiichi, 1991–1993, Tōdai, Law.

Corporate Elite

Consistent with what has already be described about Japanese elites, and consistent with studies of elite networks in other industrial nations, the more broadly defined the elites, the less dense are their interrelationships. It is the very top, where most power resides, which is most closely interlinked and often closed to those from the outside.

A 1992 survey of the presidents and board members from the largest 3,767 corporations in Japan by *Tōyō Keizai* weekly business magazine supports this generalization. Of the 3,767 presidents in the survey, only 16 percent were Tōdai graduates, while 19 percent of the 63,821 board members were Tōdai graduates.[336] Another study in 1985 of the top executive officers from the 1,817 corporations listed in the First Tokyo Stock Market Exchange, the *Nihon Keizai* business newspaper in Japan found 22.9 percent to be Tōdai graduates.[337] A survey of the 154 "top industrial elite" found almost 45 percent to be Tōdai graduates.[338]

Still, while progressively focusing on the higher elite level, the above studies have not gotten to the truly elite in Japan's corporate world. The best way to capture these people is to look at the top few corporations in each industry, and, of course, the men who are in top positions in the big business organization, Keidanren.

If we consider only the top three executive officers during the 1980s from the ten largest banks, the five largest trading companies, the five largest electronics companies, and the top five auto companies, we find almost 60 percent were Tōdai graduates.[339]

Top Ten Banks

Daiichi Kangyō Bank

Chairman. Nishikawa Seijirō, Tōdai, Economics.

Governor. Muramoto Shūzō, Tōdai, Economics.

Vice-Governor. Hanegura Shinya, Kyoto University, Economics.

Bank of Tokyo

Chairman. Yokota Shūichi, Tōdai, Business.

Governor. Kashiwagi Yūsuke, Tōdai, Law.

Vice-Governor. Watanabe Kō, Tōdai, Law.

Mitsui Bank

Chairman. Oyama Gorō, Tōdai, Law.

President. Seki Masahiko, Tōdai, Law.

Vice-President. Kaneko Yasu, Keiō University, Economics.

Mitsubishi Bank

Chairman. Nakamura Toshio, Tōdai, Law.

Governor. Yamada Haruo, Tōdai, Law.

Vice-Governor. Yamamuro Yūji, Kyoto University, Economics.

Sanwa Bank

Chairman. Miyamichi Daigo, Tōdai, Law.

Governor. Akazuka Toshio, Tōdai, Law.

Vice-Governor. Kawaguchi Kōji, Tōdai, Business.

Sumitomo Bank

Chairman. Ibe Kyonosuke, Tōdai, Economics.

Governor. Isoda Ichirō, Tōdai, Law.

Vice-Governor. Kameoka Takeo, Osaka University, Business.

Daiwa Bank

Chairman. Fukukawa Susumi, Kyoto University, Economics.

Governor. Ikeda Ichirō, Osaka University, Law.

Vice-Governor. Abekawa Sumio, Tōdai, Law.

Kyōwa Bank

Chairman. Irobe Yoshiaki, Tōdai, Law.

Vice-Chairman. Kawakami Masaichi, Waseda University, Business.

Governor. Yamanaka Tetsuo, Tōdai, Law.

Fuji Bank

Chairman. Sasaki Kunihiko, Tōdai, Economics.

Governor. Matsuzawa Shōji, Tōdai, Law.

Vice-Governor. Araki Yoshirō, Kyoto University, Law.

Tōkai Bank

Chairman. Miyake Shigeaki, Kyoto University, Law.

Governor. Katō Takaichi, no college.

Vice-Governor. Sakai Kentarō, Tōdai, Law.

Five Top Trading Companies

C. Itō

Chairman. Sejima Ryūsaburō, Rikkyo University, Business.

Vice-Chairman. Tanaka Masao, Osaka University, Business.

President. Tōzaki Seiki, Tokyo College of Business.

Mitsui Bussan

Chairman. Ikeda Yoshizō, Tōdai, Law.

Vice-Chairman. Uchida Katsu, Tōdai, Law.

2nd Vice-Chairman. Aoki Saburō, Tōdai, Law.

Mitsubishi Trading Company

Chairman. Tabe Fumiichirō, Tokyo College of Business.

Vice-Chairman. Yamada Keisaburō, Todai, Law.

President. Mimura Yohei, Keiō University, Economics.

Sumitomo Trading Company

Chairman. Shibuyama Kazuō, Tōdai, Law.

President. Uemura Akio, Tōdai, Law.

Vice-President. Hidaka Junnosuke, Tōdai, Law.

Marubeni Trading Company

President. Matsuo Yasuichirō, Tōdai, Economics.

Vice President. Kawasaki Tachifuto, Tōdai, Law.

2nd Vice President. Ikeda Matsujirō, no college.

Top Five Consumer Electronics Manufacturers

Toshiba

Chairman. Iwata Kazuo, Tōdai, Law.

President. Sanami Masaiichi, Tōdai, Engineering.

Vice President. Imai Ryūji, Tōdai, Economics.

Matsushita

Chairman. Matsushita Masaharu, Tōdai, Law.

President. Yamashita Toshihiko, no college.

Vice President. Yasukawa Hiroshi, no college.

Sony

Chairman. Morita Akio, Osaka University, Physics.

President. Iwama Kasuo, Tōdai, Physics.

Vice President. Ōga Sukeo, Tokyo College of Art and Music.

Mitsubishi Electronics

Chairman. Shindō Sadakazu, Kyūshū University, Business.

Vice-Chairman. Mizuno Shōji, Tokyo College of Business.

President. Katayama Kōji, Kyūshū University, Engineering.

Hitachi Electronics

Chairman. Yamashita Toshihiko, Tōdai, Engineering.

President. Misumasa Fumi, Tōdai, Engineering.

Vice President. Mita Katsushige, Tōdai, Engineering.

Top Five Automobile Manufacturers

Nissan

Chairman. Kawamata Katsuji, Tokyo College of Business.

Vice-Chairman. Iwakoshi Takahiro, Tōdai, Engineering.

President. Ishihara Toshio, Tōhoku University, Law.

Toyota

Chairman. Hanai Masaya, Kōbe Business College.

President. Toyoda Eiji, Tōdai, Engineering.

Vice President. Toyoda Shoichirō, Nagoya University, Engineering.

Honda

President. Kawajima Kiyoshi, Hamamatsu Technical College.

Vice President. Sugiura Hideo, Kyoto University, Physics.

2nd Vice President. Shinomiya Shigeo, Hamamatsu Technical College.

Isuzu

President. Okamura Toshio, Meiji University, Business.

Vice President. Kadoshika Tetsuya, Tōdai, Business.

2nd Vice President. Uesugi Ichirō, Tōdai, Economics.

Mitsubishi Auto

Chairman. Kubō Tomio, Tōdai, Engineering.

President. Sone Yoshitoshi, Tōdai, Engineering.

Vice President. Sugiura Kensuke, Tōdai, Economics.

Finally there is Keidanren, whose president is often called the prime minister of business, and perhaps the most powerful corporate elite in the country, if not the most powerful man in the nation. There have been eight chairmen of Keidanren since it was formed after World War II. These chairmen and their educational backgrounds are as follows[340]:

Oshidawa Ichirō, 1946–1956, Tōdai, Law.

Ishizaka Taizō, 1956–1968, Tōdai, Law.

Uemura Kangorō, 1968–1974, Tōdai, Law.

Dōkō Toshio, 1974–1980, vocational high school only.

Inayama Yoshihiro, 1980–1986, Tōdai, Economics.

Saitō Eijirō, 1986–1990. Tōdai, Economics.

Hiraiwa Gaishi, 1990–1994, Tōdai, Law.

Toyoda Shoichirō, 1994–present, Nagoya University, Engineering.

It is also worth noting that as of the early 1990s there were ten vice-chairmen of Keidanren: five were Tōdai Faculty of Law graduates, three were Tōdai Faculty of Engineering graduates, one was a Tōdai Faculty of Economics graduate, and the only non-Tōdai graduate was from the Tokyo College of Business.

In addition to Keidanren, as noted in the previous chapter, there are three other elite business organizations that are important in organizing and protecting the interests of the coroprate class. Keizai Dōyūkai, or Dōyūkai, has a leadership made up of a "representative director" (*daihyō kanji*) and five "vice-representative directors." The director and three of the five vice-directors have been graduates of Tokyo University. Presidents or chairmen of one hundred and twenty-three companies are currently members of Keizai Dōyūkai, including the head of Fujitsu, Fuji Bank, Kajima Development, etc. Just over half of the 123 men, sixty-nine to be exact, are graduates of the Tokyo University, thirty-one from the Faculty of Law and twenty-two from the Faculty of Economics.

Nikkeiren has as its more important organ Gyōyjū Bekkaiin Dantai, a council of the heads of major industries such as the paper and pulp industry association, the insurance industry alliance, the cement producers' alliance, etc. Of the fifty-three chairmen of the separate council member organizations, twenty-nine are graduates of the Tokyo University, nineteen from the Faculty of Law and eight from the Faculty of Economics.

The governing body of Nissho consists of a general secretary, five vice-general secretaries and three special advisors. There is also an advisory board made up of an additional fifty-six members. Currently the general secretary and three of the vice-general secretaries are graduates from the Faculty of Law of Tokyo University, one additional vice-general secretary is a graduate of the Faculty of engineering at Tōdai, and two of the three special advisors are as well from the Tōdai Faculty of Law. Of the members of the advisory board, fourteen of the fifty-six are Tōdai graduates, half from the Faculty of Law, four from the Faculty of Engineering and three from the Faculty of Economics.[341]

When considering the top elites from all three elite groups in Japan, but especially the government ministry and top corporations, we find that they are more closely linked through old school ties and other old boy networks than the elites from any other industrial society, including England. In the United States, for example, while Harvard, Yale, and Princeton are noted as training grounds for the elite, they create old school ties which pale in comparison to those of Japan. Considering the 52,837 executives from the corporations listed in *Standard and Poor's*, just over 3 percent are from Yale, and just over 2 percent are from Harvard or Princeton. When considering the executives and board members from only the 250 largest corporations in the United States, slightly more than 5 percent are from Yale, 4 percent from Harvard, and slightly less than 3 percent are from Princeton.

Various studies of the corporate elite in England find from 40 to 58 percent of the executives of the largest 100 or so corporations are from Oxford or Cambridge, as are perhaps 70 percent of the top civil service and judiciary.[342] As in the United States, these British elites are also connected by various social clubs and other prep school, or public school ties.[343] But there is nothing as extensive in the United States or England linking the elites in addition to the old school ties such as the *keibatsu, amakudari,* the *keiretsu,* and Keidanren.[344] Also, we must not forget that because of age ranking, the top elites in Japan are more similar in age, which means that not only did most of them graduate from Tōdai, they were there at the same time, overwhelmingly from a single academic department of that university, as classmates!

ELITE RECRUITMENT IN JAPAN

Returning to F. Scott Fitzgerald's observations: to what extent are the Japanese elite reproduced from within, from generation to generation, creating what many people would expect to be the "waste at the top," where

"great seriousness" is unlikely to be "in the same skin with great opportunity"? It is beyond question that Tōdai and just a few other elite universities are the routes to the top in Japan. But how open are these universities
to those below the elite level? Do they admit their students, and future elites
of the country, through merit criteria, through what can be called equality
of opportunity? Or can the rich buy their way into these elite universities,
therefore making it easier for the sons of the elite to attain elite positions
themselves?

The answers to some of these questions are clear. Yes, entrance into the
best universities in Japan is based upon strict achievement tests. No, you
cannot buy your way into Tōdai or the other top national universities; it is
almost equally impossible to do so at the elite private universities. The manual laborer's son and the top executive's son must take the same examination
to get into Tōdai and the other universities. If they do not score toward
the top on the exam, they do not get in, period. This is also to say, your
father cannot buy a new building for the university as a means of getting
you in. And cheating on these examinations is almost unheard of, especially
at the major national universities.[345]

Still, do the rich and better-educated have an advantage in getting their
sons and daughters into the best universities? Entrance exams based upon
strict merit and achievement are not the same as equality of opportunity.
But before we get to the tougher questions, we must describe the process
of getting into these top universities in Japan.

"Exam Hell" and Education in Japan

This is serious business in Japan. Each early spring, dreams come true, or
are dashed, perhaps within one weekend. One's whole future is on the line—
will it be possible for a future shot at a top executive position in one of the
biggest corporations, or perhaps a ministry position? Or will it be a life of
drudgery as a low-level "salaryman," or even a blue-collar worker? A single
exam is likely to determine this. When the exam results are given out, made
public, it is front page news. The exam questions themselves are in the
newspapers, with serious analysis of the questions and the correct answers.
And there is extensive media analysis of the high schools with the best records of students passing the exams to get into the top universities. It may
be difficult for Westerners to understand, especially Americans, but the results of these exams determine the life course of tens of thousands of young
people.

To begin with, it must be understood that the aged-ranked society of
Japan provides for very few deviations from the life course: you go to college
in your late teens and early twenties. There is no late life change of mind,
a return to college as an undergraduate. Walking around the Tōdai campus,

for example, one sees very few if any undergraduates who are older than twenty-three or so. Thus, if you hope for a high position in the society, you take your shot within one or two years after high school.

For the majority taking these entrance exams, it *is* one shot—this one exam, for one university. Since the late 1980s there has been some experimentation by some universities with criteria for accepting students based upon other than just the exam score. But there is still primarily one exam given by each major university during the same weekend in early spring. Each university has its own examination: there is no College Testing Service giving the equivalent of an SAT examination which can be used by almost all universities to accept or reject students—it is one exam, different for each university, given in the same week. Thus, a student must decide which university he or she has a chance to enter, take the exam in January, receive the results in February, and if successful, begin as a freshman at the university in April.

With the stakes so high, it is understandable that a billion-dollar business has developed for giving trial examinations months before the official entrance exam. In addition to the trial exam, this service provides each student with a detailed analysis of where he or she scored compared to other young people, and statistical probabilities for success in passing the exam at each major university. Thus, say your probability for success is only 50 percent for Tōdai, but 80 percent for Hiroshima University: do you go for the top, with huge potential rewards, or play it safe with a respectable but not elite university such as Hiroshima University?

If you fail in your first attempt, you can "drop out of life" for a year, and study for next year's exam: this means to become a *rōnin,* the old term for a leaderless samurai. About 25 percent of the young people taking the exam for major universities every year are *rōnin,* a few for even a second or a third year. But the chances of a *rōnin* getting in the same university the next year are not much better, and the process requires money and much family support.[346] Thus, while becoming *rōnin* for one year is not uncommon, there are few young people who can remain in that status for more than one year.

As Japan has become better known to the industrial West, "examination hell," the college entrance examinations, has also become more known. Less well understood, however, is how the process of college entrance begins much earlier in life.[347] Almost as important as the college entrance exam is the high school entrance exam. Before the high school level the Japanese public schools are quite egalitarian. There is no tracking by ability, which in the United States often means tracking by parents' class background, and all of the primary schools cover the same material at the same time. It is said that Ministry of Education officials in Tokyo can tell you at a given time of the day, week, and month what all students at a particular grade level are learning all over the country.

All of this changes after junior high school. At this point there are examinations to see which level or type of high school the student will be able to enter.[348] There are roughly four levels of high schools: in the upper rank are the college prep high schools with the best records of sending their students on to prestigious universities; then there are college prep high schools whose records for placement are not as good; followed by industrial high schools, which, though very good in contrast to the image of such institutions in the United States, provide students almost no chance to get into a university; and finally there are vocational schools, which are more likely to fit the image common in the United States of schools where students are given little training for low-skilled working-class jobs.

As one would expect, all of these exams are so important in life few people want to leave their fate in the hands of the regular public schools. One study has recently indicated that for the students who have hopes of some day going to college, 84 percent pay for extra, after-hours education, and about 60 percent of these people rely on two or more types of this extra education. Another estimate is that 55 percent of all sixth-grade students were in some form of extra educational program in 1980.[349] The most common is called *juku*, which is basically a second high school or junior high school which students may attend several days a week after the regular school lets out for the day. About 46 percent of students with college aspirations attend some form of *juku*. Then, if the student does not pass the college entrance examination the first time and chooses to become a *rōnin*, there is more intense cramming for the next year's exam at private schools called *yobiko*.

These extra educational programs vary in quality and cost. In 1965 it was estimated that 5 percent of all money spent on education in Japan went to such extra educational programs; by 1982, 20 percent of all money for education in the country went for these programs.[350] *Yobiko*, for example, can cost from $2,000 to $20,000 a year or more.

This is where the inequality of educational opportunity in Japan can come into play. Family income has a slightly greater impact upon college attendance in Japan than in the United States, and as might be expected, there is also a relationship in Japan between family income and the type of high school a student is able to get into.[351]

Japanese Education and Elite Selection

It is time to consider what all of this means for the elite selection process in Japan. The overall degree of equality of educational opportunity in a country does not necessarily imply that the degree of openness at the top is the same, but there is an important influence on elite selection.

With respect to the overall amount of equality of opportunity in Japanese education, rates of openness, or rates of social mobility, have varied from time to time.[352] There is evidence that before World War II the rate of social mobility or equality of opportunity in Japan was decreasing in contrast to other industrial nations. Pre-World War II schools had increased the use of tracking, which usually means children of higher-class backgrounds are more likely placed in a college-prep track. Soon after World War II, the rate of social mobility or equality of opportunity in Japan was higher than before the war, but also higher in comparison to other industrial nations.[353] Evidence suggests that by the 1970s the rate of mobility had slowed to become more like the average for industrial nations.

The process of elite selection in Japan, the rate of movement into the top, has followed a similar pattern. Due to the importance of Tōdai and just a few other top universities in the elite selection process, trends in the class backgrounds of Tōdai students can indicate possibilities for a more or less open elite selection process. Even though the strict entrance exams for these selective universities in Japan go back to the late 1800s, places such as Tōdai were not so open to the middle and working classes.[354] At this time, as already noted, 90 percent of the Tōdai students were from former samurai backgrounds.[355] Soon after World War II, however, reports indicate that 63 percent of Tōdai students had to work to pay for even the low Tōdai tuition, and as much as 10 to 14 percent were from working class families; quite remarkable given the elite status of the university, and when compared to other elite universities around the world.[356] With the increasing use of expensive additional educational aid to pass college entrance exams noted above, however, we might expect that this openness at universities such as Tōdai has been eroded. By 1982 over half of Tōdai students came from more expensive private high schools. And already by the middle 1960s the class backgrounds of students from the prestigious national universities, including Tōdai, were again getting higher and higher, a trend which continued in the 1970s and 1980s.[357]

As for the question of an open or closed elite selection process, the above evidence is less than conclusive. For example, Tōdai could be a rather open institution, with students from all class backgrounds, and the very top positions in the political and economic institutions still could be closed to everyone who does not have an elite family background. Not all Tōdai students make it to the very top: thus, elite selection could still be restricted to those Tōdai students from elite family backgrounds. Considering the actual backgrounds of other than educational elites, however, the Tōdai pattern seems rather similar. Before the war the top was quite closed, and dominated by people from wealthy *zaibatsu* families, or those with aristocratic titles. This drastically changed with defeat in war and the rather radical reforms in the economy, politics, and education following the war. However, by the 1970s and 1980s there were growing material inequalities, less social mobility in the society, subversions of equality of educational opportunity, and a tendency toward closing of the ranks among the elites in the form of such things as the *keibatsu* family groups.

ELITE SELECTION, LEGITIMACY, AND UNITY:
A CONCLUSION

There are three very important points to make about elite selection, legitimacy, and unity. First, Tōdai, with very few other universities, is still the route to the top: this has been a constant factor since the late 1800s in Japan. A corollary constant factor is the process of selection for Tōdai based upon merit, the passing of strict entrance examinations. Rich or poor, no matter how the mixture is found among Tōdai students, they are still among the brightest in the country. Rich kids with limited intellectual abilities do not get into Tōdai, in contrast to universities in some other industrial nations. Thus, the second major point is that no matter what the class background of Tōdai students or elites in Japan, the fact that these elites must go through universities such as Tōdai gives them great legitimacy. The general population tends to assume that even though these elites may have come from privileged backgrounds, they have faced and passed the test of meritocracy through "exam hell" like everyone else trying to get into Tōdai. No other industrial country can as confidently say as much about their own elites.

Third, and perhaps most important, it must be remembered that personal ties continue to be more important in Japan than other industrial nations. In one of those puzzling mixtures of old and new, modern and preindustrial, and perhaps East and West, Japan has created an educational system based extensively upon objective evaluation and merit, while personal relationships, or informal relations among people, continue to be very important. In what is called *jinmyaku*, personal ties of trust and mutual help continue to influence decision making, business and political influence.[358] It is in this context that the old school ties and old boy networks strongly forged in the college years, especially among Tōdai graduates, are important for elite selection and elite cooperation and unity in Japan today.

CHAPTER 9

Japan's Mass Society: People Control for Elite Power

In *The Power Elite*, C. Wright Mills employed the concept of a mass society to explain why a powerless population is not so uncommon in the present age. He used this concept of a mass society to describe a population either ignorant or confused about important issues, and/or unable to act collectively upon these issues, all of which makes the existence of a "power elite" possible. Most people who have given much thought to the subject agree today that Mills was overly simplistic in his description of the American public as a mass society. But what about Japan?

The popular conception of Japan in the West is of a nation of patient, obedient people, a people who respect the authority of the family head, corporate boss, and emperor. On occasion we still hear the Japanese referred to as "ants," and by such opinion leaders as a recent prime minister of France.[359] To the extent that any of this is correct, it would seem that Japanese elites have it rather easy: there would be little dissension against their rule, there would be little need to concern themselves with whether or not the Japanese people agree or disagree with what they do.

There is some scholarly opinion to support this view of an obedient Japanese population. In his acclaimed work on Asian cultures, for example, Lucian Pye argues that Asian cultures share "the common denominator of idealizing benevolent, paternalistic leadership and of legitimizing dependency." In particular, "paternalistic authority works in Japan because [of] the desire for dependency on the part of subordinates."[360]

Placing this idea on a more psychological plane, the respected Japanese psychiatrist, Doi Takeo, uses the Japanese concept of *amae* to explain Japanese dependency toward authority figures. Described by Doi as kin to an uncritical and unconditional love held by a mother toward her child, he argues that Japanese people are socialized into seeking *amae* because after this form of total, uncritical love is given for the first few years of life to Japanese children, it is suddenly taken away during their school years, and they long for this lost condition the rest of their lives, and seek it in other relationships. *Amae* is said to form "the actual or potential basis for the whole social system" in Japan, and thus, the basis of the willingly dependent position Japanese people place themselves in with respect to figures of authority from family head to emperor.[361]

Images supporting this caricature of the Japanese, for example, were common in January of 1989, following the death of Emperor Hirohito. Even before this time, as the emperor lay dying, beginning in September of 1988, many social activities were canceled, and even "questionably moral" television programs were curtailed out of deference to the emperor: the entertainment industry lost billions. With the emperor's death, his palace in Tokyo was surrounded with tearful people, bowing in respect to the father figure of modern Japan. Buildings all over the nation were draped with the national flag outlined in black. All normal television programming was disrupted for twenty-four hours with nothing but information about the death and documentaries of the emperor's life. Saturday morning, the day the emperor died, classes were dismissed, and shops and department stores opened one hour late out of respect for the emperor. When they did open, shop clerks wore black arm bands.

There are other facts about Japan today which seem to support this common image of an obedient population. All types of crime are very low in Japan, perhaps the lowest of any major nation. There also seems to be little overt conflict between labor and management, with average days lost to strikes in Japan only 3 to 5 percent of that found in the United States, Italy, or England throughout the 1980s.

There are, however, misleading aspects to this popular image of the Japanese, and theories such as those about the effects of *amae* have been highly criticized. For instance, the people who shed tears for the emperor were not necessarily in the majority as indicated by "man on the street" TV news interviews throughout the country; the total blackout of normal television programming brought a raid on video stores all over Japan, with pictures of these stores the next day showing completely empty shelves; and a significant minority of the Japanese people showed a less than reverent attitude toward the emperor as he lay dying. Especially on university campuses there was discussion of whether or not the emperor system should be abolished, and the extent of Hirohito's responsibility for World War II. At Hiroshima University, student protestors erected large signs in the middle of campus which read, in rough translation, "push the Emperor into hell." This is not the stuff of obedient, passive ants.

A Western visitor bringing this image of a passive, obedient Japanese population will be puzzled. Japan is brimming with protest movements and disruptive activities. The visitor's first hint that something doesn't fit the stereotype comes after landing at the main international airport—Narita has come to resemble an armed camp since the 1970s due to ongoing protest over its location. Tucked into a hotel for the night, the visitor's sleep is likely to be interrupted by the almost nightly conflicts between the police and *bōsōzoku* motorcycle gangs which populate the streets of most large Japanese cities at night.[362] Next morning the visitor is likely to walk down the street to find a protest march against pollution; or a march by ethnic minorities against discrimination, doctors against some change in the health care system, sound trucks blasting rightist political protest slogans, or the headquarters of a power company blockaded in protest over its new nuclear power plant. While it is hard to measure precisely, there are probably more active protest movements in Japan than most other industrial nations today.[363]

Looking to earlier history shatters the passive image of the Japanese even more dramatically. During the relatively quiet two centuries preceding industrialization, there were an estimated 6,889 major peasant revolts. In the 1880s there was a spreading "poor peoples' army."[364] Massive working-class riots in 1905 destroyed over 70 percent of the police stations in Tokyo, and in 1918 massive strikes brought down a government.[365] From the late 1940s to 1960, among industrial nations, Japan had one of the highest levels of disruption due to protest, with several million people protesting the 1960 treaty with the United States, and over five million workers on strike.[366] Again, these are not the actions of passive, obedient ants.

There is nothing inherent in being Japanese which leads to obedience. In fact, as noted earlier, a group-oriented society, such as Japan certainly is, can demonstrate either obedience or prolonged conflict depending upon other factors or circumstances. If Japanese elites are to have a comparatively passive society, or at least one that does not seriously threaten their rule, they must work hard at it, as they have throughout Japanese history.[367] Current Japanese elites are no more assured of a "mass society" than the elites in any other industrial nation: like their predecessors, they must work hard for it.

It is the aim of this chapter is to explain *how* and *by what mechanisms* Japanese elites today are often able to prevent serious challenge to their positions of power. A strong and expanding economy, an economy producing an ever-rising standard of living and more jobs in the decades after World War II certainly helps. But a strong economy is seldom enough in the long run, nor will such economic prosperity last unaltered, as the Japanese are beginning to realize in the 1990s. And with the many protest movements described above, it is especially interesting to consider how these movements are prevented from being very successful, or at least from posing a major threat to the status quo in Japan. Japanese cultural traditions may have significant effects upon stability and order, and there are various other noncultural and nonpsychological factors, such as the mass media, education, work organization, and the nature of the legal system, that work to maintain social order in Japan today.

CULTURE AND SELF-CONTROL

Indications of what some people call Japan's "culture of conformity" can be found in folk sayings.[368] One of the most famous is "destroy ego and serve others." Another is "the nail that sticks out gets hammered down," often cited in contrast to the Western "the squeaky wheel gets the grease." A commonly heard word, *seishin,* meaning simply spirit or will, is often used in a way suggesting self-degradation to restrain the ego for inner strength. As indicated in opinion polls, one of the most respected books in Japan is Sōseki's *Kokora,* in which the main character counsels a young boy on how to suppress his ego so as not to take advantage of others or offend group expectations.

The fact that this individual ego exists in the Japanese person no less than in people anywhere is indicated by the strain and difficulty of keeping it under control. If this ego did not exist, the moral teaching of books such as Sōseki's would not be necessary, nor would the *seishin* rituals noted above.[369] Neither would there be need for social work or psychological counseling, which in Japan is oriented toward making people accept their place and conform by suppressing the ego and individualism, in contrast to the West, where social counseling is geared to making people self-actualizing and self-reliant. Nor would there be a need for the famous corporate "basic training" camps to initiate new employees and make them conform.

No matter what the culture, there is always the self, the individual, looking out for her or his own interests, trying to attain his or her desires, as well as independence and freedom, or simply a better deal in life. In the words of the main character in another of Sōseki's novels, *Kōfu* ("The Miner"), a man who is trying to escape Japanese pressures of conformity, "Human beings are *supposed* to get angry now and then, they're *supposed* to rebel. That's how they're *made.* Forcing yourself to become a creature that doesn't get angry and never rebels is tantamount to happily educating yourself to be an idiot." Some Japanese, in fact, like to say that Japanese people are in many ways even more individualistic than Westerners. There is some truth to this, but it is more accurate to say that the Japanese are so pressured to conform in most situations that they more actively seek ways and situations where they can be individuals at other times.[370]

Conformity comes no more naturally for the Japanese than for anyone else, but there are more cultural mechanisms in Japan designed to bring about this conformity. This is also to say that ideologies stressing conformity are no more naturally accepted by the Japanese than by anyone else.

Power and Selective Culture

When saying that a nation has a particular culture, at least somewhat different from any other, we must ask why this is so. And while there are many reasons and possible answers, some of the answers involve elements of power and control. What we mean is that those with the power to do so have often been active in influencing what become elements of culture in a society, and which elements of culture already present in a society are given more importance.

Many historians argue that due to Japan's long period of feudalism, the ruling class has had more influence on what beliefs enter the country than has been the case anywhere else.[371] The Confucianism which stresses order and respect for authority was actively pushed by this early elite, then during the Meiji Restoration of the late 1800s, the new ruling elite actively promoted Confucianism again. This time, however, it was directed toward the masses who previously had less influence from Confucianism, which finally worried elites with the approach of the first constitution and voting in the 1890s. It was also at this time that the *tennōsei* ideology of emperor worship was pushed by the Meiji elites, and somewhat later the "emperor's rescript on education" was created and promoted, both as a means to enforce civil morality, which is to say obedience.[372] Finally, as a more authoritarian government emerged in the late 1920s, to remain until after the war, a Peace Preservation Law was passed in 1925 which actually created sort of "thought police" working to keep the hearts and minds of the Japanese people "clean."[373]

Restraints of the Small Group

The small groups so important in Japan, it might seem, would make "public" or interest group formation easier, thus providing the masses with a greater voice and influence in the broader society. In actuality, it is argued, there is the opposite effect: small group ties are often so strong and important that most Japanese are unable to form broader memberships outside of their small family, occupational, or other group associations.[374] There is, so to speak, a retreat within, a barrier blocking organization for broader issues affecting the masses.

A related point is made by the noted Japanese sociologist Nakane Chie, but in her view it is the vertical nature of small group organization in Japan which is important.[375] According to Nakane, work groups in Japan are vertically organized to include the higher- and lower-status members of the company or other associations. This close association among higher- and lower-status people blunts vertical conflicts, such as the socioeconomic class conflicts, more prevalent in other industrial societies. Further, because of the strong attachments to these vertical groups, horizontal groups, or groups including primarily people of equal rank, are more difficult to form. Thus, according to this argument, workers find it more difficult to organize interest groups to challenge higher corporate managers, middle-class citizens in a community find it more difficult to organize against a local corporation responsible for pollution, and so forth.

Nakane's thesis can be overused, but there is evidence supporting some of her arguments. For example, in Japanese corporations workers are more likely to socialize with their bosses than in American corporations, and there is a lower rate of joining volunteer organizations in Japan compared to Western industrial nations.[376] But criticism of these ideas, and the extent of social movement activity noted earlier, provides some skepticism about the restraining effects of small groups in Japan.

What can be said, however, is that social movements and interest groups in Japan are formed relatively easily, and thus are prevalent, but they are kept small and divided, reducing their overall potential. This is suggested by one estimate that there were some ten thousand local protest movements against pollution in Japan during the early 1970s.[377] With protest of this fragmented nature, it is relatively easy for opposing elites to isolate and weaken protestors, as we will see in more detail below.

MODERN MECHANISMS OF SOCIAL CONTROL

Despite any Japanese cultural tendency to obey or respect authority, and to remain fragmented in small groups, compliance is still not simple or assured. The number of contemporary social movements in Japan, as well as in earlier periods of strife and rebellion, makes clear that if anything there is only a somewhat greater tendency toward compliance when compared to other industrial nations. Building upon these cultural tendencies, other means of social control are needed if elites are to remain relatively unchallenged.[378]

The Mass Media

Few people watch more TV or read more popular magazines and more newspapers than the Japanese. And their information sources are much more concentrated: the top three newspapers in Japan have a daily circulation of over twenty million copies, compared to less than three million for the top three in the United States, which has twice the population. And with few television channels compared to the United States, during 1990 the Japanese watched an average of 28.5 hours of television per week, compared to

29 hours per week for the United States, the world leader in such passive activity.[379] Thus, what is presented in these media is likely to have a huge impact on what the Japanese people know, think, and understand about their society and the world.[380] This mass media, therefore, can be a force to keep the Japanese people either ignorant or confused about important issues, maintaining obedience and social order in the process.

As in the United States and other Western industrial nations, the mass media in Japan is relatively free. By that we mean there is very little *formal* government censorship in Japan (with the exception of such things as showing pubic hair on film and television), and in fact, less than in some countries such as England. But the extent to which mass media ate "free" cannot be answered so easily. In the United States, for example, a nominally free mass medium is often forced to stay away from subjects which can upset powerful interest groups, especially wealthy interest groups, for fear of losing advertising revenue or having expensive lawsuits brought against them.[381]

In Japan there is even greater pressure to stay away from subjects certain groups do not want presented, or to have these subjects presented in a way these groups prefer. One of the greatest means of influencing the media by powerful corporate interests comes through the huge advertising agency Dentsū. "Dentsū's sway over the substance of Japanese TV culture is quite unlike any kind of social control through the mass media anywhere in the world."[382] Dentsū accounts for almost one-third of all advertising on Japanese TV, "and virtually monopolizes the scheduling of sponsors during prime-time hours." Overall, Dentsū controls over one-fourth of advertising revenues in Japan, and about one-fifth of the advertising in major newspapers. This compares to the less than 3.5 percent market share held by the largest advertising agency in the United States.

Along with their power over the market, Dentsū is well connected to Japan's corporate elite, and works as their protector through what amounts to censorship of the media. In his analysis, van Wolferen lists many cases in which Dentsū has forced programs off the air that were deemed offensive to corporate interests. And with respect to news, there are many cases of intervention by Dentsū to prevent reporting of information detrimental to the corporate elite.[383] But Dentsū is certainly not alone: the second largest agency, Hakuhōdo, is also "concerned" about protecting its corporate clients, and is even more linked to the ministry elite in Japan because many of Hakuhōdo's top executives come directly from the ministry, primarily the Ministry of Finance, through *amakudari*. Still, Dentsū is by far the largest and most powerful, and holds perhaps the not so surprising distinction of being built up after the war by the former head of the wartime "thought police."[384]

Another of the important limitations to a free mass media in Japan comes from the operation of "press clubs." There are over 1,000 of these press clubs, or *kisha* clubs, organized around and controlled by the main government ministries as well as leading politicians. Membership is restricted, and only members of these clubs have the privilege of obtaining information directly from these top ministry or political officials.[385] If these officials dislike the news coverage they receive, the offending reporter or news agency will be barred from the club. Thus, when the government calls for a news blackout on some issue, or asks that the coverage be slanted in a certain way, it is quite likely to happen. But this is not necessarily professional neglect in the eyes of Japanese journalists; in journalism schools they are taught that the media is to help the government "guide the people of Japan."

Journalists from other countries who have rather different ideas about the role of journalism are seldom able to interfere. Only the Foreign Ministry, for obvious reasons, allows foreign journalists to participate in their press club and news briefings. It is journalists from other countries, or smaller presses within Japan kept out of the inner circles, who usually break stories about big scandals involving politicians or corporate elites, and only later are these stories picked up by the main Japanese media when the stories can no longer be ignored.

It would be too simple to suggest that controversial issues are covered up *only* by political elites, or by any other powerful group in the society, such as Dentsū. Many observers of Japan claim that there is something like "civil inattention" with respect to controversial subjects and that this is an aspect of Japanese culture. It is argued that more than other people, the Japanese have a propensity to accept that certain things which could cause hard feelings between people or reflect badly upon themselves and their group should be hidden.[386] As we have seen, there are even two common terms for this attitude and its opposite—*tatemae* and *honne*. *Tatemae* means to keep the true nature of a situation hidden, while *honne* refers to the actual facts of a situation. *Tatemae* does not necessarily have the negative connotation of lying; it can at times have the positive connotation of showing that you have a kind heart because you do not want to say anything that will make someone uncomfortable or feel bad.[387] Putting it more strongly, van Wolferen writes that the cultural concept of *tatemae* "provides a frame of reference in which many forms of deceit are socially sanctioned."[388]

Thus, with respect to the news media, it is important to note that much "self-censorship" is followed. In part this is because of the Japanese cultural aversion to controversy. Like many Japanese citizens who become uncomfortable and quiet when foreigners bring up controversial topics about Japan in their presence, the news media feel more comfortable neglecting such topics.[389] When writing about the outcast *burakumin* in his popular book on the Japanese society a few years ago, Robert Christopher stated, "It is a reasonable bet, for example, that when this book is translated into Japanese, this particular portion of it will be quietly omitted."[390] It has since been translated: he was right.

Limits to Japanese Education

Japanese universities are not always the best places for objective, scientific debate on social and political issues. The main problems are avoidance of controversy, at times overt suppression of controversial ideas, and what some call a weak tradition of free universal discourse in Japan. The first problem, avoidance of controversial issues, is similar to the avoidance of controversy noted above in the mass media. With respect to the second problem, a large percentage of Japanese social scientists are Marxist in orientation. Most often elites actually pay scant attention to them, and they are seen as isolated and harmless. But they are not always left alone, and there are still cases of Japanese professors being fired for teaching or doing research on controversial subjects, such as discrimination against minorities.[391] The third problem, that of a weak tradition of free discourse, requires more explanation.

Putting it strongly, as van Wolferen is apt to do, it can be said that "in Japan . . . argument is associated with conflict itself, and, since all conflict is defined as bad, arguing and debating are not usually recognized as healthy ways to settle disputes."[392] More specifically on scholars and intellectuals, "intellectuals are rarely asked to prove or disprove their hypotheses, and consequently are themselves not very good at critical evaluation."[393] For anyone who has spent time with Japanese social scientists, it is obvious that the lack of sound critical evaluation by intellectuals is overstated.[394] And it is interesting to note that in the mid-1990s the Japanese are becoming aware of this problem, with the Ministry of Education taking action by requiring debate classes in the public schools for the first time. However, the newly recognized need for such debate classes indicates some recognition of the problem.

The most important limitations to knowledge about controversial subjects in Japanese education, however, can be located in elementary and secondary schools. As most people know, Japanese high school students have the best test scores for math and science in the world. But with respect to history and aspects of their own contemporary society, there are surprisingly large gaps in their knowledge. When teaching Japanese college students, for example, it is a mistake to assume that in high school they have learned much about, or have been given complete information about, the 1930s and wartime events; an accurate and complete account of some of this history can bring surprise to these young Japanese faces. American students may be poor in math and science, and unable to locate their own state or other countries on a map, but they have a better understanding of many controversial events in their own country's history. And German students are at the other extreme. They may not know the exact involvement of their parents or other relatives, but the Holocaust and other negative events of German history are explained to them time and again in their public schools. A people ig-

norant of their history may or may not be condemned to repeat it, but they
may indeed be more easily manipulated by elites when they are ignorant.

From the beginning of modern Japanese education in the late Meiji Period, "moral values" and ideology were at the forefront of goals for education. Thus, soon after the Occupation forces arrived with the intent of
remaking Japan, education became a target. The first task was to rid the
system of such things as emperor worship, the glorification of war, and
unquestioned support for authority in the Japanese educational system.[395]
This began with the textbooks. With the country hungry and in ruins, no
new books would be forthcoming for years. In each classroom, all over the
nation, students were instructed by their teachers what to black out, page
by page, in their current textbooks before teaching could continue. Secondly, experts in education from the United States were sent to Japan to
reform education, decentralize it, and help create an educational system
which would help promote democracy and equality of opportunity.

These attempts at reform, however, were short-lived: by the mid-1950s
the Ministry of Education, the Monbusho, was taking more control and
returning education to its social control functions, and by 1956 it had rein-
troduced centralized textbook control and censorship.[396] Almost every year
this power is challenged by some group in the courts, especially in attempts
to bring about a more accurate accounting of Japanese actions in World
War II, and every time this happens the Ministry of Education wins its case.
Consequently, a detailed analysis of the contents of Japanese textbooks
shows that a very conservative ideology is stressed throughout, and while
some social problems are mentioned, these are few in number and tend to
be trivialized.[397]

What Westerners would find most surprising, however, is the extent to
which public school teachers and administrators are able to control the everyday lives of students. And many aspects of Japanese high school remain
militaristic. For example, almost all students must wear uniforms, with those
worn by boys still closely modeled after old Prussian military uniforms.
While there is some variation across high schools, most students have such
things as their hair length, pant leg size, and even size and style of girls'
panties, checked regularly.[398] And, of course, other kinds of behavior are
required—such as standing when the teacher enters, moral/inspirational lectures by the principal—while much is also prohibited. But perhaps most
unique is that such behavior is required outside of school hours as well.
Students caught in forbidden places after school hours, certain coffee shops
perhaps with a bad reputation, or doing things such as smoking, will be
reprimanded by the school authorities.[399]

Perhaps the most powerful tool of control over students by teachers and
administrators is the *naishinsho*—confidential student evaluations of each
student.[400] These records contain the opinions of teachers about students,

their behavior, character, along with test scores and grades. These records are passed along from school to school, and even to universities and potential employers, but they are confidential in that neither students nor their parents can see them. As of the late 1980s, in a famous case, the Japanese courts continued to rule that there is nothing improper or unconstitutional about such student records and their uses.

CHALLENGE TO AUTHORITY: MORE LIMITS

When confronted by strong elites resisting change, there is conflicting evidence and controversy over the extent to which protest movements versus "legitimate means" are more effective in producing social change in modern societies.[401] Clearly, however, both means *can* be effective, and under certain conditions, successful in improving the position of nonelites. Both types, however, are rather limited in Japan. We will consider first the legal means of social change, then prospects for successful protest movements in Japan.

Limits to the Legitimate Means of Social Change

In modern, democratic societies, two legal means of creating social change have been institutionalized: voting for representatives to the political system, and litigation. Limits to the first in Japan have already been considered. But the legal system and courts can be equally important.

The problem with the legal system for the average Japanese person begins with access to a lawyer. While the United States has one lawyer per 360 people, Japan has one lawyer per 9,294 people, the lowest ratio of any major industrial nation.[402] The effect of this upon consumer protection can be used as an example of how Japanese people in general find it difficult to protect themselves from powerful interests or pressure for change through the courts.

Japanese courts have ruled on 150 product liability cases in the past fifty years. In the United States there are around 1,000 such cases every year.[403] Consequently, much of what the Japanese make and sell to the United States must have extra safety features added which are not found on the same products in Japan. When there are complaints about consumer injuries in Japan, corporations are generally able to deal with them quietly, keeping others unaware of the problem, thus preventing it from becoming a broader issue generating more consumer complaints and calls for action against the corporation. But there is also a matter of the laws themselves: the laws covering consumer safety in Japan make it much more difficult for a plaintiff to prove liability. What all of this indicates is that it is difficult to acquire legal help, and when legal assistance is found, the laws are stacked against the average person.

Becoming a Lawyer

There are even more fundamental questions about the nature of the Japanese legal system than the small number of lawyers suggests. Who are the lawyers and judges, how are they trained, and what is their relation to bureaucratic elites? To begin with, the Ministry of Justice has extensive power to limit the number of lawyers in Japan, and their ability to do this is centered on the Legal Training and Research Institute run by ministry bureaucrats.[404] All future judges, prosecutors, and lawyers in Japan *must* be accepted into and trained for two years by this institute—there is no other way to become a lawyer, judge, or prosecutor. The Ministry of Justice initially keeps the number of legal professionals low through the very difficult entrance exam for the Legal Training and Research Institute. Then, during the two years of training at the institute, their trainees are "molded" into the type of lawyer, judge, or prosecutor Justice Ministry bureaucrats deem suitable for Japan.

The judicial system, of course, is of particular importance in upholding the status quo, so special precautions are taken in the selection process for judges. During the two-year training period at the Legal Training and Research Institute, those considered potentially good judges are secretly selected for special instruction and introduced to the high ranking judges currently serving the courts for further guidance. Then, once a person becomes a judge, promotions and assignments are made every three years *in secret* by the Ministry bureaucrats who run the system. At the very top of the court system, however, most Supreme Court judges are lawyers arriving through another, more familiar route. As with *amakudari* most Supreme Court Judges are retired top bureaucrats from the Justice Ministry who control the system to begin with. It is quite understandable that the Supreme Court in Japan *almost always* sides with the government in legal decisions.

We should note that some people argue that the low number of lawyers and litigation reflects Japanese culture. Lawsuits, it is said, are looked down upon by people who prefer to avoid overt conflict.[405] Stories are told such as one about a family who brought suit against a neighbor for allowing a dangerous situation that resulted in their son's death. In the end, the family who lost a son was condemned by the community more than the neighbor whose negligence caused the death. The lawsuit was interpreted as an unseemly, and wholly avoidable, stain on the image of the neighborhood. There is no doubt some truth to both sides of the argument over why Japan has so few lawyers and so little litigation, but just in case a culture of nonconfrontation is not enough to maintain the status quo and those with interests in it, there is a legal system which provides more assurance.

Prospects for Protest Movements

In one sense, the average person's potential for winning some concessions through organized protest in Japan is not so limited. As Susan Pharr found in her analysis of contemporary social movements in Japan, specific but limited gains are at times achieved by particular protest groups in Japan more often than in Western industrial nations.[406] Authorities, however, see these concessions as tactical. They are used to isolate protest groups and keep their voices from a wider audience through "buying off" protestors quickly before the protest can spread. From this perspective one is better able to understand why there are so many protest movements in Japan, while at the same time not much seems to change. Protest can pay off in a limited way, but the pay-off is usually far short of significant change that may affect many people, and thus it falls short of correcting the situation which brought about the protest in the first place. Even in this description, however, we may be creating an inaccurate impression that most protest movements in Japan win anything at all.

From her case studies of several specific protest movements in Japan, Pharr describes the steps through which authorities usually control protest movements, thus limiting any gains the protestors might otherwise achieve.[407] First, when faced with protest, authorities respond by ignoring it. If this does not work, there is an attempt to keep protestors from existing channels of resolution, such as the courts, arbitration, and so forth. This helps to isolate the protestors, prevent them from attaining any legitimacy, and keep others from joining the movement. If necessary, only when all else has failed, authorities can give concessions to protestors, as limited as possible, to buy them off and allow protestors to give up the protest with a feeling something has been done.

This is not to say authorities in other countries do not follow the steps outlined by Pharr. The difference is that in Japan authorities are more willing to make small concessions, and more willing to do so more quickly to eliminate confrontation that can do more damage to their interests. Most important in the end is to avoid "solutions that generate principles having broad applicability across cases." Holding out simply for some principle on their part seems to make less sense to most Japanese authorities.

TAMING JAPANESE WORKERS

A central problem in all capitalist industrial societies is that of somehow gaining the cooperation of workers. For elites in preindustrial agrarian societies it was, and is, less difficult, and also less important. It is less difficult because peasants tend to be more isolated from each other, less organized, and especially centuries ago, they were less aware of how their lot in life could be changed for the better.[408] And peasant cooperation with the lord was less important than employee cooperation in industrial societies.

While physical coercion continues to be employed from time to time, there has been an evolution of other, less costly mechanisms for inducing worker cooperation in the twentieth century. At first there was "Fordism" assembly line control and increased supervision, along with a proliferation of bureaucratic rules; then "welfare capitalism" to try to "buy" more worker commitment; and finally the "work teams" for which the Japanese have become famous.[409] There is also the option of bringing workers into the management of the company, thus making employees equal partners, with an equal stake in the company's profitability, but only some European nations have moved in this direction, and certainly not Japan.

On no other issue concerning the nature of modern Japan has there been more disagreement than about the issue of worker control, even as the "Japanese management style" is exported around the world. Have Japanese managers found the more efficient system to create worker commitment and contentment, or has Japan simply found a more efficient means of controlling workers through "quality control circles" in which the workers become tools of their own (and coworkers') control and exploitation?[410] The Japanese have been able to create more worker cooperation certainly than they had before World War II, and more than most countries today. But it must be recognized that this creation has occurred in a much more complex manner than most people outside of Japan understand. To make the point most clearly it will be useful to consider briefly the situation of post-war Germany, a country like Japan that has extensive labor-management cooperation and fewer strikes than other industrial societies, but for very different reasons than Japan.

Labor in Post-War Germany

Two defeated and devastated powers, Germany and Japan, in many ways took different roads in rebuilding their respective societies after World War II. But the contrast could hardly be more divergent with respect to labor relations. In the immediate years after World War II, both Germany and Japan allowed unions destroyed by pre-war dictatorships to rebuild. The rebuilding process in Japan, however, was quickly retarded by the "Red scare" fueled by events in China and by the Korean War, while attempts to retard the development of unions and labor power in Germany failed dramatically.

The term "dual system" is used to describe the form of German labor representation that has evolved since World War II. What this dual system involves is (1) labor representation on the company shop floor by legally mandated "works councils," as well as in the corporate board rooms where by law one-half of directors must usually come from labor, and (2) the continued presence of powerful labor unions representing workers in wider issues above the individual plant level.[411]

What was originally a conservative government idea to weaken labor unions through more isolated worker representatives in each corporation backfired when unions in fact did not decline, but learned to cooperate with works councils in each corporation for influence on two fronts. With a more liberal government in the 1970s, these labor laws, or codetermination laws, were expanded in 1972, giving workers even more rights of "codetermination" about what happens in the work place. A division of labor has developed between unions and works councils: the unions work for wage and other agreements affecting German workers generally—often through political action and threats of strike—while the works councils see that these wider agreements and already existing labor rights are upheld on each individual shop floor.[412]

None of the above should be seen as an idealized description of German labor relations: the nation is not without serious labor conflict and discontent over many issues. However, compared to most other industrial nations, the German codetermination laws and dual system of works councils and union representation present a situation which fosters worker commitment and cooperation with management. This dual system is now even supported by most managers because it promotes long term planning and the introduction of new technology for greater productivity, in large part because employees feel more secure about the future of their company and jobs when they have a say in all of this.[413] To some extent, this sounds much like outcomes of Japanese management styles: but the means of achieving these outcomes are quite different in Germany.

Labor in Post-War Japan

As in Germany, Japanese unions destroyed before and during the war made a comeback, but unlike German unions, the Japanese unions never gained as much strength (though labor is stronger in Japan than most people outside of Japan believe). The image of Japan in the West is of "company unions" with passive, controlled workers. For example, when meeting their Japanese counterparts, along with Japanese corporate executives, union leaders of the powerful IG Metall in Germany told us of their surprise over the extent to which the Japanese union leaders spoke out against and challenged their company managers.[414]

The new constitution forced upon Japan by General MacArthur and the Occupation gave unions even more freedom than found in the United States. Union activity mounted quickly, membership rose rapidly, and many strikes took place. But this all changed with the "spread of the Communist menace" in Asia.[415] Even before the Korean War there were dramatic and often bloody struggles going on over union recognition in Japanese companies. But after the Korean War and Occupation withdrawal, the tide turned in favor of corporate managers. Methods used to break unions were varied. For example, in the famous struggle of the 1950s and early 1960s over union representation in the Miike mines owned by Mitsui, right-wing assassins imprisoned during the 1930s were employed to help break the miners' union through force. Workers were then required to join a counter-company union.[416] The U.S. Central Intelligence Agency through conservative branches of the AFL-CIO, helped fund many of the counter-company unions. Rightist union leaders from the industrial Ruhr area of Germany were also financed to come to Japan and help organize company unions all over Japan, with much more success than they were eventually able to do back in Germany. Company unions, with the inherent weaknesses they tend to have for labor, became the standard for all big Japanese corporations by the 1960s. Corporations are able to require things of workers, without effective union challenge, that would not be found in most other industrial nations.

Still, it is misleading to suggest that these company unions are completely powerless and that labor has no influence in post-war Japan. What must be recognized is that political leaders and corporate managers badly needed stability and a national consensus soon after World War II if they were to rebuild Japan. Further, Japanese elites seemed to realize that the level of labor exploitation and inequality that existed before the war was detrimental to Japan's future development. And, not least in importance, there was still the matter of the Socialist Party in Japan: while often ideologically impractical, poorly organized and poorly led, they have been the second largest party throughout post-war Japanese history, and thus a party to be reckoned with for the trouble they can make in the Diet. What transpired were some key compromises along the road to rebuilding Japan, sometimes forced upon Japanese corporations by political and bureaucratic elites, and also the formation of a powerful national union confederation, today called Rengō.

One of the major compromises forced upon corporations by the government was the "densen wage system," a system of minimum wages based upon worker need and seniority, which helped reduce income inequality.[417] Then, beginning in 1955, there has been the annual *shuntō*, or "spring offensive," organized by the national labor confederation, with quiet agreement from the government. In this annual "spring offensive" the national federation of unions targets certain industries for wage increases and strikes if needed. When the wage settlement is made, the Japanese government then uses this agreement as the standard for that year, suggesting and pressuring other corporations in other industries to make similar wage settlements. Through the annual *shuntō* Japanese labor has been able to focus its resources to pressure for wage concessions, and like German labor, has been consistently successful, year after year, in keeping wages moving upward, in a big contrast to the efforts of American workers since the early 1970s.[418] As we have already seen, Japan today has one of the lowest, if not *the* lowest, income inequality of all industrial nations, certainly much lower than in the United States. Labor unions as weak as those many outsiders believe exist in Japan would not be able to maintain such low inequality.

Taming the "Salaryman"

As in all other industrial societies, the working class, which is to say the people doing manual labor, is steadily shrinking. Today this class is smaller in Japan than anywhere else in the world. Far more than 50 percent of Japanese employees are white-collar workers, now the backbone of the Japanese economy, and using a Japanese version the English word, they are referred to generally as "salarymen." These are the people glorified in the Japanese hit musical of 1993 called *The Salaryman's Gold Medal* and in television programs about such employees as the "storeman" and the "hotelman." These programs make salarymen today's heroes in Japan, praising their hard work and sacrifice, much as military heroes were praised in the past. And it is here that we find the most intense process of indoctrination and social control over individuals to assure that people turn out to be what the image suggests.

In large Japanese corporations, most new employees start all at the same time, soon after graduation from college in March, making up what can be referred to as the company "freshmen class." In the first weeks of employment this freshmen class goes through something which is more like army boot camp than job training or a company orientation found in the West. Some companies, in fact, have created for their new employees real boot camps run by former military personnel. But whether or not it is in a real boot camp, in all of these big companies the employees must learn such things as the company philosophy, the company song, how to respect those ranked above them, the proper dress, and the finer points of bowing, in between attendance at rallies to hear pep talks from executives.

It is at this point that the Japanese corporation, at least for its young employees, is a little like what sociologists call a "total institution."[419] In total institutions—such as prisons, military basic training camps, mental hospitals, and religious communities—there are controls over much of the person's life, and all the needs of the person are obtained from within the institution to prevent influence from outsiders. There are also important "degradation ceremonies"—rituals in which people are humbled and depersonalized to show the power of the organization over them, and to show they no longer can have the individual self-identity they once had.[420] This is not to say that freshman training in most Japanese corporations fits the example of total institutions perfectly. There is a close enough fit, however, to allow corporate managers to brag often about how the increasingly "independent and lazy young people" in Japan are still made into the good company men that Japan has always had since World War II.

It seems that C. Wright Mills might have been writing about the Japan of which he knew little, instead of the United States: "The white-collar man is the hero as victim, the small creature who is acted upon but who does not act, who works along unnoticed in somebody's office or store, never talking loud, never talking back, never taking a stand." For these people overall, "What must be grasped is the picture of society as a great salesroom, an enormous file, an incorporated brain, a new universe of management and manipulation." As for the effects upon the individual: "In many strata of white-collar employment, such traits as courtesy, helpfulness, and kindness, once intimate, are now part of the impersonal means of livelihood. Self-alienation is thus an accompaniment of his alienated labor."[421]

Culture, the success of the Japanese indoctrination process, and glorification of the salaryman in pop musicals such as *The Salarymlan's Gold Medal* may make many Japanese see it differently. Freedom and individuality are not missed by people who are living in a manner they have come to believe is right and proper. Trends in the Japanese "business novel," however, suggest that the feeling of alienation is often there, and perhaps growing.[422] This is also suggested by the growing discussion and anger in Japan over *karōshi*—death by overwork. In 1991 there were some 597 claims of *karōshi*, with thirty-three of these claims won in the courts—a small number, but one which is still remarkable given the bias in the court system already described. Other estimates put the real number of *karōshi* at perhaps 10,000 per year.[423]

How the Japanese feel about what they experience and how they must behave, however, is less important for the point we are making: the point is that salarymen of Japan have been comparatively more passive toward the powers that be in their everyday work world, which makes it easier for an elite to maintain order and perpetuate the status quo.

JAPAN'S MASS SOCIETY—A CONCLUSION

In one of the most famous cases of many since the end of World War II, a Japanese soldier, former Lt. Onoda Hirō, was finally enticed into surrendering in a Philippine jungle in March of 1974. Lt. Onoda had been hiding out since 1944, ready to continue the fight, because he never received word of Japan's surrender or the emperor's call to lay down arms. Although Hirō was seen a few times in the jungle, it was not until 1974 that his old commanding officer from the war was brought in with a loudspeaker to convince him that the war was indeed over and the emperor had asked that fighting stop. Onoda Hirō is something of a folk hero in Japan today. He has recently been featured in advertisements for camping gear, no doubt because of his years of experience with such matters. The obedience and loyalty of the Japanese people, of course, is seldom this extreme.

Continuing with wartime examples, there is also the case of "Japan's Schindler," Sugihara Chiune. In July of 1940, Sugihara was the Japanese government envoy in Lithuania as thousands of Jews were in that country trying to flee death in Nazi Germany. Again and again he asked permission from the Foreign Ministry in Tokyo to issue visas to these people in order to save their lives. Repeatedly told no, Sugihara told interviewers before his death in 1986, "I had to look at it from the standpoint of humanity. I could only be fired and returned to Japan. What else were they going to do?"[424] For twenty-eight days and nights, before the Japanese government forced him back to Japan, he wrote as many visas as he could. Finishing the last visa as the train was taking him from the country, Jewish survivors say, Sugihara bowed and said, "Please forgive me. I can't write any more. I will pray for your safety."

In the end Sugihara had written an estimated 1,600 visas, which the Israeli government estimates saved perhaps 8,000 Jews when counting family members included in the visas. Back in Japan, Sugihara was fired, and suffered from that degradation in Japan's status-ordered society for the rest of his life. In recent years the Sugihara family and other governments have been pressuring the Japanese government to recognize Sugihara as a hero, and admit that it was wrong to fire him. But as of the mid-1990s the Japanese government still refuses to do so: the implied reason is that Sugihara disobeyed orders and therefore showed disrespect for his superiors.

Whether or not Japan has more or fewer people than other countries who would disobey orders as did Sugihara, there is still much less obedience and conformity in Japan than the common image of the country has it. Still, the status quo is more firmly in place for two basic reasons we have touched upon in this chapter. First, when there is discontent, protest for change, or even all-out rebellion, the Japanese people have fewer means in their hands to push successfully for change, and there are many ways that change is blocked by those in authority. Second, much information about what is happening in the country, why it might be happening, and perhaps who is responsible, does not get to the public. This is one reason Japanese people often refer to politics in their country as a "black box." Or even when facts damaging to elites become known, there is always counter-information to confuse the issue, making it difficult to know what can be done to change the situation.

There are perhaps more people in Japan like Sugihara than Onada. But passive disobedience and quiet resistance is not enough to produce basic change in a society where elites have so much influence.

Elites and the Future of Japan: Some Final Thoughts

There is little disagreement that an "iron triangle" of corporate elites, bureaucratic ministry elites, and to a lesser degree, political elites, has ruled Japan since World War II. The institutional positions held by these individuals make their rule possible. The extent and degree of unity among these elites is found nowhere else in modern industrial societies, despite the fact that these elites had rather diverse backgrounds before they became elites. Japanese elites today are primarily selected through highly competitive entrance exams at major universities, primarily Tokyo University, and in some respects can be called a "meritocracy." The process of elite selection creates an old boy network of elite college graduates, further enhancing elite unity and cooperation in later life, along with *keibatsu* family ties and other means of unity and cooperation. Japan has many aspects of a mass society, with a general population often kept ignorant or confused about many important issues and otherwise prevented from effectively challenging Japanese elites.[425] Some implications of all this may now be reconsidered.

We must not forget that Japan is the first, and as yet only, advanced industrial nation in Asia. Whether or not this fact is now appreciated by the Western world, it will be. Until quite recently the world economy has been a European-centered world economy. Yes, the twentieth century has primarily been dominated by the United States, but this North American economic power is only an extension of the dominant European core that began around the 1500s as the European countries started to develop and expand around the world.[426] With the continuing economic strength of Ja pan, and the rapid economic growth of Japan's neighbors in Asia, the coming centuries could well be Asian-centered.

It is not simply the fact that Japan and other Asian countries are becoming economic powers, which is important at this point, but how they are doing it. According to much economic theory, all established in the West, Japan should not be a dominant economic power.[427] How Japan has become an economic power, and how some other Asian nations are following suit, is to a large degree related to the nature of elites and elite institutions in these countries.[428]

IMPLICATIONS OF ELITE POWER IN JAPAN

As if demonstrating the potential for elite power and who has it were not hard enough, there remains the really hard part—what does all of this mean for Japan, and the rest of the world?

Since the end of the Cold War the world appears to be much more complex. Gone are the simple answers about how societies should be organized. We in the West were told that communism is bad, and capitalism, if not perfect, is certainly better. That seemed simple enough, and, for the communist societies which existed at *the time*, certainly true.

But now that communism is basically gone, we have discovered capitalism*s*. While we in the West used to think it was "them," them being the Soviet Union and their allies, and "us," us being all of the other industrial nations, we find it is no longer so clear. The three largest industrial nations—the United States, Japan, and Germany—have very different forms of what we used to think of as democratic capitalism. Furthermore, one of these countries, Japan, has elites who are more unified and influential than anywhere else. And, according to our modern Western ideals and concepts, powerful elites are supposed to be bad for us.

In trying to consider what all of this may mean, some of these old ideas about elites may act as guides and present one conclusion for this book. Then another conclusion, if you will, follows some new ideas about the nature of the state and elites in economic development. Finally, we can consider where Japan seems to fit in all of this.

"Elites are Bad"

The old saying familiar in the West sums it up: "power corrupts, and absolute power corrupts absolutely."[429] The extensive power held by the relatively few elites in Japan may be blamed for a host of problems. Certainly among these problems is political corruption, which reached new heights in Japan during the 1980s. The image of Kanemaru's home safe with $50 million in illegal gold bars and securities is vivid. But there is much more, and it is no longer only the politicians who are corrupt.

During the stock market fall in the early 1990s many Japanese were out-raged to find that the losses of big corporate clients were reimbursed by stock brokerage firms such as Nomura, while the small investors, a big per-centage of whom were housewives, took the losses. The Ministry of Finance, it was learned, had been secretly allowing this to go on for many years.

There are also complaints about the comparatively low standard of living for the average Japanese person—as they say, "Japan is an economic super-power without a superpower standard of living." Wages are no longer so low, but costs for many consumer items, as well as food and necessities in general, are very high—often illogically high.

There are many, many examples of how ministry elites in collaboration with corporate executives have regulated an economy that favors corpora-tions, merchants, and producers over consumers, thus, among other things, keeping costs high for Japanese people. And there are also the many other examples of abuse, such as how workers must work very long hours to the detriment of their health, move to a new location when told to do so, often having to leave their families behind. In many ways, workers, students, mothers, housewives, and even the elderly in a society that seems to give much respect to the aged, all have a tough life compared to most North Americans and Europeans. As one veteran Japanologist has put it, "I have spent a third of a century studying Japanese culture. Admiration for the Japanese has not diminished, nor has fascination with their culture. . . . Yet I have spent much of my time being glad that I am not Japanese."[430]

With respect to the Japanese economy, it can be said that it is overly regulated by interlocked corporate *keiretsu* in cooperation with the ministry elite and political elite. Japan experienced rapid development and recovery after World War II because of protection and help from the United States. But with such help and protection fading, Japan is in for big economic trouble. There is less Adam Smith-style economic competition than there should be, and repressive regulation by ministry officials stifles innovation.

"Elites Made Japan's Economic Miracle"

There are many problems with the above view of elite exploitation in Japan.[431] One is quite obvious: to have exploitation there must be exploiter and exploitee. With the exception of some politicians in recent years, a clear distinction as to who is who becomes difficult to make.[432] And in most Asian societies the place of the individual is different than in the West: what West-erners might see as repression and exploitation may be seen in Japan as fulfilling group responsibilities.

Overall inequality is relatively low in Japan, and elites in general have much less wealth and income than elites in the United States. There is very little of a capitalist class that owns the major corporations and takes most of the profits for their personal gain. Workers may be experiencing *karoshi*, death by overwork, but so are their bosses. And as we have seen, much has been written about a general senseof dedication and concern for the general welfare of the nation among post-war elites.

With respect to the post-war economic "miracle" in Japan, the influence, unity, and cooperation among elites of the iron triangle has contributed to economic planning and the ability of Japan to look to the long term. Japanese corporate elites have not been looking for "a quick buck," a scam to get rich quickly and get out, nor have they been interested in the business of buying and selling corporations only to break them up for short-term profits at the expense of productivity and jobs. It is the capitalist development state, said to be at the center of this economic planning, which is also related to the elite unity and cooperation in Japan.

And it is no longer just Japan: the capitalist development state that Japan is said to have perfected is now the reality for many rapidly developing Asian nations. What has been written about Japan's capitalist development state is related to much respected writing about what developing nations must do to develop their own economies and improve standards of living.

The situation for developing countries now is much different from that experienced when the developed countries of today were first developing.[433] In essence, the industrializing countries back then did not have already developed nations to contend with. They did not have to worry about how the multinational corporations from richer nations might harm their development chances by taking profits and resources out of the country, and in other ways reducing development chances. And these industrializing nations did not have to worry that the short-term improvements in the standard of living for their middle and upper classes, due to ties to richer nations, and their ability to buy relatively cheap imported goods, would hurt long-term economic development for domestic industries. Thus, much like Japan's capitalist development state, developing countries need a "hard state" that is willing and powerful enough to make the decisions that will improve the general long-term welfare at the expense of short-term benefits for the middle and upper classes.[434]

With economic expansion all over Asia fueled by little capitalist development states, and with East and Southeast Asia soon accounting for more of the world's GNP than any other region, it may well be that this form of capitalism, far different from that of the United States, will be the wave of the future.

DANGER SIGNS FOR JAPAN

These two sides of the argument are presented here in a rather simplistic fashion, and certainly there is more to say about both. However simplified, though, the second of the two arguments above, citing the Japanese development state and post-war elites as responsible for the economic miracle and comparative lack of social problems, seems most accurate, at least for the post-war period.

To return to a basic point: Japan has many common Asian traditions, built over the centuries, wherein elites tend to have more responsibility toward the common people.⁴³⁵ This has not always been so, and all Asian countries are certainly not alike in this respect—but compared to other nations of the world, the traditions of elite responsibility in Asia are striking. Will Japan hang on to this sense of elite responsibility? Such responsibility was much less evident in Japan before World War II.

As the twenty-first century approaches, however, there are danger signs for Japan. To the extent that the nature of Japanese post-war elites has contributed to rapid economic development, rising standards of living, and a sense of fairness in the society, the Japanese people should be worried. Significant change in the nature of these elites can pose a threat to it all.

In addition to the salient characteristics of these post-war elites—their power, unity, and so forth—there are also indications of change for the worse. There is evidence, and certainly a feeling among the Japanese people, that the degree of self-sacrifice and concern for the average person once found at the top of the iron triangle is melting away. *Inequality* seems to be increasing, *corruption* is certainly increasing, and the *route* to *the top* has become *somewhat less open*. As noted in Chapter 1, there is a tendency for all revolutions to slow, to reach a point where the new elites try to hang on to too much, to grab too much power.

Is this what Japan is going through in the final years of the twentieth century? Has the image of paternalistic, responsible elites been overestimated, at least for Japan? Or, looking back from a few decades in the future, will we find that the corruption, growing inequality, and arrogance among Japanese elites was only a temporary outcome of the 1980s "bubble economy"?

If these negative characteristics are not simply a short-term problem of the Japanese bubble economy of the 1980s, then Japan is in real trouble. Powerful elites with a high sense of responsibility to the people is one thing: powerful elites without such responsibility will quickly become more corrupt and oppressive, likely putting an end to the relative social order and rapid development of the post-war period. It must be one way or the other— elites with a strict sense of responsibility, or more democracy and less power in the hands of elites in all sectors of the society.

Herein is found the dilemma for Japanese elites that is not contradictory to democracy—how is more democracy achieved when elites have so much power? Without extensive pressure from non-elites, elites with such power have seldom if ever had a change of heart, saying in effect, "we are sorry, we have become corrupt, taken too much, and will now give up our power." This dilemma is similar to one of the most striking inaccuracies in Marxian ideas. Marx believed that a dictatorship of the proletariat would be necessary as the transition from a capitalist to a communist society is made. There must be social order after the revolution, and besides, there are many messy jobs to be done. But once all of this was finished, the dictatorship and the state would wither away, leaving equality and freedom. The problem has been that these men never seem to go away once they get all that power. They start to like it, and want to keep it. And they do keep it, at least until the society deteriorates to the point of dysfunction as did the Roman Empire in the end, or there is bloody revolution, as in France.

What will it be for Japan? Elites who remain responsible? Or more democracy, with a reduction of elite power? If it is neither, Japan will likely return to the levels of inequality, exploitation, and hardship experienced before World War II, and that economic miracle will not last.

Notes

1. We must comment on our use of "elites," ruling class, "upper class," "power elites," and related terms. Technically there are differences between all of these terms, with elites being the most general concept. For example, a ruling class implies, rule over people, either politically or economically, and often both. Upper class usually refers to people and families in a dominant economic position, usually because of wealth. And since the work of C. Wright Mills (1956), the term power elite generally refers to a combination of all the above, in industrial societies. This book favors the more generic term elites.

The term elite in Japan does not have the negative connotations it does in Western countries such as the United States. Elites are not necessarily considered exploitive, selfish, and undeserving of admiration in Japan. In fact, the term *eriito* often has a very positive connotation, and readers should be aware of alternative views on the subject of elites in Asian nations more generally.

2. See Kerbo and Nakao (1991).

3. We follow the Japanese custom of listing the family name first. Thus, Hirose is the family name, and Gen is the given name. Most of this biographical information about Hirose Gen comes from Hayakawa (1983) and Jin (1989).

4. Information such as this is easily found in the useful *Japan Company Handbook* published every year by Tōyō Keizai Shinpōsha.

5. See the *Japan Times Weekly*, July 6–12, 1992, p. 18.

6. See Rohlen (1983, p. 91).

7. See Usui and Colignon (1994).

8. See Burstein (1988, p. 197).

9. Another member of the bureaucratic elite, Mieno Yasushi, who heads the Bank of Japan, created the problem when he changed interest rates specifically to burst the "bubble economy" that worked in favor of land developers and financial

firms, but hurt the average person in Japan. The bubble, however, deflated considerably more than expected.

10. For a summary of some of these activities by the Ministry of Finance in English, see the *Los Angeles Times*, February 1, 1993, p. D-3.

11. See the *Los Angeles Times*, February 1, 1993, p. D-3. This statement was most likely made by one of the three ministry officials we have discussed here, but they seldom go on record officially. Throughout American and Japanese newspapers one is likely to read something like, "the Ministry of Finance says. . . ." This is consistent, of course, with the Japanese way of presenting a group rather than an individual as in charge or standing out. Politicians are the exception, as they must be everywhere to get votes.

12. See *The New York Times* (March 10, 1993, p. A-1), and the *Los Angeles Times* (March 10, 1993, p. A-1).

13. The existence and nature of these *keibatsu* family groups is just now being examined by Japanese social scientists. Among the most recent books by Japanese on this subject, we will be citing most often the books by Jin (1989), Sato (1987), and Hayakawa (1983).

14. See, for example, Pfeiffer (1977), Lenski (1966).

15. For more details on these kinds of questions in the study of elites and why they are important, see Domhoff (1970, 1979, 1983) and the classic work on the American power elite by C. Wright Mills (1956).

16. For example, studies have shown that corporate personnel ties bring more unity and cooperation for political action than do simple common economic interests among corporations without such ties. See Mizruchi (1992).

17. See the World Bank (1986) and Kerbo (1991, p. 39). For an interesting analysis of Japan's low inequality since World War II as unique in that it is not due to a welfare state or state redistributive policies, see Verba et. al. (1987).

18. See, for example, Kerbo and Inoue (1990).

19. These and similar data will be discussed more fully in coming chapters. But for estimates noted here, see *Time*, January 20, 1992, and the *Los Angeles Times*, February 7, 1992.

20. There have been numerous studies of income inequality between workers and corporate executives in Japan, the United States, and other leading industrial nations such as Germany. While the figures differ somewhat due to the number of industries included and time periods, all of the studies agree that the pay gap is much lower in Japan than in the United States, with Germany quite close to Japan in the worker to chief executive pay gap. See, for example, Abegglen and Stalk (1985, p. 192), the *Wall Street Journal* (April 18, 1984), the *Wall Street Journal Europe* (October 9–10, 1992), and the *Los Angeles Times* (March 2, 1993).

21. See Verba et al. (1987, pp. 76–85).

22. Of the top 113 bureaucratic elite in 1984, 70 percent earned incomes between $48,000 and $79,000. In fact, about nine percent of these 113 individuals made incomes below $48,000 a year. These figures are taken from Miyake et al. (1985), and will be discussed more fully in Chapter 5.

23. See Kerbo and Nakao (1991), Dore (1987, p. 112).

24. Increasingly, parents with money can help give their sons and daughters additional education so they can pass the college entrance exam. But the cost of going to a university in Japan is not great (except for some of the private universities

that are not well rated), nor can you buy your way in through contributing money to the university.

25. There has been a recent case study of one of these *keibatsu* recently published by an American sociologist in English (Hamabata, 1990). However, the author seems to be unaware of how widespread and important these *keibatsu* are in Japan today, in contrast to several recently published studies by Japanese social scientists. See especially Jin (1989) and Hayakawa (1983).

26. See Lenski (1966), pp. 2–10).

27. See Antonio (1979); Wells (1971, pp. 415–433); MacMullen (1974).

28. For example, see Kennedy (1987), Skocpol (1979), Wallerstein (1989), and Soboul (1974).

29. Solzhenitsyn (1973, p. 272).

30. See especially Reischauer (1987), and Halliday (1975).

31. Figures such as these can be found in Johnson (1982), Dore (1987), and Lincoln (1988).

32. It should be noted that everything in the Peace Park implies that Japan was only the victim in the bombing and the war more generally. Until 1994, efforts by Japanese peace activists to include information about and memorials to the many thousands of Chinese killed by the Japanese, and even to the hundreds of Korean forced laborers killed in Hiroshima, have failed.

33. The information in this paragraph is based upon personal interviews conducted in 1993.

34. Based upon personal interviews conducted in 1989.

35. See especially Skocpol (1979).

36. See Alletzhauser (p. 108), Halliday (p. 180).

37. See Abegglen and Stalk (1985, p. 191).

38. See Hane (1982).

39. See Hane (1982, 1988); Bowen (1980); Gluck (1985).

40. Dore (1987), for example, describes this sense of fairness as a key ingredient in the cooperation and economic success of the post-war years.

41. See Koh (1989, pp. 227–229), and Johnson (1983).

42. See Keisai Kikaku Cho Hen (1988).

43. It is interesting to note that in 1990 Japanese businessmen spent more money from their expense accounts on "wine, women, and song," about $38.3 billion, than the government spent for the military, about $32 billion. See the *Los Angeles Times*, Dec. 3, 1991, p. H-12.

44. See for example the classic work of de Tocqueville (1955) on the French Revolution, written about 150 years ago, and the more recent works by such people as Brinton (1965) and Skocpol (1979).

45. Currently there are some conflicts of interest between the heads of many big corporations in Japan and bureaucratic elites over the issue of government regulation of the economy. Upon assuming the chairmanship of the big business organization, Keidanren, in 1994, for example, Toyoda Shōichirō has said that one of his chief goals will be "drastic deregulation" of the economy. (See *The Japan Times*, June 6, 1994.) To the extent that Keidanren is serious about this issue, therefore, the others in Japan pushing for such deregulation may be able to achieve some reform. But given the extensive power of the government ministry, as we will show in Chapter

5, it is very likely that any deregulation will be limited, brought about very slowly, and not exactly the kind of "deregulation" many other groups have in mind.

46. A Dutch journalist, Karl van Wolferen, has recently written a book devoted in part to the subject of power in Japan. Van Wolferen published *The Enigma of Japanese Power* in 1989, after several years of living in Japan and covering the subject of Japanese politics for Western news media. A central thesis from van Wolferen's book is basically, that "no one rules."

The Enigma of Japanese Power is a book rich in detailed examples of the workings of the Japanese society. With respect to the main thesis of the book, however, our view is that van Wolferen is not only wrong, but very wrong. In addition to the inaccurate perspective of the van Wolferen book, there are three general problems related to the main thesis of van Wolferen's book.

First, even though van Wolferen mentions the fact that it is sometimes difficult to apply Western concepts in understanding Japan, he has not paid close attention to his own advice. While it can be overstated, it is true that Japan has a more collectively, or group oriented society. Decisions must be made in groups, and often without an outside audience. True, it is hard to find a Henry Ford character in Japan, a powerful person who makes quick independent decisions, though "Papa" Honda does come to mind. But this is a far cry from saying that "no one rules." It reflects rather a different leadership style, and more of leadership by groups.

Second, it seems to us that van Wolferen has an inaccurate view of the West as well. There are, in fact, few Henry Fords in the real world today, even in the contemporary West. An American president may say "the buck stops here," but more often than not, he never even sees the buck. American presidents, German chancellors, British prime ministers, for example, have many powerful forces shaping what they can and cannot do behind the scenes they construct for public consumption. It is true that American presidents can act more quickly, appear more decisive, and create the illusion that they individually are in charge in a way that would be considered dictatorial and arrogant for a Japanese leader. But again, quickness of decisions, or the appearance of quickness, must not be equated with power, or the lack thereof. Many presidents have told the American people and/or foreign leaders what will be done, only to have Congress tell them otherwise when the president's policies are not supported by Congress. And in the corporate world of the West, again there are very few, if any, Rockefellers, Morgans, Carnegies, or Vanderbilts, anymore: corporations also are run by committee, with few particular individuals or families having enough stock votes to control corporations on their own. As for chief executives of corporations, the economist John Kenneth Galbraith is fond of pointing out there are very few times when the value of a corporation's stock has dropped due to the death of its CEO.

Third, van Wolferen's examples and focus are most often on Japanese politics. We will see that compared to Western governments, and particularly the United States, Japanese politicians do seem powerless. They have less control over even what legislation is written, they have very few resources for staff or aides, and they spend most of their time trying to get reelected.

47. See Massarella (1990, pp. 13 and 65).

48. See Kapitza (1990, vols. 1, 2, and 3).

49. Popular writings in Japan today of the genre called *Nihojinron* ("the study of the Japanese"), often make wild claims about how and why Japan is so "unique."

It is interesting to note that even many of the ideas found in these contemporary writings were first suggested by Europeans. For example, these eighteenth-century European scholars were interested in the question of whether or not nations had what in German is called *ingenium* or *iudicium*. The first word means something like creative intuition, the second something like the ability for critical, sound judgement. These early European scholars concluded that Japan certainly didn't have the first, and one French scholar wrote that this was due to Japan's climate. See Kapitza (1990, vol. 3, p. 9).

50. It is also from this time that among intellectuals in Europe, Japan was becoming a curiosity, as suggested by Puccini's opera and the *Madame Butterfly* "Japonisme" fad among leading artists such as Monet, Girard, Manet, Degas, and Whistler.

51. See, for example, the biography by Rosenstone (1988). It is worth noting that for the most part the Japanese greatly admire Lafcadio Hearn and what he had to say. Today his old home in the city of Mitsue, on the Japan Sea, has been turned into a museum that honors his life and works.

52. For example, see Hearn (1956, 1962, 1976).

53. See Golzio (1985), Minear (1980), Mouer and Sugimoto (1986).

54. We can clarify the point using one example: explanations of high birth rates in some countries most often refer to culture or traditions leading women to aspire to give birth to several children. Put in other words, what this type of explanation for higher birth rates says is, "women in some societies have more children *because they want to have more children*." But we are left with more questions: most simply, why? Why do some women want more children? The explanation is circular unless we ask, "So why do cultures differ in that respect?" What has caused some countries to develop and maintain cultural beliefs leading them to have more children, and what has led other countries to reject these beliefs? It is precisely this type of simple cultural explanation most often found in Japanese studies.

55. For an account of all this, see Mouer and Sugimoto (1986, pp. 28, 47).

56. See especially Bellah et al. (1985), Vogel (1979), and Dore (1987). For an excellent discussion of the Western individualistic bias in these theories, see Pye (1985) and Hwang (1987).

57. See Morgan and Hiroshima (1983) for this analysis of the Japanese family.

58. Quite often values follow necessity or what would be rational behavior to promote survival or prosperity. To return to an earlier example, studies show that women in countries with high birth rates have had more children, at least in the past, because it made economic sense to do so, not simply or only because culture told them they should. At least in the long run, economic change usually brings change in the birth rate.

59. See, for example, Hane (1988).

60. It is this value orientation of "radical individualism" that is increasingly cited as partially responsible for many of our social problems— from the highest divorce rate and ra⁺˒ of single parent families among industrial nations, to high crime rates and low edu ˙ional success compared to other nations. See especially Bellah et al. (1985) and Etzioni (1984).

61. For more detailed explanation of this type of historical and comparative research and the effects of the material environment, see Gouldner and Peterson

(1962); Heise et al. (1976); Lenski (1978); Lenski and Nolan (1986); and Lenski (1966).

62. See Reischauer (1987, p. 17).

63. See Bendix (1978), Reischauer (1987, p. 52), and Reischauer and Craig (1978).

64. See Lincoln and Kalleberg (1990, pp. 92, 109–110, 144, 235).

65. For example, see results from national polls conducted by the Japanese government and published in *The Japan Times*, Dec. 23, 1991; and Aug. 27, 1992. Also see Lincoln and Kalleberg (1990, pp. 63, 152).

66. Nakane (1970). For a critique, see, for example, Mouer and Sugimoto (1986).

67. See, for example, Lincoln and Kalleberg (1990, pp. 91, 98, 108–111, 142).

68. See *The European*, June 7–9, 1991, May 17–19, 1991, and *The International Herald Tribune*, June 17, 1991.

69. Quoted in Smith (1983, p. 69).

70. See Smith (1983, p. 102).

71. For examples of this from Japanese history, see Pharr (1990), Bowen (1980), Hane (1982, 1988), Apter and Sawa (1984), Mouer and Sugimoto (1986).

72. See for example the classic works of Simmel (1955), and the more recent works of Coser (1956, 1967), Collins (1975), Kanter (1972), and Sherif (1966).

73. See especially the work of Pye (1985).

74. See Pye (1985, pp. 34–38, 65, 80, 170).

75. See especially Pye (1985, pp. vii–xi).

76. And, we can add, to some degree the same can be said for European nations that had old traditions of feudal rule, with rights and obligations between peasant and lord, in contrast to the countries lacking a feudal past. It is this line of reasoning followed by those who see a greater sense of "moral economy" in Europe, with state and corporate elites feeling more responsibility toward the welfare of the general population compared to elites in the United States (see Piven and Cloward 1982). Also, it is argued, this Asian concept of power and responsibility is in part behind the greater success with economic development in Asian nations as opposed to Latin American and African nations (see Vogel 1991, Pye 1985, and Myrdal 1970, and 1968, vols. 1, 2, and 3).

77. Pye (1985, pp. ix, 37–38, 52–69).

78. See van Wolferen (1989, p. 202).

79. Pye (1985, p. xii).

80. See Pye (1985), Hendry (1987), Smith (1983).

81. Baltzell (1958, p. 26).

82. The private detective agencies for this purpose are quite numerous and profitable in Japan. Their main job is to check the family background of potential marriage partners for any scandals, mental illness, birth irregularities, or the existence of *burakumin* (the old outcastes), Korean, or other blood lines in the family. If any of the above are found, the marriage is likely out of the question, whether or not it was a romantic love match or *omiai*. There are many tragic novels and movies in Japan today about love destroyed by such family background information. For more information see McKinstry and McKinstry (1991).

83. We do not have any survey research telling us exactly how common these arranged marriages are among Japanese elites today, but several indicators, such as

how often elite families are in fact merged through marriage, and qualitative studies of Japanese elite families suggest they are rather common. For example, see Hamabata (1990).

84. See Kerbo, Wittenhagen, and Nakao (1994 a, b).

85. For descriptions of the problems in the United States and England from books we feel are overstated, but useful, see, Milkman (1991), and Garrahan and Stewart (1992).

86. See especially Doi (1986) and Hendry (1987), also Smith (1983) and Christopher (1983).

87. See Mouer and Sugimoto (1986) for a discussion of much of this, clearly for the side that Japan is not different or unique.

88. For example, van Wolferen (1989), Prestowitz (1989), Fallows (1989), and Choate (1990) are in this group of revisionists, who also claim Chalmers Johnson (1982), though his main works are more scholarly and less politically charged. It is interesting to note that the best-selling novel and movie, *Rising Sun*, by Michael Crichton, is clearly in this group. In contrast to normal procedure for a novel, Crichton has taken effort to make a political point by also using a reference list and a discussion of these revisionist works in an appendix to his book.

89. It is said by revisionists that this group includes older, highly respected Japan scholars such as Reischauer (1987), Dore (1987), and Vogel (1971, 1979, 1985).

90. Most of this information can be found in Roberts (1976, especially pp. 5, 245–246), Hayakawa (1983), and Morikawa (1992).

91. See Roberts (1976, p. 410, with earlier figures on pp. 382–384).

92. Bowen (1980); Halliday (1975, p. 12); Gibney (1953).

93. See Gluck (1985).

94. See, for example, Weber (1947).

95. Roberts (1973, p. 12).

96. Roberts (1973, p. 13).

97. See Johnson (1982).

98. See Morikawa (1992).

99. These short biographical descriptions of the largest *zaibatsu* founders are summarized from Morikawa (1992, pp. 10–24).

100. Morikawa (1992, p. 20).

101. See Morikawa (1992, pp. 51–52).

102. Roberts (1973, p. 331).

103. Roberts (1973, p. 100).

104. See Morikawa (1992).

105. Morikawa (1992, p. 105).

106. Kerbo (1991, pp. 195–196).

107. See de Tocqueville (1969).

108. See Domhoff (1970, 1979, 1983); C. Wright Mills (1956).

109. Reischauer and Craig (1978, p. 141).

110. See Satō (1990, pp. 12–14).

111. See for example, Roberts (1976, pp. 144, 224; Halliday (1975, pp. 36–37); Fairbank, Reischauer, and Craig (1965, pp. 292–296).

112. Hayakawa (1983); Jin (1981, 1989); Satō (1987, 1990); Haru Reischauer (1986); Roberts (1976).

113. For the American side, see Amory (1960), Baltzell (1958, 1964), Domhoff (1970, 1983). For the Japanese side, see Alletzhauser (1990), Roberts (1976, pp. 203, 245), Morikawa (1992, pp. 125, 226), Halliday (1975, p. 127).

114. For the following biography, and especially these figures, see Alletzhauser (1990, pp. 3–14). Also see Morikawa (1992).

115. Alletzhauser (1990, p. 65).

116. See Roberts (1973, pp. 304–305); Hane (1982, pp. 11, 46); Abegglen and Stalk (1985, pp. 191–192).

117. See especially Hane (1982) for much of what follows about peasant conditions.

118. Gluck (1985, p. 175); Hane (1982, pp. 182-184). Some of the best descriptions of terrible working conditions can be found in Roberts (1973, pp. 204–207).

119. See Hane (1982, pp. 210–211; 1988, p. 10).

120. Hane (1982, pp. 22–23, 104).

121. Hane (1982, p. 21; also see pp. 108–113); Bowen (1980).

122. Hane (1982, 1988).

123. Halliday (1975, p. 80); Bowen (1980); Hane (1982, 1988); Roberts (1973, pp. 204–208).

124. Roberts (1973, p. 373).

125. Morikawa (1992, pp. 237–240); Roberts (1976, pp. 373–379, 390).

126. See Halliday (1975, p. 192).

127. Johnson (1983).

128. See Okumura (1983, pp. 86–87).

129. Roberts (1973, pp. 396–399).

130. See Roberts (1976, pp. 392–393), Halliday (1975, p. 182), and Alletzhauser (1990) for accounts of how and why American corporate elites were against many of the planned changes in Japan.

131. Hayakawa (1983); Jin (1981, 1989); Satō (1987, 1990).

132. See Roberts (1976, p. 410).

133. Hayakawa (1983); Jin (1981, 1989); Satō (1987).

134. Solzhenitsyn (1973, p. 272).

135. Morikawa (1992, p. 39).

136. C. Wright Mills, *The Power Elite*, published in 1956.

137. Dore (1987, p. 116).

138. See, for example, Halliday (1975, p. 110), Dore (1987, p. 110).

139. See, for example, the essay by Chieko Mulhern (1991) introducing one of the popular novels written by a Sumitomo executive, Shinya Arai, *Shoshaman: A Tale of Corporate Japan.*

140. A late-night walk through popular weekend night spots around Tokyo, such as Shibuya or Shinjuku, may likewise reveal the status of the new corporate elite. Such a walk will likely bring you upon inebriated college students waving the Japanese flag and chanting "Japan is number one!" Drunk college students, and especially the flag-waving, can be found in the United States. These college students in Tokyo, however, are referring not to military power or Olympic medals, but to economic might, which by implication includes their business heroes.

141. The family name is still Toyoda, but they thought Toyota sounded better for their cars, and many of us thus drive Toyotas instead of Toyodas today.

142. Most of this information about the Toyoda family is taken from Satō (1987), Hayakawa (1983).

143. See, for example, the discussion of this by Hamabata (1990, p. 5).

144. See *The Japan Times*, 1992, May 18–24, p. 16.

145. There are, however, a few corporate elites and their families among the *Forbes* list of the most wealthy fifty people in Japan in 1991. Among the best known are the Morita family of Sony with $1 billion, the Matsushita family with $1 billion, the Otani family of the hotel chain with $5 billion, and most notorious, Mr. Kyoshi Sagawa, of the Sagawa Express Company involved in the 1992 bribery scandal, with $2.7 billion.

146. For information of the family background of the Tsutsumi family see, for example, Hayakawa (1983).

147. See, for example, *The Economist* (December 30, 1978), and Kerbo (1991, pp. 173–176).

148. See Berle and Means (1932), *The Modern Corporation and Private Property.*

149. We should note here that the rule of thumb is that if a family or individual owns as little as 10 percent of a corporation's stock this family or individual in most cases can be said to control the corporation. However, each situation must be studied because it may take only 5 percent of the stock, or much more than 10 percent, especially if someone else owns more than 10 percent. All of this is of little importance for most corporations, as we will see, because it is seldom that any individual or family even owns as much as 1 percent, especially in Japan today.

150. See, for example, Kerbo and Della Fave (1983); U.S. Senate (1978).

151. Among these 21 institutional investors in the United States, only one can be listed as family-controlled, the Allegheny Corporation, controlled by the Kirby family (U.S. Senate 1978; Kerbo and Della Fave 1983).

152. See Alletzhauser (1990, p. 108); Halliday (1975, p. 180).

153. See, for example, Kitahara (1980, 1985); Miyazaki (1982, 1985).

154. See, for example, Dore (1987, p. 113), Morioka (1991, p. 155).

155. Or, rather, these Japanese stockholder meetings have been quite boring at least since the late 1980s, when laws were passed to prevent *sokaiya* sponsored by *yakuza* (organized crime) from disrupting the proceedings to demand "protection money." The *sokaiya* acquired millions of dollars in protection money from major corporations to "insure" that stockholder meetings were not disrupted, usually by themselves, after they bought just a few shares of a company's stock, which allowed them to attend the annual meeting. See van Wolferen (1989, p. 105), and Alletzhauser (1990, p. 284).

156. See the *Los Angeles Times*, June 29, 1992, p. D-3, and Clark (1979, p. 103).

157. There are, of course, pension funds and trust funds in Japan. But unlike the figure for the United States (where the trust funds put 90 percent of their investments in corporate stock), the figure for Japan is only 35 percent. And because of the underdevelopment of pension programs in Japan (both public and private programs) the Japanese have traditionally been forced to do their own saving for retirement, which in part helps explain the Japanese household savings rate of about 20 percent, compared to less than 5 percent for the United States. (See, for example, Alletzhauser 1990, p. 17.)

158. See Kerbo and Nakao (1991).

159. To make these data comparable to the data on stockholding among the 122

largest corporations in the United States described earlier, we also looked at the
pattern of the top five stock voters in the largest 100 industries and the largest
twenty-five banks in Japan. The findings were similar to those reported in Table 4.1:
For the 100 industrial corporations, 44 percent of the top five stock voting positions
were held by insurance companies and other financial firms, 34 percent held by banks,
9 percent by other industrial corporations, and only 8 percent by individuals or families. For the twenty-five largest banks, 66 percent of the top five positions were held
by an insurance company or other financial company, 13 percent by other banks, 20
percent by industrial corporations, and zero percent by individuals or families.

160. See Gerlach (1992).

161. One important effect of the long-term holding of stock by the big investors
in Japan (usually other companies) is long-term planning for growth and productivity, rather than a focus on year-to-year profitability and stock dividends. Japanese
companies do not pay dividends based upon yearly profitability, but rather on a set
percentage of the value of the stock held, which is usually a very low 1 percent (Dore
1987, p. 115; Abegglen and Stalk 1985, p. 168). The big institutional investors in
the United States are motivated by yearly appreciation of stock and dividends paid
yearly. Thus, an American company has less freedom to defer profits for long-term
growth and development because their stock will be sold, reducing its value and the
company's ability to finance expansion. There is certainly buying and selling of stock
in this manner in Japan as well, but there are big blocks of secure stock held by other
companies who are more interested in the long-term growth and development for
their investment. For example, we have seen the top stockholders in Japanese companies in Table 4.1: we can compare this to an American company in some trouble
in 1992. In 1991 and 1992 IBM had to make cuts in staff and investments and
sacrifice some profits to pay dividends to keep stockholders from selling. In 1992
IBM's biggest stockholders were institutional investors, thinking of selling off IBM
stock if dividends and profits in IBM declined further (see the *Los Angeles Times*,
Dec. 16, 1992, p. D-1).

162. See Lincoln (1992).

163. Some have suggested that what we find in Japan can no longer be called free
enterprise capitalism in the old sense. One Japanese social scientist suggests the term
"corporate capitalism" to indicate that the corporations mainly own each other
(Okumura 1984), while another calls it a "corporation-centered system" (Morioka
1991, p. 155). The respected scholar of Japanese corporations, Ronald Dore (1987,
p. 12), suggests the terms "managerial production-oriented capitalism" for Japan
and "shareholder-dominated capitalism" for England and the United States. But
whatever we choose to call it, there are major differences between the Japanese corporate structure and those of the Western capitalist nations. These differences have
important implications for Japan's economic performance *and* who is located among
the corporate elite.

164. The term *keiretsu*, however, is rather imprecise, and interestingly is a term
projected upon Japan by Americans. Before U.S. trade negotiators started popular-
izing it to describe groups of Japanese companies charged with keeping out foreign
competition, the term *keiretsu* was used less often, and only for one type of corporate
grouping.

165. Since World War II, the Japanese have typically referred to the big six *keiretsu*
as *gurūpu*, which comes from the Japanese spelling of the English word "group" in

the phonetic syllabary *katakana*. (See especially van Wolferen, 1989, p. 46.) Earlier, some people continued to refer to these big groupings as *zaibatsu*, in reference to the pre-war family groupings of corporations. And still other Japanese have referred to these big groupings as *kigyō shūdan*. But it has become more common in recent years (especially by non-Japanese) to call these big groupings *keiretsu*, often further specified as horizontal *keiretsu* (Gerlach 1992a, 1992b; Lincoln, Gerlach, and Takahashi 1992).

166. But even here there is a vagueness in the definition of *keiretsu*. For example, who is to be included? How strong do the ties need to be to say the company is included with others in a vertical or horizontal *keiretsu*? Thus, by one definition there are 187 companies within the big six horizontal *keiretsu*, while the most broad definition leads to including 577 companies (Geriach 1992b, pp. 88–87). And the vagueness of the definition is in part behind the dispute over whether or not the *keiretsu* are breaking down, thus doing more business with outside companies (especially foreign companies, as the American trade negotiators are pushing for). The Japanese government has produced data for 1991 suggesting the *keiretsu* are breaking down and becoming less exclusive. The American government and most researchers are not convinced, and produce counter-evidence (see *The Japan Times*, March 9–15, 1992, p. 19; Gerlach 1992a,b; Lincoln, Gerlach, and Takahashi 1992).

167. There is a huge literature on how all of this transpired. For descriptions in English, see for example, Johnson (1982, pp. 160, 206, 251), Dore (1987, p. 113), Halliday (1975, pp. 182–183), Alletzhauser (1990, p. 122), and van Wolferen (1989, p. 389).

168. Most of this biographical information comes from Hayakawa (1983) and Jin (1989).

169. See Gerlach (1992, p. 88).

170. Translated from Ōsono (1991).

171. Most importantly, see Ōsono (1991); Gerlach (1992, p. 87); Morioka (1989, p. 49); and *The Japan Times*, March 9–15, 1992, p. 19.

172. From Clark (1979, p. 75).

173. From Ōsono (1991).

174. See Okumura (1978, p. 112).

175. Okumura (1978, p. 121).

176. See Jin (1981, 1989), Roberts (1973).

177. See Lincoln, Gerlach, and Takahashi (1992).

178. See Okumura (1983, p. 90).

179. See Okumura (1983, p. 86).

180. See Okumura (1978, 1983).

181. For example, the top 250 corporations have been shown to have an average of ten interlocks with other top corporations, while big banks have an average of almost seventeen interlocks. In another part of the Senate study of corporate ownership and institutional investors mentioned earlier, the largest thirteen corporations were found to have 240 direct interlocks with the other 117 largest corporations in the study. (See Allen, 1974; U.S. Senate, 1978.)

182. See especially, Useem (1984); Mintz and Schwartz (1985).

183. See, Ueda (1989, 1990), Abegglen and Stalk (1985, p. 185), Clark (1979 p. 100).

184. See Gerlach (1992a,b); Gerlach and Lincoln (1992); Abegglen and Stalk (1985).

185. See Abegglen and Stalk (1985 p. 92), Lincoln and Kalleberg (1990).

186. See Florida and Kenney (1991).

187. Research in the United States has located what is called the "inner group" of the corporate elite. This inner group consists of top executives and board members with multiple positions (interlocks) among the largest American corporations. It is this inner group which is in a position to help organize and unify the corporate elite to protect its common interests. Members of this inner group are likely to be board members of the largest corporations, most often major banks, and belong to elite social clubs where the corporate elite gather. Members of this inner group have also been found to represent general corporate interests as board members in other institutions such as research foundations, social and cultural organizations, universities (as trustees), and in non-elected government positions (such as the president's cabinet, special commissions, and as other advisors). For example, between 1897 and 1973, over 75 percent of all presidential cabinet members have been associated in some way with large corporations (most often coming from top executive positions or corporate boards to serve on the president's cabinet). And in one of the most useful writings on this subject, Useem was able to show that in response to declining profits and other corporate problems in the 1970s, the inner group organized corporate resources and personnel to help elect Ronald Reagan as President of the United States. There is a long tradition of this type of research on the corporate elite and the inner group of this elite. The information discussed in this paragraph can be found in the following studies: Useem 1984; Akard 1992; Domhoff 1970, 1979, 1983; Soref 1976; Mariolis 1975; Freitag 1975; Mintz 1975; Mintz and Schwartz 1985.

188. Johnson (1982, p. 68).

189. See Koh (1989, pp. 227–229).

190. Most of the biographical information on Mieno is from Atsuta (1992).

191. Atsuta (1992, p. 229).

192. See Mulhern (1991, p. xii); much of this information about Sahashi Shigeru can be found in Johnson (1982, pp. 242–245).

193. As an authority on the Japanese bureaucracy, Chalmers Johnson points out that "English novelists sometimes choose bureaucrats as subjects . . . but economic bureaucrats in America or Britain are rarely as interesting as spies or politicians. The opposite is true in Japan, where the power and influence of economic bureaucrats make fictional portrayals of their lives and struggles intriguing" (Johnson 1982, pp. 81–82).

194. See Putnam (1976, p. 50), and Dietrich (1991, p. 277).

195. See Vogel (1979, pp. 58–59).

196. Whether one sees this inexperience as good or bad is another question. Given the need for talented government officials and some state autonomy from outside special interest groups in the more competitive world economy, however, we would argue that the Japanese system gives Japan many advantages over the United States. These points will be considered in more detail later.

197. See Freitag (1975).

198. See the *Los Angeles Times*, June 22, 1992, p. D-1.

199. See van Wolferen (1989, p. 146), and Johnson (1982, p. 52).

200. Pye (1985, p. 171).

201. See Kitagawa and Kainuma (1985, p. 96).

202. See Miyake et al. (1985, p. 43). This survey was based upon "tax-reported income," and, Japan being similar to other capitalist nations where the rich are able to avoid paying income taxes in various ways, the income of the corporate elite is no doubt deflated. But this is not the case with the bureaucratic elite, who receive a straight salary without perks and rewards that can be hidden from the tax auditor. The actual income gap between these two most powerful elite groups in Japan is, therefore, even larger.

203. See Vogel (1991), and Johnson (1982, p. 19).

204. See Johnson (1982, p. 36); Koh (1989, pp. 12–13); and Gluck (1985, p. 44).

205. Quoted in Halliday (1975, p. 37).

206. See Halliday (1975, pp. 38–39).

207. See Halliday (1975, pp. 173–174).

208. See Johnson (1982, pp. 44–45).

209. Koh (1989, p. 19).

210. See Halliday (1975, p. 39); Koh (1989, p. 86).

211. Most of the information about the selection and promotion of the ministry elite comes from the excellent book by Koh (1989) on this subject.

212. See *Japan Times Weekly International*, January 18–24, 1993.

213. See especially Koh (1989, pp. 132, 174).

214. We have specified "these men" with reason. The top corporate world as well as the top bureaucratic world in Japan belong almost exclusively to men, though this is changing slowly, very slowly. In 1986, for example, of individuals in the highest elite tracks in all the government ministries in Japan, 2.5 percent were women (Koh 1989, p. 105).

215. See Schoppa (1991, p. 79), and especially Johnson (1975) for a basic summary of bureaucratic power.

216. Major proponents of the *zoku* power arguments include Park (1986), and to some extent van Wolferen (1989). For a review of these arguments see Allinson (1989) and Schoppa (1991).

217. A number of issues can be discussed concerning this question of who has most power. For example, much depends upon the policy area, for in some cases, such as education and agriculture, it can be said that the LDP is more in control (see Koh 1989, pp. 204–218; Schoppa 1991).

218. One of the best sources for information on this subject of the Japanese government, the Constitution, the ministries, and other government functions is by Kishimoto Kōichi (1988), a longtime Japanese journalist and writer on governmental affairs. This book is used as a teaching tool in many Japanese universities, and the third edition has recently been translated into English.

219. The other ministries include Education; Health and Welfare; Agriculture, Forestry, and Fisheries; Transport; Posts and Telecommunications; Labor; Construction; and Home Affairs. Not among the main twelve it is interesting to note, and considered only as agencies, are Defense, the National Public Safety Commission, and the Economic Planning Agency (Kishimoto 1988, p. 82).

220. See Kishimoto (1988, p. 66); Koh (1989, p. 206).

221. Johnson (1982, p. 267).

222. Abegglen and Stalk (1985).

223. See Johnson (1982, pp. 205–217), Vogel (1979, pp. 73–75).

224. See the *Los Angeles Times*, February 1, 1993; *The New York Times*, February 1, 1993.

225. For discussion of the lack of U.S. competitiveness in the areas see Thurow (1992), and Dietrich (1991).

226. See Okumura (1978, pp. 136–141).

227. Most of the information about Gōtō Keitarō can be found in Jin (1989).

228. See Usui and Colignon (1994).

229. *Japan Quarterly*, July-September, 1992, p. 414.

230. Most of this discussion is based upon the work of Okumura (1978, 1983). But also see Johnson (1982) and Koh (1989, pp. 235–251).

231. See Okumura (1978, p. 150).

232. From Okumura (1978).

233. From Johnson (1982, p. 72).

234. See *The Japan Times*, April 19–25, 1993.

235. See *The Japan Times*, June 28–July 4, 1993.

236. See *The Japan Times*, July 26–August 1, 1993.

237. Benedict (1946, p. 81).

238. Gluck (1985, pp. 42–70).

239. Gibney (1992).

240. Pempel (1989).

241. See *The Japan Times*, July 26, 1993, for election results and party strengths.

242. Some of the best work on this subject can be found in Curtis (1988).

243. Nakane (1970, pp. 26–84).

244. Okimoto (1988).

245. Kitagawa and Kainuma (1985).

246. Johnson (1986).

247. Japanese politicians seem to spend most of their time running for reelection. The legal time allotted to actual campaigning in Japan has been only a few weeks for many years, and there are more restrictions on campaign activities in Japan than almost any other nation—a large percentage of which are ignored. Most of this information can be found in the classic study by Curtis (1971) and his new work on the subject (1988). Also see Kishimoto (1988), and Woronoff (1986).

248. *The Japan Times*, Sept. 13, 1993.

249. Mori (1992); Kerbo and Inoue (1990).

250. *The New York Times*, March 28, 1993.

251. Koh (1989, pp. 206–207).

252. See especially Kitagawa and Kainuma (1985, p. 212).

253. Jin (1989); *The New York Times*, April 23, 1994.

254. See Maki (1987, p. 60).

255. Kitagawa and Kainuma (1985); Jin (1989).

256. See Woronoff (1986, p. 84).

257. For the most recent survey see *The Japan Times*, June 21, 1993.

258. See *The Japan Times*, August 15, 1994, p. 1.

259. See *Mainichi Shimbun* (1991).

260. Okumura (1978, pp. 136–141).

261. See *Mainichi Shimbun* (1991).

262. Morikawa (1992); Okumura (1978, pp. 136–141).

263. *The Japan Times*, December 6, 1993.

264. See especially an excellent summary article by Teresa Watanabe (*Los Angeles Times*, February 5, 1994); also *The Japan Times*, April 11, 1994.

265. *The Japan Times*, April 11, 1994, pp. 10–11.

266. See *The Japan Times*, August 22, 1994, p. 1.

267. *The Japan Times*, September 13, 1993.

268. *The Japan Times*, January 3, 1994.

269. *The Japan Times*, November 8, 1993; *Japan Times*, November 15, 1993.

270. *Shūkan Bunshun*, July 9, 1992.

271. Jin (1989); Hayakawa (1983).

272. The above information was constructed from *keibatsu* listings in Hayakawa (1983).

273. Kitagawa and Kainuma (1985, p. 144), translation ours.

274. As discussed in Chapter 3, before the war the upper levels of the Japanese economy and politics were divided into *zaibatsu* factions and by bureaucratic turf battles, and could never really work together as effectively as elites can today. Of course, the Japanese economy was able to develop well through the first half of the twentieth century, but without these divisions and conflict, it can be argued that they might have done much better. Some historians, in fact, have argued that World War II would likely have lasted longer and the Japanese would have been more difficult to defeat by the Allied Powers had there been more elite unity at the time. Just as one example, Japan never placed its economy on a war footing, compared to the United States (which by 1943 was producing a new airplane every five minutes and a new ship every day), because the *zaibatsu* factions could not cooperate in such coordinated war production. See Okumura (1983, pp. 86–87); Kennedy (1987, p. 355).

275. For a summary of some of this research see Mintz and Schwartz (1985); Bottomore and Brym (1989); and Kerbo (1991, chapters 7 and 8).

276. For a summary from a psychologist who specializes in this subject, see Domhoff (1974, pp. 89–96). Key points of this research, however, are the following: (1) Physical proximity is likely to lead to group solidarity; (2) The more people interact, the more they will like each other; (3) Groups seen as high in status are more cohesive; and (4) The best atmosphere for increasing group cohesiveness is one that is relaxed and cooperative. And, of course, none of this even considers the more extreme situation in Japan among an elite that has extensive family ties through intermarriage, and what these familial binds produce in the way of unity and common worldviews.

277. See especially the many works of Domhoff (1970, 1974, 1983); Mills (1956); Baltzell (1958); Dye (1979); and Amory (1960).

278. See Lundberg (1968, p. 65); Cookson and Persell (1985).

279. Domhoff (1983, pp. 34–36).

280. See Dye (1979, p. 184); Domhoff (1970, pp. 22–26).

281. *The Japan Times*, September 13–19, 1993.

282. This has been the experience of the present authors as well as other researchers we have been in communication with, such as James Lincoln and Michael Gerlach.

283. See, for example, Roberts (1973, pp. 440–446); Okumura (1983); Atsuta (1992).

284. Okumura (1983, pp. 81–86: 1978, pp. 136–141).

285. Keidanren is made up essentially of two categories of members: the heads of all of the major industrial organizations (about 100 in 1981) such as the Metal Industry Alliance, Organization of Electronic Products Manufacturers, etc.; and a few members from each of the largest private companies.

Keidanren has one chairman and ten vice-chairmen. During most of the 1980s and 1990s almost all of these men have been graduates of the Tokyo University. For example, during one period in the 1980s, the chairman (Inayama Yoshihiro) and all but two of the eight vice-chairmen were Tōdai graduates, five from the Faculty of Law, three from the Faculty of Economics, two from the Faculty of Engineering. (Six of these eleven men were graduates from the numbered Tokyo high schools, two from Number One High School and one each from numbers Two, Three, Five, and Eight schools.)

The organization of Keidanren is further divided into many committees which vary in number over time. During most of the past ten years or so there have twenty-nine committees which oversee specific areas of the Japanese economy. There is a committee that concentrates on energy policy, one for production policy, a committee which oversees political contributions, one for tax policy, one for relations with foreign corporations, another which deals with relations with foreign governments and so on. Recent chairmen have all been committee chairmen prior to assuming that post. Of the twenty-nine committee chairmen in recent years, the majority have been Tokyo University graduates. A sample year in the 1980s showed fourteen of the twenty-nine men to be Tōdai graduates, six from the Faculty of Law and six from the Faculty of Economics, with two others coming from the Faculty of Engineering. See Kakuma (1981, pp. 139–144, 195–197).

286. See Atsuta (1992); Woronoff (1986, pp. 151–153).

287. Keizai Dōyūkai, or Dōyūkai, differs from Keidanren, besides being much smaller and certainly less powerful, in that it is "a place where top industrialists can address problems as individuals, unencumbered by affiliatory restrictions."

In recent years the leadership of the Dōyūkai has consisted of a representative director (daihyō kanji) and five vice-representative directors. The director and three of the five vice-directors have been graduates of the Tokyo University. Presidents or chairmen of one hundred and twenty-three companies are currently members of Keiza Dōyūkai, including the head of Fujitsu, Fuji Bank, Kajima Development, etc. Just over half of the one hundred and twenty-three men, sixty-nine to be exact, are graduates of the Tokyo University, thirty-one from the Faculty of Law and twenty-two from the Faculty of Economics.

Nihon Keieisha Dantai Renmei, or Nikkeiren, is a sister organization to Keidanren, in that it is made up in part by prefectural and regional industrial organizations. One of its main missions is to deal with problems of labor relations and working conditions in a way that Keidanren cannot.

Nikkeiren has as its more important organ Gyōjū Bekkaiin Dantai, a council of the heads of major industries such as the paper and pulp industry association, the insurance industry alliance, the cement producers' alliance, etc. Of the fifty-three chairmen of the separate council member organizations, twenty-nine are graduates of the Tokyo University, nineteen from the Faculty of Law and eight from the Faculty of Economics.

Nihon Shōkō Kaigisho, or Nissho, is an organization based on legal issues. It is not restricted to very large businesses but has members from medium and small businesses as well. Representatives are based on regional representation. It does not deal so much with national policy, but concentrates rather on details of specific business operation.

The governing body of Nissho consists of a general secretary, five vice-general secretaries and three special advisors. There is also an advisory board made up of an additional fifty-six members. Currently the general secretary and three of the vice-general secretaries are graduates from the Faculty of Law of Tokyo University, one additional vice-general secretary is a graduate of the Faculty of Engineering at Tōdai, and two of the three special advisors are as well from the Tōdai Faculty of Law. Of the members of the advisory board, fourteen of the fifty-six are Tōdai graduates, half from the Faculty of Law, four from the Faculty of Engineering, and three from the Faculty of Economics.

See Kakuma (1981, pp. 143–145, 245–248, 273–279).

288. Roberts (1973, pp. 224, 235).

289. Lebra (1993, p. 197).

290. See Hayakawa (1983); Jin (1989).

291. Morikawa (1992).

292. Kitagawa and Kainuma (1985, pp. 144–145). Translation ours.

293. For example, see Jin (1981, 1989); Hayakawa (1983).

294. Morikawa (1992); Roberts (1973).

295. Hayakawa (1983).

296. Lebra (1993); Jin (1981, 1989); Okumura (1983).

297. And it is also worth noting that the tendency of Westerners to lump all Asian societies together and assume they are all basically alike is very misleading here as well. In many Asian societies, such as Thailand, women hold a relatively high percentage of managerial and professional positions, especially in universities and the business world.

298. Alletzhauser (1990, pp. 142–145).

299. Domhoff (1970, pp. 34–35).

300. Torregrosa (1992, p. 110).

301. Baltzell (1958, p. 26).

302. Hamabata (1990).

303. Hamabata (1990, p. 127).

304. Hamabata (1990, pp. 41–43, 126–127, 140); Vogel (1961); Tahara (1980).

305. Hamabata (1990, pp. 127–128).

306. Hamabata (1990, p. 147).

307. Much of this research can be found in Domhoff's groundbreaking work, some of which will be noted below.

308. Further, of the top twenty-five banks in the United States, twenty-five had top executives in one or more of these fifteen clubs, as did twenty-five of the top twenty-five industrial corporations, twenty-three of the top twenty-five insurance companies, twenty-four of the top twenty-five transportation companies, and twenty-four of the top twenty-five retail corporations. For another example, 29 percent of these top 797 corporations in the United States had at least one member present during one two-week annual retreat of the Bohemian Club during a year for which the membership list was obtained. See Domhoff (1974).

309. Roberts (1973, p. 144).

310. Torregrosa (1992, p. 96).
311. See Verba, et al. (1987).
312. Torregrosa (1992, p. 100).
313. Ishida (1993, p. 217).
314. Most of the following information on clubs comes from a recent book by Satō (1990).
315. Satō (1990, p. 226). Translation ours.
316. At this point, however, we should perhaps note that it is claimed by some that these days important people (elites in Japan) tend to be too busy to keep to the leisurely pace of the old British-style club life. Recently American-style athletic clubs have come into vogue in Tokyo for the elite who are really "with it." They are mostly located in luxury hotels like the Okura and New Otani and the Royal Hotel in Osaka. It has become a real status symbol to have a membership in one of these athletic clubs, although they are not nearly as difficult to join as clubs such as Kō-junsha. These clubs are conveniently close to the ministries and to Nagata-chō (site of the seat of government) and to corporate headquarters. The initial joining fee is from three to four million yen, with about a million yen per year after that, which while not a staggering amount, is of course in addition to the private golf club fees which are essential for elite role playing. See, for example, Harada (1988).
317. Usui and Colignon (1994).
318. Maki (1987).
319. Satō (1990).
320. *Mainichi Shimbun* (1991, p. 36).
321. See *Mainichi Shimbun* (1991); Morioka (1989).
322. See Reischauer (1988, p. 46); Reischauer and Craig (1978, p. 18).
323. See for example, Reischauer (1988, p. 168), Gluck (1985, p. 19).
324. See for example, Rohlen (1983, p. 59).
325. See Gluck (1985, p. 85), Halliday (1975, p. 36–39).
326. See Halliday (1975, pp. 39, 119).
327. See Halliday (1975, pp. 25, 119).
328. See for example, Featherman and Hauser (1978); Featherman, Jones, and Hauser (1975); Grusky and Hauser (1984).
329. The most comprehensive research on this has recently been done by Ishida (1993). Also see Ishida, Goldthorpe, and Erikson (1991).
330. See Koyama (1981), Ishida (1993), and *The Japan Times* (March 9–15, 1992, p. 6).
331. See Kitagawa and Kainuma (1985, pp. 117–119). In another study of the "113 top bureaucrats" in the early 1980s, ninety-one were Tōdai graduates (see Miyake, Watanuki, Shima, and Urashima 1985, p. 41).
332. See Rohlen (1983, p. 89).
333. See Koh (1989, p. 142).
334. See *The Japan Times* (March 9–15, 1992, p. 6).
335. Taken from Kitagawa and Kainuma (1985), with updated material from Jin (1989) and Hayakawa (1983) on elite backgrounds.
336. See *The Japan Times* (Oct. 26–Nov. 1, 1992, p. 21).
337. See Ishida (1993, p. 153).
338. See Miyake et al. (1985, p. 41).
339. These data are compiled from Kakuma (1981a, 1981b).

340. Taken from Atsuta (1992).

341. All of the above can be found in Kakuma (1981a, pp. 143–145, 245–248, 273–279).

342. These studies have been compiled by Ishida (1993, pp. 155–158); from Useem and Karabal (1986); Fidler (1981); Whitley (1974); and Boyd (1973).

343. See, for example, Domhoff (1983, 1970, 1974); Scott (1991).

344. And as we have already considered in our look at Japanese elites in history, while most of the country's wealth and corporate assets were controlled by just a few families before the war, these old elites were much more divided in many ways, and found it more difficult to come together compared to the cooperation found among Japanese elites today.

345. See Woronoff (1980, pp. 120–121).

346. See, for example, Stevenson and Baker (1992) for a recent analysis of this process.

347. One of the best descriptions of what follows can be found in Rohlen (1983), but also see the useful examinations by White (1987) and Duke (1986).

348. This process of division can, in fact, start earlier if parents are so motivated, and have the money to do so. There are private preschools, which are attached to private schools that provide elementary through college educations. Some of these institutions have reasonably good reputations. Thus, there are examinations to get into preschool, and even what can be called preschool *juku*. If the preschooler gets in, the track is set through college.

349. See Stevenson and Baker (1992); also Rosenbaum and Kariya (1989); Rohlen (1983); Ishida (1993, p. 52).

350. See Ishida (1993, p. 52).

351. See Ishida (1993, p. 67); Rohlen (1983, pp. 129–130).

352. Again, see Ishida (1993) for one of the best recent studies and summaries of other studies on comparative rates of social mobility. Also, see Grusky and Hauser (1984); and Hauser and Grusky (1988).

353. See especially Ishida (1993, p. 69); Rosenbaum and Kariya (1989, p. 1349); Tominaga (1969, 1970, 1973, 1979); Mouer and Sugimoto (1986, pp. 279–281); Reischauer and Craig (1978, p. 283).

354. See Rohlen (1983, p. 59).

355. See Halliday (1975, p. 119).

356. See Halliday (1975, p. 249); Vogel (1979, p. 120); Reischauer (1977, p. 175).

357. See Rohlen (1983, pp. 129–137, 313).

358. For example, see van Wolferen (1989, p. 110).

359. See the *International Herald Tribune* (June 17, 1991), and *The European* (June 7–9, 1991).

360. Pye (1985, pp. vii, 176).

361. See especially Doi (1981, p. 57); also, Doi (1986).

362. See the interesting new account by Satō (1991).

363. See, for example, descriptions by Pharr (1990), Mouer and Sugimoto (1985), and Apter and Sawa (1984).

364. See Bowen (1980, pp. 49, 73); Hane (1982); Walthall (1991).

365. See Halliday (1975, pp. 68–76).

366. See Apter and Sawa (1984, p. 120); Mouer and Sugimoto (1985, p. 106).

367. Gluck (1985), for example, provides one of the best descriptions of how Japanese elites have worked to maintain social order throughout history.

368. See Smith (1983, p. 101).

369. Related to this is the popularity of characters in novels and movies who are often alienated outsiders, fighting to be free of social constraints, but who also often "get it in the end" by having to pay a high price for their independence. See Iijima (1987).

370. Even the untouchables in ancient India, possibly the most oppressed group in the history of human societies, had to have their individuality and desires considered by the society seeking to maintain their oppression. Given the horrible conditions of these untouchables it is rather surprising to humans in modern societies that they seldom revolted against their condition. But they did not revolt, because the Hindu belief system took care to hold out a "deal" for the ever-present egg, which will not give itself completely to the group: the untouchables would be rewarded in their next life by being reincarnated into a higher position if they conformed in the present life. See Moore (1978, p. 62); Dumont (1970).

371. For example, see van Wolferen (1989, p. 18); Gluck (1985).

372. See especially Gluck (1985, pp. 3–14, 102); Halliday (1975, p. 263).

373. Mitchell (1976).

374. The famous Japanese sociologist, Fukutake (1981), for example, had a chapter in one of his most important books on the subject of mass society in Japan. What he called "my-homeism" is related to this isolation within small groups.

375. See Nakane (1970).

376. See Lincoln and Kalleberg (1990): Woronoff (1980, p. 36): Fukutake (1981).

377. See Krauss and Simcock (1980): Pharr (1990, p. 3).

378. In the past, of course, there was always violence and physical force to maintain order. The shogun and their samurai were seldom hesitant to spill blood when it was in their interests. But violence in modern Japan is quite rare compared to other industrial nations, especially the United States. There are some right-wing extremists who sometimes employ violence—the mayor of one of Japan's medium-size cities was shot by one of these people in 1989 for criticism of the emperor, and a few journalists have been injured. But overall, indicators of violence such as the murder rate in Japan are very low. The police do carry guns, but it is extremely rare for these guns to be drawn. The Japanese find American movies about the Japanese *yakuza* (organized crime) rather humorous because from these movies one would think that the *yakuza* have more firepower than the Japanese Self-Defence Force, whereas in reality they possess very few guns. And despite the massive protests involving millions in the streets during 1960, only one protestor was killed, accidentally. The contrast to the violence used by police and demonstrators in similar protests just across the Japan Sea in Korea and by the military in China could not be greater.

379. See Japan Foreign Press Center (1985): Shapiro (1992, p. 166).

380. According to C. Wright Mills, "The media not only give us information; they guide our very experience. Our standards of credulity, our standards of reality, tend to be set by these media rather than by our own fragmentary experience." With respect to information, "The media provide much information and news about what is happening in the world, but they do not often enable the listener or viewer truly to connect his daily life with these larger realities. They do not connect the infor-

mation they provide on public issues with the troubles felt by the individual" (1956, pp. 310–315). Many writers since have agreed with Mills, and have expanded upon his idea with further explanation and research. For example, see Marcuse (1964); Habermas (1984); Herman and Chomsky (1988); Gans (1979).

381. For example, see the many cases cited by Herman and Chomsky (1988).

382. See van Wolferen (1989, pp. 176–180).

383. Included among these are interventions to downplay news about arsenic contamination by the largest dairy company in Japan, and deaths from a cold medicine produced by one of the largest pharmaceutical companies. See van Wolferen (1989, p. 178).

384. See van Wolferen (1989, pp. 386–387).

385. See van Wolferen (1989; *The Japan Times*, Dec. 16, 1991): *Los Angeles Times* (Nov. 12, 1992, p. A): *The Japan Times* (March 16, 1992): Alletzhauser (1990, pp. 157–158): *The Japan Times* (March 7–13, pp. 10–11, 1994).

386. Doi (1986).

387. Doi (1986, p. 43).

388. See van Wolferen (1989, p. 235).

389. However, fear and intimidation by groups large and small, powerful or even rather weak, are often reasons for the avoidance of "sensitive issues" in the Japanese media. Since World War II "there have been hundreds of incidents in which politicians, businessmen, labor leaders, publishers, teachers, writers, and other public figures were harassed, beaten, kidnapped, stabbed, bombed, or subjected to arson" because of voicing controversial issues. For example, see Roberts (1976, pp. 467–468).

390. Christopher (1983, p. 50). Many foreign scholars have complained that their works critical of some aspect of Japan will not be published in Japan, or that portions of their works dealing with what the Japanese view as controversial (such as discrimination against *burakumin*, Koreans, Chinese, or Japanese organized crime—*yakuza*) are omitted from their works when translated into Japanese. For example, authors of a highly respected book on the *yakuza* have yet to find a Japanese publisher. See Kaplan and Dubro (1986).

391. For example, see the American Sociological Association newsletter, *Footnotes* (June, 1991), about the firing of three professors for such activities at Hiroshima Shūdō University in 1990.

392. Van Wolferen (1989, p. 333).

393. Van Wolferen (1989, p. 237).

394. It is clear that many if not most Japanese scholars are less than comfortable with open debate over their theories and research. Scholarly meetings in Japan are comparatively orderly and highly regulated. A paper is given, then the floor is open for questions. However, the meeting organizer usually controls the questioning, making sure that the senior, ranking scholars in the room are able to ask their questions (seldom threatening), one after another, moving down the rank order. Serious questions may be asked, but overly negative comments are rare, and best saved for other close colleagues in private. In contrast to this, a Japanese sociologist attending an American Sociological Association meeting for the first time commented on the "rudeness" of the debate, with everyone trying to argue with each other to prove they are right.

395. See Rohlen (1983); White (1987); Mouer and Sugimoto (1985).

396. Halliday (1975, p. 246); Rohlen (1983, pp. 247–249); Mouer and Sugimoto (1985, p. 260).

397. Rohlen (1983, p. 254).

398. For example, on national television news one night in 1989 there was a story, reported quite positively, about a study done by one high school suggesting that bikini panties on girls did, in fact, cause more stomach aches, and therefore the rules are justified.

399. Mouer and Sugimoto (1985, p. 245).

400. Mouer and Sugimoto (1985, p. 258).

401. See for example, Gamson (1975); Goldstone (1980); Piven and Cloward (1977).

402. See van Wolferen (1989, p. 214). In one respect, some people argue that these figures are misleading because there are more people in Japan who are not formally lawyers but who do legal work, though even when these people are considered, the United States has 310 lawyers per 1,000 population and Japan has ninety-three. See, for example, Shapiro (1992, p. 136). However, the point we are making here continues to be valid because the people performing these legal functions in Japan are more likely doing jobs such as tax accounting rather than defending people's rights in court.

403. Much of what follows comes from a long investigative article in the *Los Angeles Times* (Feb. 6, 1993, p. A-1).

404. See van Wolferen (1989, pp. 214–225); Koh (1989, p. 98).

405. Hendry (1987, p. 191); Smith (1983, pp. 43–44). For counter arguments, see van Wolferen (1989, pp. 213–215).

406. Pharr (1990).

407. See Pharr (1990, pp. 149, 208–209).

408. Variation in these factors, usually associated with the types of crops grown in the area, in fact explain much about the likelihood for peasant revolts or revolutions in agrarian societies throughout history and around the world today. See, for example, Paige (1975).

409. For a history of this see Edwards (1979); Lincoln and Kalleberg (1990).

410. The first view, of course, reflects the popularity of Japanese management techniques such as "Theory Z" (see Ouchi 1981), while the opposite view is held by some labor leaders and leftist academics (see Garrahan and Stewart 1992).

411. See Thelen (1992) and Turner (1992) for excellent histories of labor development in Germany since World War II.

412. For example, works councils must be consulted on any changes in policies affecting work time arrangements, overtime, work breaks, vacation times, plant wage systems, the introduction of new technologies and any other alterations in the work environment, as well as the hiring, transfer, reclassification, or firing of workers. Corporate managers "must secure (in advance) the consent of the works council on a range of personnel decisions affecting individual workers, including job assignments, classifications and reclassifications, and transfers [paragraph 99 of the Works Constitutions Act]." After consulting with the works council on these issues, it is sometimes possible for managers to go against a vote of the works council, but to do so is very time consuming because of extensive rights for challenge given workers in a labor court system in Germany. See Thelen (1991, p. 101).

413. When first confronted with the array of German labor laws, legal rights, and

labor costs, American, British, and Japanese corporate executives are likely to assume these are harmful to business, and wonder how German corporations are able to survive. But German corporations certainly do survive, and there is convincing evidence that German labor laws, unions, and works councils actually help the competitiveness of German companies. *And*, interviews from several studies with executives from major German corporations indicate these executives now agree that codetermination laws have helped their business.

For example, in a four-year, ongoing study of the attitudes of German corporate executives toward codetermination laws and works councils, a majority of the executives supported these laws and works councils, and agreed they and their companies are better off because of them. Most executives in this study agreed that works councils are: (1) more practical and easier to work with than the highly ideological unions of the past; (2) often reduce tension between labor and management; (3) are more likely to get workers to go along with agreements; (4) and were very helpful in times of change, especially in helping workers to understand the need for change to protect profits and jobs. These German executives were also likely to say they were proud of the system of worker-manager relations, especially in contrast to what exists in the United States. See Wever (1993).

414. Personal interviews in Dusseldorf, Germany: see Kerbo, Wittenhagen, and Nakao (1994a, 1994b).

415. See van Wolferen (1989, pp. 65–72); Halliday (1975).

416. See Roberts (1973, pp. 447–460).

417. See especially Halliday (1975, pp. 211–222).

418. Also, see Lincoln and Kalleberg (1990, p. 230).

419. See for example the analysis of total institutions and their functions in Goffman (1961).

420. Also see Garfinkel (1956).

421. See Mills (1951, pp. xii–xvii).

422. See the long essay on this subject by Chieko Mulhern for the preface to her translation of the novel, *Shoshaman: A Tale of Corporate Japan*, by Shinya Arai (1991); also, *The New York Times* (May 17, 1993, p. C-1).

423. See for example, the *Los Angeles Times* (Jan. 14, 1992, p. H-6).

424. See the excellent essay by Teresa Watanabe in the *Los Angeles Times* (March 20, 1994).

425. We have not, of course, exactly measured the power held by these elites in Japan. Such power can only be measured on a case by case basis: that is, when A comes into conflict with B over some issue, if A finally wins, then we can say A is more powerful. More of this type of analysis is needed, but what has been done follows what we have suggested about the power of Japanese elites in this book (Broadbent 1989). What we have shown in this book is the potential for power—who has it due to position in the society, and why.

426. Wallerstein (1974, 1980, 1989); Chirot (1986); Kennedy (1987).

427. We like the following observation with respect to these Western economic theories: in 1992, when the Nobel Prize for economics was awarded—as usual to someone from the United States or Europe, and never Japan—one international journalist noted "it makes you wonder."

428. For a short summary of this, see Vogel (1991).

429. Few people who think seriously about the subject would reject the argument

that elites in some form will always exist, and this is especially so in large, complex industrial societies. Thus, the major question is not whether there will always be elites: rather, major questions pertain to such issues as the extent to which elites are accountable to others in the society, and the degree of unity among these elites. Some elite unity, it can be argued, is even necessary for democratic institutions (Higley and Burton 1989; Prewitt and Stone 1973). But there is also basic agreement that an elite so unified and interrelated becomes too powerful and unaccountable to others in the society.

With respect to the United States, for example, the debate is over exactly how unified elites have been: are there "strategic elites" in somewhat separate groups which result in checks and balances, reducing and taming elite power? Or is there a highly unified elite that is so powerful as to be unaccountable to the mass of others in the society? Such questions have led to one of the most lively debates in the social sciences (see Keller 1963; C. Wright Mills 1956; Domhoff 1970, 1974, 1983; Dye 1979).

But not all sides in the debate agree that unified elites are bad. One argument which most Westerners would find offensive to their democratic values, is made by a member of the American upper class (Baltzell 1958, 1964). In this view, for industrial societies, including the United States, elites made up of an hereditary upper class have ruled, and should rule—the rest of us, furthermore, are better off for it. As the argument goes, because of their upbringing, traditions, moral values, and education, as well as their cooperation and unity, this upper class is most suited to rule. It is only this group who is said to have a sense of "noblesse oblige," the tradition of self-sacrifice and concern for the common people to ensure freedom, prevent corruption, and guard against the abuse of power.

The biggest danger, in this view, is rule by a new rich which lacks such morality, a proper upbringing, and thus the sense of noblesse oblige. Following this line of reasoning, with a new rich in power, there will be corruption and short-sighted and self-serving actions which enrich this elite, but threaten the long-term survival of the society.

An argument can be made that post-war Japanese elites were in some ways close to Baltzell's ideal of responsible elites with the unity and talent to rule for common national interests. But these post-war Japanese elites developed in ways far different than described by Baltzell. Then again, Baltzell's view of what happens when newly rich, greedy elites obtain power without such moral responsibility may fit where Japan is headed. Baltzell's problem, however, is in assuming that an elite such as the one he describes in such positive terms can ever last very long in history without much democratic pressure and extensive circulation from below.

430. Edward Seidensticker, "Preface" to Taylor (1985, p. 13).

431. When writing about elites and dominance, Western languages such as English box us into concepts and images which are at times too narrow and imply only self-interests. The word "elite" tends to have this negative connotation, and implies exploitation of the many by and for the few, but it is not necessarily so in Japan. While this may in fact be the case, we must try to dispel such simplicity in the concepts.

432. We suggest three main issues are involved in deciding whether or not there is a high degree of elite exploitation that is harmful to the interests of others in the society: (1) to what degree are the interests of the elites and masses divergent or

convergent? (2) how equal is the distribution of benefits and profits between the elites and masses? and (3) how equal is the distribution of effort and contribution to the society, and the economy more specifically, between the elites and masses?

We have argued that the destruction caused by the war brought the interests of the elites and masses together far more than had been the case before the war, and to a larger extent than can be found in many other industrial nations, and this convergence of interests stands in particular contrast to the United States. The post-war years in Japan created a society more equal than it had been before the war, and a more equal society than that of almost any other industrial nation. The contribution and effort has not differed so greatly between the elites and masses in the years since World War II.

433. Chirot (1986); Bornschier, Chase-Dunn, and Rubinson (1978).
434. Myrdal (1968, 1970); Gold (1986); Barrett and Whyte (1982).
435. Pye (1985).

References

Abegglen, James C., and George Stalk, Jr. 1985. *Kaisha: The Japanese Corporation*. New York: Basic Books

Akard, Patrick J. 1992. "Corporate Mobilization and Political Power: The Transformation of U.S. Economic Policy in the 1970s." *American Sociological Review* 57: 597–615.

Allen, Michael. 1974. "The Structure of Interorganizational Elite Corporations: Interlocking Corporate Directorates." *American Sociological Review* 39: 339–406.

Alletzhauser, Albert J. 1990. *The House of Nomura: The Inside Story of The Legendary Japanese Financial Dynasty*. New York: Arcade.

Allinson, Gary D. 1989. "Politics in Contemporary Japan: Pluralist Scholarship in the Conservative Era—A Review Article." *Journal of Asian Studies* 48: 324–332.

Amory, Cleveland. 1960. *Who Killed Society?* New York: Harper and Row.

Anderson, Stephen J. 1993. *Welfare Policy and Politics in Japan: Beyond the Development State*. New York: Paragon.

Antonio, Robert. 1979. "The Contradiction of Domination and Production in Bureaucracy: The Contribution of Organizational Efficiency to the Decline of the Roman Empire." *American Sociological Review* 44: 895–912.

Apter, David E., and Nagayo Sawa. 1984. *Against the State: Politics and Social Protest in Japan*. Cambridge, Mass.: Harvard University Press.

Arai, Shinya. 1991. *Shoshaman: A Tale of Corporate Japan*. Berkeley: University of California Press.

Atsuta Masanori. 1992. *Shinzaikai jinretsuden* (Biography of the new financial world lineup). Tokyo: Yomiuri Shimbunsha.

Baltzell, E. Digby. 1958. *Philadelphia Gentlemen: The Making of a National Upper Class*. New York: Free Press.

———. 1964. *The Protestant Establishment: Aristocracy and Caste in America*. New York: Random House.

Barrett, Richard, and Martin King Whyte. 1984. "Dependency Theory and Taiwan: Analysis of a Deviant Case." *American Journal of Sociology* 87: 1064–1089.

Bellah, Robert, et al. 1985. *Habits of the Heart: Individualism and Commitment in American Life*. New York: Harper and Row.

Bendix, Reinhard. 1978. *Kings or People: Power and the Mandate to Rule*. Berkeley: University of California Press.

Benedict, Ruth. 1946. *The Chrysanthemum and the Sword: Patterns of Japanese Culture*. New York: Houghton Mifflin.

Berle, Adolf, and Gardiner Means. 1932. *The Modern Corporation and Private Property*. New York: Macmillan.

Bornschier, Volker, Christopher Chase-Dunn, and Richard Rubinson. 1978. "Cross-National Evidence of the Effects of Foreign Investment and Aid on Economic Growth and Inequality: A Survey of Findings and a Reanalysis." *American Journal of Sociology* 84: 651–683.

Bottomore, Tom, and Robert J. Brym. 1989. *The Capitalist Class: An International Study*. New York: New York University Press.

Bowen, Roger W. 1980. *Rebellion and Democracy in Meiji Japan*. Berkeley: University of California Press.

Boyd, David. 1973. *Elites and Their Education*. Windsor, Ontario: NFER Publishing.

Brinton, Mary C. 1989. "Gender Stratification in Contemporary Urban Japan." *American Sociological Review* 54: 549–564.

Broadbent, Jeffery. 1986. "Environmental Politics in Japan: An Integrated Structural Analysis." *Sociological Forum* 4: 179–202.

———. 1989. "Strategies and Structural Contradictions: Growth Coalition Politics in Japan." *American Socological Review* 54: 707–721.

Burstein, Daniel. 1988. *Yen: Japan's New Financial Empire and Its Threat to America*. New York: Fawcett Columbine.

Chirot, Daniel. 1986. *Social Change in the Modern Era*. New York: Harcourt Brace Jovanovich.

Choate, Pat. 1990. *Agents of Influence: How Japan Manipulates America's Political and Economic System*. New York: Simon and Schuster.

Christopher, Robert. 1983. *The Japanese Mind: The Goliath Explained*. New York: Simon and Schuster.

Clark, Rodney. 1979. *The Japanese Economy*. Tokyo: Tuttle.

Collins, Randall. 1975. *Conflict Sociology*. New York: Academic Press.

Cookson, Peter W., Jr., and Caroline Hodges Persell. 1985. *Preparing for Power: America's Elite Boarding Schools*. New York: Basic Books.

Coser, Lewis. 1956. *The Function of Social Conflict*. New York: Free Press.

———. 1967. *Continuities in the Study of Social Conflict*. New York: Free Press.

Curtis, Gerald L. 1971. *Election Campaigning Japanese Style*. New York: Columbia University Press.

———. 1988. *The Japanese Way of Politics*. New York: Columbia University Press.

de Tocqueville, Alexis. 1969. *Democracy in America*. New York: Doubleday.

Dietrich, William S. 1991. *In The Shadow of the Rising Sun: The Political Roots of*

American Economic Decline. University Park, Pa.: Pennsylvania State University Press.

Doi Takeo. 1981. *The Anatomy of Dependence*. Tokyo: Kōdansha.

————. 1986. *The Anatomy of Self: The Individual Versus Society*. Tokyo: Kōdansha.

Domhoff, G. William. 1970. *The Higher Circles*. New York: Random House.

————. 1974. *The Bohemian Grove and Other Retreats*. New York: Harper and Row.

————. 1979. *The Powers that Be*. New York: Vintage Press.

————. 1983. *Who Rules America Now?: A View for the 80s*. Englewood Cliffs, N.J.: Prentice-Hall.

Dore, Ronald. 1987. *Taking Japan Seriously*. Palo Alto, Calif.: Stanford University Press.

Duke, Benjamin. 1986. *The Japanese School: Lessons for Industrial America*. Westport, Conn.: Praeger.

Dumont, Louis. 1970. *Homo Hierarchieus: The Caste System and Its Implications*. Chicago: University of Chicago Press.

Dye, Thomas R. 1979. *Who's Running America?* Englewood Cliffs, N.J.: Prentice-Hall.

Edwards, Richard. 1979. *Contested Terrain: The Transformation of the Workplace in the Twentieth Century*. New York: Basic Books.

Etzioni, Amitai. 1984. *An Immodest Agenda: Rebuilding America Before the 21st Century*. New York: McGraw-Hill.

Fairbank, John K., Edwin O. Reischauer, and Albert M. Craig. 1965. *East Asia: The Modern Transformation*. Boston: Houghton Mifflin.

Fallows, James. 1989. *More Like Us: Making America Great Again*. Boston: Houghton Mifflin.

Featherman, David L., and Robert Hauser. 1978. *Opportunity and Change*. New York: Academic Press.

Featherman, David L., F. Lancaster Jones, and Robert Hauser. 1975. "Assumptions of Social Mobility Research in the U.S.: A Case of Occupational Status." *Social Science Research* 4: 329–360.

Fidler, John. 1981. *The British Business Elite*. London: Routledge and Kegan Paul.

Fligstein, Neil, and Kenneth Dauber. 1989. "Structural Change in Corporate Organization." *Annual Review of Sociology* 15: 73–96.

Florida, Richard, and Martin Kenney. 1991. "Transplanted Organizations: The Transfer of Japanese Industrial Organization to the United States." *American Sociological Review* 56: 381–389.

Freitag, Peter. 1975. "The Cabinet and Big Business: A Study of Interlocks." *Social Problems* 23: 137–152.

Fukutake, Tadashi. 1981. *Japanese Society Today*. Tokyo: Tokyo University Press.

Gamson, William. 1975. *The Strategy of Social Protest*. Homewood, Ill.: Dorsey Press.

Gans, Herbert. 1979. *Deciding What's News*. New York: Pantheon.

Garfinkel, Harold. 1956. "Conditions of Successful Degradation Ceremonies." *American Journal of Sociology* 61: 420–424.

Garrahan, Philip, and Paul Stewart. 1992. *The Nissan Enigma: Flexibility at Work in a Local Economy*. London: Mansell Publishing.

Gerlach, Michael L. 1992a. *Alliance Capitalism: The Social Organization of Japanese Business*. Berkeley: University of California Press.

———. 1992b. "Twilight of the Keiretsu?: A Critical Assessment." *Journal of Japanese Studies* 18: 79–118.

Gibney, Frank. 1953. *Five Gentlemen of Japan: The Portrait of a Nation's Character.* New York: Farrar, Straus, and Young.

———. 1979. *Japan: The Fragile Superpower.* Tokyo: Tuttle.

———. 1992. *The Pacific Century.* New York: Random House.

Gluck, Carol. 1985. *Japan's Modern Myths: Ideology in the Late Meiji Period.* Princeton, N.J.: Princeton University Press.

Goffman, Erving. 1961. *Asylums.* Garden City, N.Y.: Doubleday.

Gold, Thomas B. 1986. *State and Society in the Taiwan Miracle.* Armonk, N.Y.: M. E. Sharpe.

Goldstone, Jack. 1980. "The Weakness of Organization: A New Look at Gamson's 'The Strategy of Social Protest.'" *American Journal of Sociology* 85: 1017–1042.

Golzio, Karl Heinz. 1985. "Max Weber on Japan: The Role of the Government and the Buddhist Sects." In Andreas E. Buss (ed.), *Max Weber in Asian Studies,* pp. 90–101. Leiden: E.J. Brill.

Gouldner, Alvin, and Richard A. Peterson. 1962. *Notes on Technology and Moral Order.* Indianapolis: Bobbs-Merrill.

Grusky, David, and Robert Hauser. 1984. "Comparative Social Mobility Revisited: Models of Convergence and Divergence in 16 Countries." *American Sociological Review* 49: 19–38.

Habermas, Jurgen. 1984. *Reason and the Rationalization of Society.* Boston: Beacon Press.

Halliday, Jon. 1975. *A Political History of Japanese Capitalism.* New York: Monthly Review Press.

Hamabata, Matthew Masayuki. 1990. *Crested Kimono: Power and Love in the Japanese Business Family.* Ithaca, N.Y.: Cornell University Press.

Hane, Mikiso. 1982. *Peasants, Rebels and Outcasts: The Underside of Modern Japan.* New York: Pantheon.

———. 1988. *Reflections on the Way to the Gallows: Voices of Japanese Rebel Women.* New York: Pantheon.

Harada Norio. 1988. *"Nihon no meimon kurabu"* (Prestigious clubs of Japan). In *Jimbutsu Ōrai Who's Who,* pp. 151–158. Tokyo: Shinjimbutsu Ōraisha.

Hauser, Robert, and David Grusky. 1988. "Cross-National Variations in Occupational Distributions, Relative Mobility Chances, and Intergenerational Shifts in Occupational Distributions." *American Sociological Review* 53: 723–741.

Hayakawa Takashi. 1983. *Nihon no jōryū shakai to keibatsu* (Japan's upper strata social groups and their family connections). Tokyo: Kadokawa Shoten.

Hearn, Lafcadio. 1956. *Japan: An Interpretation.* Tokyo: Tuttle.

———. 1962. *Kokoro: Hints and Echoes of Japanese Inner Life.* Tokyo: Tuttle.

———. 1976. *Glimpses of Unfamiliar Japan.* Tokyo: Tuttle.

Heise, David, et al. 1962. "Further Notes on Technology and Moral Order." *Social Forces* 55: 316–337.

Hendry, Joy. 1987. *Understanding Japanese Society.* London: Crom Helm.

Herman, Edward S., and Noam Chomsky. 1988. *Manufacturing Consent: The Political Economy of the Mass Media.* New York: Pantheon.

Higley, John, and Michael G. Burton. 1989. "The Elite Variable in Democratic Transitions and Breakdowns." *American Sociological Review* 54: 17–32.

Hwang, Kwang-kuo. 1987. "Face and Favor: The Chinese Power Game." *American Journal of Sociology* 92: 944–974.

Iijimas, Takehisa. 1987. "Criticism of Twentieth-Century Civilization in *Wagahai wa Neko de Aru.*" In Takehisa Iijima and James M. Vardaman (eds.), *The World of Natsume Sōseki*, pp. 125–151. Tokyo: Kinseidō Ltd.

Ishida, Hiroshi. 1993. *Social Mobility in Contemporary Japan.* Palo Alto, Calif.: Stanford University Press.

Ishida, Hiroshi, John H. Goldthorpe, and Robert Erikson. 1987. "Intergenerational Class Mobility in Postwar Japan: Conformity or Peculiarity in Cross-National Perspective." Paper presented to the Research Committee on Social Stratification of the International Sociological Association, Berkeley, August 23.

Japan Company Handbook. Annual. Tokyo: Tōyō Keizai Shimpōsha.

Japan Foreign Press Center. 1985. *Fact and Figures of Japan.* Tokyo: Foreign Press Center.

Jin Ikko. 1981. *Nihon eriito gundan* (Japan's elite corps). Tokyo: Guriin Arō Shuppansha.

———. 1989. *Keibatsu—shin tokken kaikyū no keifu* (Genealogy of the new privileged class). Tokyo: Mainichi Shimbunsha.

Johnson, Chalmers. 1982. *MITI and the Japanese Miracle.* Palo Alto, Calif.: Stanford University Press.

Kakuma Takashi. 1981a. *Nihon no shihai kaikyū, jōkan* (Japan's ruling class, Part One). Tokyo: PHP Kenkyūjo.

———. 1981b. *Nihon no shihai kaikyū, jōkan, gekan* (Japan's ruling class, Part Two). Tokyo: PHP Kentyūjo.

Kanter, Rosabeth Moss. 1972. *Commitment and Community.* Cambridge, Mass.: Harvard University Press.

Kaplan, David, and Alec Dubro. 1986. *Yakuza.* London: Futura.

Keisei Kikaku Cho Hen. 1988. *Kokumin seikatsu hakusho* (White paper on national life). Tokyo: Okura Sho.

Keller, Suzanne. 1963. *Beyond the Ruling Class: Strategic Elites in Modern Society.* New York: Random House.

Kennedy, Paul. 1987. *The Rise and Fall of the Great Powers: Economic Change and Military Conflict from 1500 to 2000.* New York: Random House.

Kerbo, Harold R., 1991. *Social Stratification and Inequality: Class and Conflict in Historical and Comparative Perspective.* New York: McGraw-Hill.

Kerbo, Harold R., and Richard Della Fave. 1983. "Corporate Linkage and Control of the Corporate Economy: New Evidence and a Reinterpretation." *Sociological Quarterly* 24: 204–218.

Kerbo, Harold R., and Mariko Inoue. 1990. "Japanese Social Structure and White-Collar Crime: Recruit and Cosmos and Beyond." *Deviant Behavior* 11: 139–154.

Kerbo, Harold R., and Keiko Nakao. 1991. "Corporate Structure and Modernization: A Comparative Analysis of Japan and the United States." *International Review of Sociology* 3: 149–174.

Kerbo, Harold R., Elke Wittenhagen, and Keiko Nakao. 1994a. "Japanische Unternehmen in Deutschland: Unternehmenstruktur und Arbeitsverhaltnis." *Ver-*

oeffentlichungsliste des Instituts fur Arbeit und Technik, Gelsenkirchen, Germany.

———. 1994b. "Japanese Corporations in Germany: Corporate Structure and Employee Relations." *Duisburger Beitiage zur Soziologischen Forschung,* Duisburg, Germany.

Kishimoto Kōichi. 1988. *Politics in Modern Japan: Development and Organization.* Tokyo: Japan Echo, Inc.

Kitagawa Takayoshi and Kainuma Jun. 1985. *Nihon no eriito* (Japan's elite). Tokyo: Otsuki Shoten.

Kitahara Isamu. 1980. "Ownership and Control in the Large Corporation." *Keio Economic Studies* vol. 8, no. 2: 19–34.

———. 1985. *Gendai shihonshugi ni okeru shoyū to kettei* (Ownership and decision in contemporary capitalism). Tokyo: Iwanami Shoten.

Koh, B. C. 1989. *Japan's Administrative Elite.* Berkeley: University of California Press.

Lebra, Takie Sugiyama. 1993. *Above the Clouds: Status Culture of the Modern Japanese Nobility.* Berkeley: University of California Press.

Lenski, Gerhard. 1966. *Power and Privilege.* New York: McGraw-Hill.

———. 1978. "Marxist Experiments in Destratification: An Appraisal." *Social Forces* 57: 364–383.

Lenski, Gerhard, and Patrick Nolan. 1986. "Trajectories of Development: A Further Test." *Social Forces* 64: 794–795.

Lincoln, Edward J. 1988. *Japan: Facing Economic Maturity.* Washington, D.C.: The Brookings Institution.

Lincoln, James R., Michael Gerlach, and Peggy Takahashi. 1992. "Keiretsu Networks in the Japanese Economy: A Dyad Analysis of Intercorporate Ties." *American Sociological Review* 57: 561–585.

Lincoln, James R., and Arne L. Kalleberg. 1985. "Work Organization and Work Force Commitment: A Study of Plants and Employees in the U.S. and Japan." *American Sociological Review* 50: 738–750

———. 1990. *Culture, Control, and Commitment: A Study of Work Organization and Work Attitudes in the United States and Japan.* New York: Cambridge University Press.

Lundberg, Ferdinand. 1968. *The Rich and the Super-Rich.* New York: Bantam Books.

MacMullen, Ramsay. 1974. *Roman Social Relations.* New Haven: Yale University Press.

McKinstry, John A., and Asako McKinstry. 1991. *Jinsei Annai: "Life's Guide," Glimpses of Japan Through a Popular Advice Column.* Armonk, New York: M. E. Sharpe.

Maki Tarō. 1987. *Nagatachō no jōryū kazoku* (Leading families at the center of national politics). Tokyo: Kanki Shuppan.

Marcuse, Herbert. 1964. *One-Dimensional Man.* Boston: Beacon Press.

Mariolis, Peter. 1975. "Interlocking Directorates and the Control of Corporations: The Theory of Bank Control." *Social Science Quarterly* 56: 425–439.

Massarella, Derek. 1990. *A World Elsewhere: Europe's Encounter with Japan in the Sixteenth and Seventeenth Centuries.* New Haven: Yale University Press.

Milkman, Ruth. 1992. *Japan's California Factories: Labor Relations and Economic Globalization.* Los Angeles: UCLA Institute of Industrial Relations.

Mills, C. Wright. 1956. *The Power Elite.* New York: Oxford University Press.

Minear, Richard. 1980. "Orientalism and the Study of Japan." *Journal of Asian Studies* 30: 507–517.

Mintz, Beth. 1975. "The President's Cabinet, 1897–1972: A Contribution to the Power Structure Debate." *Insurgent Sociologist* 5: 131–148.

Mintz, Beth, and Michael Schwartz. 1985. *The Power Structure of American Business.* Chicago: University of Chicago Press.

Mitchell, Richard. 1976. *The Korean Minority in Japan.* Berkeley: University of California Press.

Miyake Ichirō, Watakuki Jōji, Shima Sumi, and Urashima Ikuo. 1985. *Byōdō o meguru eriito to taikō* (Equality, the elite, and the counterelite). Tokyo: Sōbunsha.

Miyazaki Yoshikazu. 1982. *Gendai shihonshugi to takokuseki kigyō* (Contemporary capitalism and multinational corporation). Tokyo: Iwanami Shoten.

———. 1985. *Gendai kigyōron njyūmon* (An introduction to the theory of the modern corporation). Tokyo: Yuhikaku.

Mizruchi, Mark. 1992. *The Structure of Corporate Political Action: Interfirm Relations and Their Consequences.* Cambridge, Mass.: Harvard University Press.

Moore, Barrington. 1978. *Injustice: The Social Basis of Obedience and Revolt.* Armonk, N.Y.: M. E. Sharpe.

Morgan, S. Philip, and Kiyosi Hirosima. 1983. "The Persistence of Extended Family Residence in Japan: Anachronism or Alternative Strategy." *American Sociological Review* 48: 269–281.

Mori Hideki. 1992. "Greasing the Wheels of Power." *Japan Quarterly* 39:303–310.

Morikawa, Hidemasa. 1992. *Zaibatsu: The Rise and Fall of Family Enterprise Groups in Japan.* Tokyo: Tokyo University Press.

Morioka, Koji. 1989. "Japan." In Tom Bottomore and Robert J. Brym (eds.), *The Capitalist Class: An International Study*, pp. 140–176. New York: New York University Press.

Mouer, Ross, and Yoshio Sugimoto. 1985. *Images of the Japanese.* New York: Routledge and Kegan Paul.

Mulhern, Chieko. 1991. "Introduction: The Japanese Business Novel," pp. vii–xxv. In Arai Shinya, *Sho Sha Man: A Tale of Corporate Japan*. (Translated by Chieko Mulhern.) Berkeley: University of California Press.

Myrdal, Gunnar. 1968. *Asian Drama: An Inquiry into The Poverty of Nations.* Vols. 1, 2, 3. New York: Pantheon.

———. 1970. *The Challenge of World Poverty.* New York: Pantheon.

Nakane, Chie. 1970. *Japanese Society.* Berkeley: University of California Press.

Okimoto, Daniel I. 1988. *Between MITI and the Market: Japanese Industrial Policy for High Technology.* Palo Alto, Calif.: Stanford University Press.

Okumura Hiroshi. 1978. *Kigyō shūdan no keieisha* (Leaders in an era of industrial groups). Tokyo: Nikei Shinsha.

———. 1983. *Shin-Nihon no roku dai kigyō shūdan* (Six great industrial groups of later day Japan). Tokyo: Nihon Jitsugyō Shuppansha.

Orloff, Ann Shola, and Theda Scocpol. 1984. "Why Not Equal Protection? Explaining the Politics of Social Spending in Britain, 1900–1911, and the United States, 1800s–1920." *Sociological Review* 49: 726–750.

Ōsono Tomokazu. 1991. *Kigyō keiretsu to gyōkai chizu* (Map of industrial *Keiretsu* and other big business circles). Tokyo: Nihon Jitsugyō Shuppansha.

Ouchi, William G. 1981. *Theory Z*. Reading, Mass.: Addison-Wesley.

Paige, Jeffrey. 1975. *Agrarian Revolution*. New York: Free Press.

Pempel, T. J. 1989. "Prerequisites for Democracy: Political and Social Institutions." In Takeshi Ishida and Ellis S. Krauss (eds.), *Democracy in Japan*, pp. 17–38. Pittsburgh: Pittsburgh University Press.

Pfeiffer, Richard. 1977. *The Emergence of Society: A Prehistory of the Establishment*. New York: McGraw-Hill.

Pharr, Susan J. 1990. *Losing Face: Status Politics in Japan*. Berkeley: University of California Press.

Piven, Frances Fox, and Richard Cloward. 1988. *The New Class War: Reagan's Attack on the Welfare State and Its Consequences*. New York: Pantheon.

Poulantzas, Nicos. 1973. *Classes and Contemporary Capitalism*. London: NLB.

————. 1976. *The Comparative Study of Elites*. Englewood Cliffs, N.J.: Prentice-Hall.

Prestowitz, Clyde V. 1989. *Trading Places: How We Are Giving Our Future to Japan and How to Reclaim It*. New York: Basic Books.

Prewitt, Kenneth, and Alan Stone. 1973. *The Ruling Elites: Elite Theory, Power, and American Democracy*. New York: Harper and Row.

Putnam, Robert. 1976. *The Comparative Study of Elites*. Englewood Cliffs, N.J.: Prentice-Hall.

Pye, Lucian W. 1985. *Asian Power and Politics: The Cultural Dimensions of Authority*. Cambridge, Mass.: Belknap Press/Harvard University Press.

Reischauer, Edwin O. 1988. *The Japanese Today*. Tokyo: Tuttle.

Reischauer, Edwin O, and Albert M. Craig. 1978. *Japan: Tradition and Transformation*. Boston: Houghton Mifflin.

Reischauer, Haru Matsukata. 1986. *Samurai and Silk: A Japanese and American Heritage*. Cambridge, Mass.: Harvard University Press.

Roberts, John G. 1973. *Mitsui: Three Centuries of Japanese Business*. New York: Weatherhill.

Rohlen, Thomas P. 1983. *Japan's High Schools*. Berkeley: University of California Press.

Rosenbaum, James, and Takehiko Kariya. 1989. "From High School to Work: Market and Institutional Mechanisms in Japan." *American Journal of Sociology* 94: 1334–1365.

Satō, Ikuya. 1991. *Kamikaze Biker: Parody and Anomy in Affluent Japan*. Chicago: University of Chicago Press.

Satō Tomiyasu. 1987. *Monbatsu* (Family cliques). Tokyo: Rippu Shobō.

————. 1990. *Nihon no royaru fuamirii* (The royal family of Japan). Tokyo: Rippu Shobō.

Schoppa, Leonard J. 1991. "Zoku Power and LDP Power: A Case Study of the Zoku Rule in Education Policy." *Journal of Japanese Studies* 17: 79–106.

Scott, John. 1991. "Networks of Corporate Power: A Comparative Assessment." *Annual Review of Sociology* 17: 181–203.

Shapiro, Andrew L. 1992. *We're Number One*. New York: Random House.

Sherif, Muzafer. 1966. *In Common Predicament: Social Psychology of Intergroup Conflict and Cooperation*. Boston: Houghton Mifflin.

Shūkan Bunshun. 1993. "Hosokawa Morihisa no saidai jyakuten—uyoku to kane" (Hosokawa Morihisa's greatest weakness—the right wing and money), July 9.

Simmel, Georg. 1955. *Conflict and the Web of Group Affiliations*, ed. Kurt H. Wolff and Reinhard Bendix. New York: Free Press.

Skocpol, Theda. 1979. *States and Social Revolutions: A Comparative Analysis of France, Russia and China*. New York: Cambridge University Press.

Skocpal, Theda, and Edwin Amenta. 1985. "Did Capitalism Shape Social Security?" *American Sociological Review* 50: 572–575.

Smith, Robert J. 1983. *Japanese Society: Tradition, Self and the Social Order*. Cambridge: Cambridge University Press.

Soboul, Albert. 1974. *The French Revolution, 1787–1799: From the Storming of the Bastille to Napoleon*. New York: Random House.

Solzhenitsyn, Aleksandr. 1973. *The Gulag Archipelago*. New York: Random House.

Soref, Michael. 1976. "Social Class and a Division of Labor within the Corporate Elite: A Note on Class, Interlocking, and Executive Committee Membership of Directors of U. S. Firms." *Sociological Quarterly* 17: 360–368.

Stevenson, David Lee, and David P. Baker. 1992. "Shadow Education and Allocation in Formal Schooling: Transition to University in Japan." *American Journal of Sociology* 97: 1639–1657.

Tahara Sōichirō. 1980. *Nihon no pawaa eriito* (Japan's power elite). Tokyo: Kōbun-sha.

Taylor, Jared. 1983. *Shadows of the Rising Sun: A Critical View of the "Japanese Miracle."* Tokyo: Tuttle.

Thelen, Kathleen A. 1991. *Union of Parts: Labor Politics in Postwar Germany*. Ithaca, N.Y.: Cornell University Press.

Thurow, Lester. 1992. *Head to Head: The Coming Economic Battle between the United States, Japan, and Europe*. New York: Morrow.

Tominaga, Kenichi. 1969. "Trend Analysis of Social Stratification and Social Mobility in Contemporary Japan." *Developing Economics* 7: 471–489.

———. 1970. "Studies of Social Stratification and Social Mobility in Japan: 1955–1967." *Rice University Studies* 56: 133–149.

———. 1973. "Social Mobility in Japan—Prewar and Postwar." *Japan Interpreter* 8: 374–386.

———. 1979. *Nihon no kaisō kōzō* (The structure of Japanese social stratification). Tokyo: Tokyo University Press.

Torregrosa, Luisita Lopez. 1992. "Ginzan Poses." *Vanity Fair* (November): 94–116.

Turner, Lowell. 1992. *Democracy at Work: Changing World Markets and the Future of Labor Unions*. Ithaca, N.Y.: Cornell University Press.

Ueda, Y. 1989. "Similarities of the Corporate Network Structure in Japan and the United States." *Ryūtsu-Kagaku Daigaku ronshū* 21: 49–61.

———. 1990. "The Structure of 'Japan, Inc.' " *Ryūtsu-Kagaku Daigaku ronshū* 23: 93–102.

U.S. Senate Committee on Government Affairs. 1978. *Interlocking Directorates Among the Major U.S. Corporations*. Washington, D.C.: U.S. Government Printing Office.

Useem, Michael. 1984. *The Inner Circle: Large Corporations and the Rise of Business Political Activity in the U.S. and U.K.* New York: Oxford University Press.

Useem, Michael, and Jerome Karabal. 1986. "Pathways to Top Corporate Management." *American Sociological Review* 51: 184–200.

Usui, Chikako, and Richard Colignon. 1994. "Amakudari (Descent from Heaven): The Cement between the Japanese Polity and Economy." Paper presented at the annual meeting of the Midwest Sociological Society, St. Louis, Missouri. March 29.

van Wolferen, Karel. 1989. *The Enigma of Japanese Power.* New York: Knopf.

Varley, H. Paul. 1977. *Japanese Culture: A Short History.* New York: Holt, Rinehart and Winston.

Verba, Sidney, et al. 1987. *Elites and the Idea of Equality.* Cambridge, Mass.: Harvard University Press.

Vogel, Ezra. 1961. "The Go-Between in a Developing Society: The Case of the Japanese Marriage Arranger." *Human Organization* 20: 112–120.

———. 1971. *Japan's New Middle Class.* Berkeley: University of California Press.

———. 1979. *Japan As Number One: Lessons for America.* Cambridge, Mass.: Harvard University Press.

———. 1985. *Comeback: Building the Resurgence of American Business.* New York: Simon and Schuster.

———. 1991. *The Four Little Dragons: The Spread of Industrialization in East Asia.* Cambridge, Mass.: Harvard University Press.

Wallerstein, Immanual. 1974. *The Modern World System.* New York: Academic Press.

———. 1980. *The Modern World System II: Mercantilism and the Consolidation of the European World Economy, 1600–1750.* New York: Academic Press.

———. 1989. *The Modern World-System III: The Second Era of Great Expansion of the Capitalist World-Economy, 1730–1840s.* New York: Academic Press.

Walthall, Anne. 1991. *Peasant Uprisings in Japan.* Chicago: University of Chicago Press.

Weber, Max. 1947. *The Theory of Social and Economic Organization,* ed. Talcott Parsons. New York: Free Press.

Wells, H. G. 1971. *The Outline of History.* New York: Doubleday.

Wever, Kirsten. 1991. "Co-determination and Competitiveness: What German Employers Think." Paper presented at the Industrial Relations Research Association, Anaheim, California, January 12.

White, Merry. 1987. *The Japanese Educational Challenge.* New York: Free Press.

Whitley, Richard. 1974. "The City and Industry." In P. Stanworth and A. Giddens (eds.), *Elites and Power in British Society,* pp. 65–80. Cambridge: Cambridge University Press.

Woodiwiss, Anthony. 1992. *Law, Labour and Society in Japan: From Repression to Reluctant Recognition.* London: Routledge.

World Bank. 1986. *World Development Report.* New York: Oxford University Press.

Woronoff, Jon. 1980. *Japan: The Coming Social Crisis.* Tokyo: Lotus Press.

———. 1986. *Politics the Japanese Way.* Tokyo: Lotus Press.

Index

About the Authors

HAROLD R. KERBO is Professor of Sociology and Chairman, Department of Social Sciences, California Polytechnic State University. He is the author of the widely used textbook, *Social Stratification and Inequality: Class Conflict in Historical Perspective*, which is now in its third edition.

JOHN A. MCKINSTRY is Professor of Sociology at California Polytechnic State University. He is the coauthor of *Japan's Last Secret: Fortunetelling and Divination in Contemporary Japanese Society*.

Both Kerbo and McKinstry have lived in Japan for a number of years and have taught at several Japanese universities.